The Umbrian Thursday Night Supper Club

Marlena de Blasi is the internationally bestselling author of *A Thousand Days in Venice*, as well as four further bestselling memoirs and a novel, *Amandine*. She has been a chef, a journalist, a food and wine consultant and a restaurant critic. She is also the author of two internationally published cookbooks of Italian food. She and her Venetian husband, Fernando, live in Orvieto in Umbria, Italy.

The Umbrian Thursday Night Supper Club

MARLENA DE BLASI

✸ WINDMILL BOOKS

9 10

Windmill Books
20 Vauxhall Bridge Road
London SW1V 2SA

Windmill Books is part of the Penguin Random House group of companies
whose addresses can be found at global.penguinrandomhouse.com.

Copyright © Marlena de Blasi 2015

Marlena de Blasi has asserted her right to be identified as the author of this Work
in accordance with the Copyright, Designs and Patents Act 1988.

First published by Hutchinson in 2015
First published in paperback by Windmill Books in 2016

www.penguin.co.uk

A CIP catalogue record for this book is available from the British Library.

ISBN 9780099591856

Internal design by Christa Moffitt, Christabella Designs
Set in 10.57/16pt Minion Pro buy Bookhouse, Sydney

Printed and bound in Great Britain by Clays Ltd, St Ives Plc

Penguin Random House is committed to a
sustainable future for our business, our readers
and our planet. This book is made from Forest
Stewardship Council® certified paper.

CONTENTS

PREFACE

Linked by culture, blood, tradition, compassion, empathy and love, four rural women compose the Thursday Night Umbrian Supper Club. Their ages ranging from fifty-two to somewhere beyond eighty, they gather each week in a derelict stone house in the hills above Orvieto to cook, to eat, to drink and to talk. In another epoch – less distant in these parts than one might imagine – they would have been the women who gathered by a river to scrub clothes on stones or sat among meadow weeds to mend them, waiting for the weekly bread to bake in a communal oven. The four are linked, too, by their work, each one having earned her bread by making it. More specifically, the four are or were professional cooks who practise – or practised in the past – genuine Umbrian culinary traditions.

Inclined to things practical which, in their hands, somehow become also things romantic, the women say that gathering together by the fire and around the table is where one finds antidotes to life's caprice. A good supper, they are convinced, restores to us the small delights that the day ransacks. Through crisis and catastrophe and rare moments of uninterrupted joy, it's this round, clean and imperishable wisdom that sustains them: cook well, eat well and talk well with people who are significant to your life.

Long after I'd come to live in Orvieto and been befriended by the club's matriarch, she risked making room for me at the Thursday table. The only 'stranger' among them, it wanted only time before I became *of them*, foraging, harvesting, making do, listening, watching, learning, enacting a few of my own ways and means upon them.

The narrative has a dual thrust: in exuberant detail it recounts what we cooked and ate and drank and, in at least as exuberant detail, it tells the stories of the women's lives: fidelity, aging, men and aging, sexuality, aging men and sexuality, aging women and sexuality, children, abandonment, destiny, death, the Mafia and Mother Church being among the subjects explored.

'*Vivi per sempre*, live forever,' we'd say, as we set to work on the preparations for a meal. 'Live forever,' we'd say again, holding each other's hands around the table, passing around loaves of still-warm, wood-baked bread, pouring out jug after jug of our own chewy, teeth-staining red, benevolence setting the scene for dining but, as much, for storytelling, invigorating memory, soothing rancour and even, once in a while, illuminating a fear long stuck in the heart tight as the stone in an unripe plum.

Spoken by Miranda one evening, maybe it's these lines that can best introduce you to the Thursday Night Umbrian Supper Club:

I don't know how much more I could have learned about the point of life had I wandered farther away than the eight kilometres from where I was born and have lived for all my life to where I'm sitting right now. I think that wherever I might have gone I would have found you. Souls like you. We are magnificently the same. Not only us, all of us. Without pain, without fear, who would any one of us have become, what would we have to show for having lived? Any five women, wherever, whomever, put them together at supper around a fire and, *ecco, ci saremo*, there we'll be. The point of life is to do what we're doing right now. What we did yesterday, what we'll do with what's left of our time. Surely we are not barren of fantasy or dreams and yet none of us seem to be swanking about, reaching for *great things* or, worse, perceiving ourselves to be doing *great things*. There are no great things. After the myth of security, the second greatest myth ever inflicted on humans is the myth that we were meant to triumph. How wonderful it is to be content with holding hands around this mangled old table, with some nice bread, some wine, a candle and a fire. A blessed sleep waiting.

The narrative is set in the years 2004 through 2008.

PART I

MIRANDA

HAVING POURED OIL INTO A LARGE, DEEP POT, AND SET IT over a quiet flame, she sets out for a quick tour of the garden and the meadow just as we are arriving. Shedding coats and shawls, greeting one another as though years have passed since last Thursday night, we see to the table, to the filling of the wine jugs from the demijohn of red sitting in the corner. One of us lays uncut loaves of new bread on the table, another pokes about to see what it is that Miranda has cooking over the hearth fire though none of us dares to put a hand to anything without her command.

Her breath a bit short from fervour for her mission, Miranda returns holding her apron together with two hands and in its hollow there are what must be the last of the string beans – green and yellow – the first of the brussels sprouts, the chopped-off long leafy heads of celery, apples, zucchini blossoms, sage. Two brown-skinned pears she has stuffed into her sweater pockets for tomorrow's breakfast.

'Out of my way, *via, via,*' she says, pushing us aside, bussing cheeks as she passes each one, then sets to the tasks of rinsing and drying and trimming, preparing her bounty for glory. All of us familiar with her frying dance, we surround her, hungry children in her thrall.

Starting with the celery leaves, dragging the branches a few at a time into a batter no thicker than cream, she slips the dripping things into the hot oil, letting them be until they rise to the surface of the now bubbling oil, the force of which turns them over – without a prod – to crust the other side of them. Her feet anchored in place, the whole of Miranda's generous upper body sways, her hands flying over the leaves and the blossoms and the beans to the batter, to the pot, lifting batch after batch from the oil with a wide skimmer, turning the gilded stuff out to rest on a long, flat pan lined with a tea towel. We pass the pan among us, devouring the fritters out of our hands, burning fingers, burning mouths, and have barely placed the empty pan back to her reach – we still chewing and sipping and moaning – as Miranda piles it with another batch. And another. She saves apple peelings and sage leaves for the last, since these are what she, herself, craves most. As she lifts these onto the pan and moves the frying pot off the heat, she turns to us, taking a long pull from the glass of white someone slaps into her hand. Then Miranda eats, drinks.

'Pan-to-hand-to-mouth food, I like the wine cold, nearly gone to ice following the hot shattering crust in my mouth, the contrast sending one's whole body into ecstasy,' she tells us. 'I don't think I've ever served a *frittura* at the table. No time to get it there since I'm always on to the next round of dragging things through the batter, slipping them into the oil, lifting them out dark and crisp. I prefer everyone gathered around the pot, waiting.'

Sighing and laughing and crunching and sipping, Miranda asks for more wine. The three bottles of white (a rare luxury is 'bought wine' on Thursday nights), which she'd cooled in a tub of supermarket ice, are dead soldiers. Someone suggests we drink the bottle of Champagne that has been lying on its side in some cupboard for months, a bottle from some lesser-known house in Reims, which was gifted – read: *lifted* – by one of the truckers among Miranda's admirers.

'Shouldn't it be drunk cold?' she wants to know but two of the men are already fiddling with the foil, the wire, shouting *'Attenzione, attenzione,'* though the cork slides out with a quiet plunk. We pour it, flat and sour, into one another's tumblers, toasting Miranda and the thieving trucker. They go quiet, all of them, searching for some motive to compliment their first taste of 'real French' when Miranda says, 'Yeasty stuff, we might better have made bread with it.'

I begin a cliffs-notes version of the story of Dom Pérignon and the sometime glories of what came to be *la méthode champenoise* but Miranda couldn't be less interested. She says, 'Leave a monk in a cellar and there's bound to be a travesty.'

Flailing her toasting fork now, she bosses us into our places at table, stoops down then to the small hearth on the wall behind it to turn the thick, spluttering slabs of pancetta, which have been slowly crisping on a grate over olivewood embers and branches of wild sage. Sitting deep in the red-hot ash below the grate is a long, shallow terracotta baking dish of potatoes, small as a thumbnail, and the luscious sage-smelling fat drips over them. From the pocket of her pinafore she takes a handful of dried wild fennel flowers, rubs them between her palms over the potatoes, and the maddening perfumes they send up cause sighs of longing from us. Struggling to rise from her bent position, steadying herself with one hand on the mantel, once she is upright, Miranda-of-the-Bosoms is flushed with delight. For the pancetta, for the potatoes. For her frying dance and because it's Thursday. Likely for much more than that.

'*Quasi, quasi* – almost, almost,' Miranda laughs over her shoulder, her great beautiful form juddering back behind the faded flowery bedsheet that secludes the kitchen from the dining room in the tiny derelict and woodsmoked house she calls her *rustico*.

It's a Thursday in a long-ago October. And in this squat stone building, which sits on the verges of the Montefiascone road, we are nine still-hungry souls awaiting supper. Four women – five including myself – form the core group and, tonight, we are joined by four men: two husbands, the widower of a former member, and a lover, the last being Miranda's long-time friend, Filiberto.

The ten small tables at which Miranda's guests sit to dine on other evenings in the week have been pushed together into one, the diversity of their heights and widths smoothed over in green-checked oilcloth. Under sheaves of dried olive branches that hang from the slouching, split-beamed ceiling barely a metre above our heads, we sit on plank benches and half-broken chairs along its length. A merry troupe, having our way with Miranda's purple wine, passing along a thin-bladed knife and a two-kilo round of her crusty sourish bread, still warm from the wood-fired oven in the back garden, each of us saws off a trencher, passes it to the person on their right. When everyone has bread, we tear it into pieces, wet the pieces in the wine, and chew the fine pap with gusto. *Pane e vino*, bread and wine.

We slide further into our cups, wet more bread in more wine until Miranda parts the bedsheet curtain – keeping it pinned to the wall with a tilt of her hip – and comes forth holding a great steaming basin of wild porcini braised in red wine and tomato. Into small deep white bowls she spoons the mushrooms with their dark potent juices and directs someone to fetch more bread and another to remove the pancetta from the grate and lay it over the potatoes where it'll stay warm without burning. She asks if the wine jugs are full, then serves herself. We raise tumblers and voices in *buon appetito* and the house goes silent as stone save for low-pitched salacious murmurings.

We share in the clearing of plates and the resetting of others. One of the Thursday night rules is: *Once the supper begins, Miranda will not leave her chair at the table until the meal is finished.* And so, with two kitchen towels against its heat, I lift the pan of pancetta and potatoes from the embers and take it round the table for everyone to serve themselves. Next, one of us fetches from the kitchen two large chipped Deruta platters piled with chicken crusted in wild herbs – rosemary, oregano, fennel seeds, fennel flowers and thyme – and roasted with crushed tomatoes and olive oil, the whole of it doused in white wine toward the end of its cooking time. We fight over the pan juices and before we're ready to surrender the platters – crusts poised for a last swipe – someone whisks them away behind the curtain. Coitus interruptus. We suffer the noise of furtive slurpings. Then frenzied scrapings of the roasting pan left behind in the sink.

'The chicory is outside in the bread oven,' Miranda says to no one in particular, knowing that someone will run to get it. This between-course bustle with too many of us trying to help seems always a four-minute farce, everyone bent on getting back to the table.

To complete the savoury part of the supper, Miranda has rolled steamed chunks of autumn squash in cornmeal and pan-fried them in olive oil. Only a whisper of sea salt and a grinding of pepper scent them, consenting to yet more sage leaves – sautéed in oil this time – which exalt the natural richness of the squash rather than conceal it with sugar and spices. Nothing much gets a mask in Miranda's kitchen. This reprise of sage – first, battered and fried, then to scent the pancetta and the potatoes and now with the squash – is an example of Miranda's theory of the *filo conduttore*: literally, the conducting thread. Often she uses an element more than once in a meal, thus connecting the various dishes, coaxing them into a harmonious whole. *The whole is greater than the sum of its parts.* Aristotle knew.

Though Miranda almost never prepares a traditional dessert on Thursday nights, sometimes, when she's set ewe's-milk ricotta in a sieve to drain overnight, she'll place a lush, creamy pat of it on a yellow plate, a big hunk of honeycomb and a pepper mill beside it, and everyone will take a tablespoonful or so in a teacup, break a piece of the comb over the ricotta, and grind on pepper with a heavy hand. Without fail, ricotta or not, she always reaches into the armoire where she keeps flour and sugar and dried beans, and takes out a fine old metal tin. Oval in shape, its pale blue and silver paint left only in patches, it's always filled with

8

tozzetti, hard, twice-baked biscuits made with whatever nuts or fruit or seeds she has to hand. These and a good ambered *vin santo* in which to wet them, that's how Miranda ends Thursday nights. We began our supper by dipping bread in wine and end with the same gesture. Amen.

Patting his chin with a napkin, Filiberto then lays the square of tattered blue cloth flat on the table; after smoothing and folding it into a small triangle, he places it in the pocket of his woollen shirt. Another of the Thursday night rules is: *Anyone who wants one brings their own napkin.* He rises then, walks to Miranda's place, takes her hand in his and, in the style of the old cavaliers, brings it close to his lips without touching it. Turning from her, he strides the few metres to a chair set near the hearth and takes up his waiting mandolin, and begins plucking the strings in a minor key. One of the two shepherds who tend the flocks on the far-flung meadows of this parish on the Montefiascone road, Filiberto sings, his voice a cracked whisper. Hoarse, ragged.

Miranda shuts her eyes, totters her chair back on its hind legs and, as though all of us and even the little room itself have fallen away, she is alone with Filiberto and his tender wail. His voice, his music, are her after-supper prize on Thursday nights. Miranda-of-the-Bosoms, goddess of abundance, *la Madonna* of the burners in a kitchen-towel turban, Juno-esque breasts, soft and brown, bursting from the bodice of a white pinafore as she rocks her chair like a cradle, its creaking keeping time with Filiberto's plucking. When he stops, she rouses, and her old rheumy eyes are drenched blue-black flowers flitting from one to another of us with what seems like regret. She sips the heel of her *vin santo*, runs a hand across her cheek, pinches her upper lip, pats her kitchen-towel turban. Miranda has been consenting to the age seventy-six for several years now but I think one of her recent birthdays was her eightieth.

It was a cold January night when I first met Miranda, six years ago now. While still living in the stable in San Casciano, Fernando and I were in the thick of our search for our 'next house'; somehow we found ourselves accidental guests at a festival to honour *Sant'Antonio Abate* – Saint Anthony the Abbot – in a tiny Umbrian village near the hilltown of Orvieto. A wooden crate of just-baked bread balanced picturesquely on her head, Miranda had gone about the little *festa* swinging her prosperous hips, causing the men to pause in their quaffing and orating whenever she passed by. I remember one man in particular would bite the side of a forefinger each time she came near. A forceful gesture this, indicator of many sentiments. But that man's motive for finger-biting was undeniably desire.

As it turned out, we soon found our 'next house' – in Orvieto – and waited out the two years it wanted to restore it; for all that time and ever since, Miranda has been an affectionate and generous presence in our lives. My first Umbrian friend, my enduring one. When I was too-long kitchenless she put the keys to the rustico in my hand, invited me to complete the work of testing recipes for a manuscript perilously overdue. And when Fernando and I finally moved into Number 34 Via del Duomo, again it was she who swanned me through the markets, introduced me to the farmers, helped me – the first American ever to set up in Orvieto full-time – to slash a path through the spiny cultural labyrinth of the *centro storico*, the town's historic centre. Always there, Miranda was. Always near in the Umbrian way of being near. Close by but not too close.

Miranda and I have spent untold hours – we two, alone, and in the company of others – working and talking, laughing ourselves to tears and then weeping ourselves back to laughter, cooking and baking and sitting down to supper. And when she asks, I give a hand in preparing the suppers she serves in the rustico on three or four nights other than Thursday when Miranda hosts twelve or so people. Her guests on those nights are mostly locals who live alone, truckers passing through or couples living on '*caffe latte* pensions' – a sum that barely allows them to put supper on their own tables and would prohibit any thought of dining out. For all of them the handwrought sign – *Miranda* – swinging from a metal arm above her old green door and backlit by a flame in an iron lantern announces a kind of sanctuary, the broken-down castle keep on the Montefiascone road.

Miranda cooks whatever she has, whatever others have brought to her. No bill is brought to the tables at the end of the evening. People leave what they can, be it a few euros, eggs wrapped in newspaper, a sack of just-dug potatoes smudged in wet red earth, or a crate of artichokes, their round barbed heads lolling on thirty-centimetre leafy stems. The arrangement works. Miranda makes it work.

I think of all this and wonder what troubles Miranda-of-the-Bosoms this evening, why her eyes shine with tears that won't fall.

Still sitting by the hearth, Filiberto wonders, too. '*Amore mio*,' he says, looking over at her, 'are you not feeling so well?'

'*Sto bene. Sto veramente bene ma,*' she says. 'I'm well, truly well, but . . .'

'Well then, what is it?' asks Gilda. A delicate fifty-something beauty, Gilda's face seems made of white silk in which her amber eyes have burned great round holes. 'I can also see you are a bit down.'

'I think it's a matter of fatigue. Our little Miranda is doing too much. Maybe there should be a nice interval in our Thursday nights,' says Ninuccia, a stout red-haired women with gorgeous grey eyes and a tendency to rule. The tribe's *portatrice della verità*, the carrier of truths, Ninuccia knows what is and what isn't and rarely is she disputed.

All' Italiana, everyone around the table begins to speak at once, each one hearing only themselves. No one wants to surrender the Thursday suppers nor do they disagree that Miranda should be doing less. At least for a while. The rumpus builds until she commands quiet.

'My nephews have promised to do a bit of work on this old place. Not much, mind you – shoring up the beams, laying down a truckload of antique tiles one of them bought from an auction in Viterbo. Some paint. Even though they'll be working only in the evenings, I should think a month would be enough. Sometime after the *raccolta* they should be finished. The olives will be ripe enough to harvest by mid-November this year, wouldn't you say?'

A murmur of accord. 'Yes, after the harvest and before the first snow, the boys should be finished.'

'*Benissimo*. And then we will resume our rhythm,' says Pierangelo, who is Ninuccia's husband. The last words he tilts upward in question.

'Actually, I had more than an *intervallo* in mind,' Miranda says, not looking up. 'I've been thinking to close down the rustico.' Crushing a crust of bread against the green and white oilcloth, she lifts her empty glass to her lips, trying to sip from it.

Thunder rumbles the room.

'No, no, I mean close it down *except* for our Thursdays,' she hastens to explain. 'I won't be opening up on the other nights. That's what I mean.'

Over the others who chant praises to the saints, Miranda is still trying to be heard. 'But if we do start up again . . . *when* we start up again, I won't be cooking. I want you to know that. I'll be here to help. We'll keep the same system, everyone contributing what they can to make the supper. For a while there'll be little enough growing in anyone's *orto* save pumpkins and black cabbage and cauliflower, but persimmons will be ripe by November, and pomegranates. If everyone would leave a few porcini to dry, we'd have a windfall for winter suppers. But dry them right. Better, bring them to me and I'll string them up, let them swing from the beams in my attic.'

'I'll have leeks even after the snow,' says Ninuccia. 'And I've a cellarful of apples and potatoes. Everyone's got chestnuts.'

'Good. *Bravissimi*. But remember, only what's *fine*,' Miranda cautions.

A Thursday night rule: *Humble or rich, always offer only the best of what you have.*

'And whoever can spare something from his hunt, well, feel free to hang the haunches, or the beasts entire, in the cheese hut out back. Birds, hare, boar. Remember to wrap a hoof or a foot or a wing with the date, written legibly, so we'll know the order in which to use them.'

'No need to date a bird, Miranda. Once it's putrid, it speaks for itself.'

'You're just about reaching the putrid stage yourself, Iacovo,' Miranda assures a handsome man in a hand-knitted black sweater, navy basque and grey canvas trousers tucked into knee-high boots – the same hand-knitted black sweater, navy basque and grey canvas trousers tucked into the same knee-high boots he's been wearing summer and winter, it's been observed, since the day his wife passed away half a decade before.

'For the last years of his life, Michelangelo never took his boots off, my darling girl,' Iacovo tells her. 'It's in deference to him that keeps me night and day in mine.'

'Bah. Where was I? Yes, the wine and the oil will be here, wood for the fire, for the bread oven.'

'And the pecorino,' Filiberto says. 'There'll always be cheese.'

Miranda looks at Filiberto, blows him a kiss.

'*Certo, certo*, you've done more than your share and now we'll . . . we'll take over. Take turns.' As usual, it's Ninuccia who decides for all of us.

Once again, everyone speaks at the same time, all of them agreeing that Miranda should indeed retire from her stance in front of the old iron stove. 'Yes, yes, of course, *è giusto, giustissimo*, it's right, very right,' they repeat again and again though their voices and the pace of their words wane, their conviction a diminishing chord. A tentative whistle in the dark. They are bewildered babes who've lost their piper.

A soft but unshy voice makes a small rip in the silence.

'I'll cook.'

The voice is mine.

I have just offered to prepare supper for as many as fourteen people once a week in a place with no electricity or gas. I shall cook over the three holes of a wood-and-coal-fired stove and a length of chicken wire stretched between the andirons of a Lilliputian hearth. The people who will come to eat what I cook – some of them of a certain age – are culinary traditionalists, old-school Umbrians who work the land, shepherd flocks, raise courtyard animals, hunt birds and wild boar, and have never in their impressively long existences eaten an egg plucked from a carton but always from under the warm derrière of a hen. Rigid are their gastronomic formulas: a rabbit is either tugged through a small hill of flour and fried in bubbling lard or wrapped in pancetta, roasted with rosemary and splashed stintingly with white wine once it's been carried to the table; this last ceremony giving up luscious vapours, which settle back to rest deep in the beast's soft, hot flesh. Chicken is chopped into small pieces, roasted with crushed tomatoes, olive oil and handfuls of wild herbs. It gets its white-wine sousing halfway through the cooking. A Sunday chicken can be pan-sautéed with yellow capsicums and fat black olives. Oregano is the prescribed herb to scent it. Lamb, a leg or a shoulder, is roasted with potatoes. Its tiny ribs are charred fast over a wood fire. The only sauce is olive oil – green as sun-struck jade – splashed in small, lustrous puddles through which one skates the flesh, the fat, the bones, the potatoes, the bread. In the last best drops, one skates a finger. Pig, suckling or mature, is roasted with sage and rosemary and often, but not always, with wild fennel, or, yet more ubiquitously, it is boned, stuffed with a poultice of its innards, run through with a metal rod and rotated over a slow fire until its skin, glistening like rubbed mahogany, is brittle as caramel gone cold.

The rural folks' bible is long, its codes chiselled in Umbrian stone. I am not Umbrian. My own bible is a crucible, a composite of riches gathered from all the places where I've lived and worked and cooked. Even for these canonical Umbrians, I know I shall be wilfully tempted to blasphemy. I might sauté a rabbit with wild thyme and shallots in the rich, salty fat rendered from wild herb-perfumed lard, splash it with good black beer, braise it until its plump flesh goes bronze as August wheat and, if barely prodded with a single tine of a fork, falls from its bones in succulent heaps. Worse than this, I will likely serve the same black beer to drink as the one in which the rabbit was drowned. In other words, I shall cook for these Umbrians in the way that is natural for me. This feels right. In fact, it feels wonderful.

It must feel right to Miranda as well, her broad smile making glittering blue-black slits of her eyes. She's laughing now, her kitchen-towel turban – singed in some earlier combat with the flames – sits askew and wilting in the smoky mists of the dying fire. I notice that it's only Miranda who laughs.

'I thought you would, Chou,' she says. 'In fact, it's you I've had in mind to . . . ever since Rai Uno showed that old film, *La*

Festa di Babette. Since then, well, I've been thinking that we're like those locals who'd lived on salt cod and water and that you could be her, that Babette woman, sitting us down to some strange supper on a Thursday. *La Festa di Babette.*'

'You've hardly fared on fish and water all these years,' I say, raising my glass. Everyone follows suit and we drink to the health and joy of the goddess of Buonrespiro.

'*Brava, Miranda, bravissima, bravissima.*' Everyone's on their feet, coming to surround her, kissing, embracing, placing their hands on her sweat-shined cheeks. Miranda has ruled her tribe justly and so merits their love. But the brio quietens perhaps too quickly and, once back at their places, they resume a collective sulk, one fidgeting with his ring, one flicking a middle finger and thumb against errant crumbs. Some fix a perplexed gaze in my direction, as though I was someone else, someone new. Which, in a way, is what I am. Being *someone new* is who an expatriate is always.

Though I've known these souls who compose Miranda's famous Thursday suppers for all the years I've lived in Orvieto – at least to greet in the markets or wherever our paths cross – it was only last spring that she first invited Fernando and I to join the ranks of her inner circle. But more than the longevity I lack, it's my *straniera*, my stranger, status that worries them. How, oh how, can *l'Americana* slip into the old white clogs of their beloved Miranda?

I know better than they that I can't. But what I know that they don't is that I have no wish to. It's not Miranda's shoes I'll try to fill; I've got shoes of my own. I like that Miranda sensed I would offer to cook. So often I have made her privy to this longing of mine for a large family around my table. I suspect she, too, knows the others would make a muddle of taking turns. 'A good hearth has only one *Vesta*,' she always says when, unbidden, someone dares insist upon her territory.

The fire's gone cold and the little room is nearly dark save the last flames hurled up by the guttering candles. One of the Thursday night rules says: *When the candles are spent, the evening is over.* No one moves to leave.

The deeper the dark, the looser their tongues. A triangular dialogue prevails among Ninuccia, the woman called Paolina, and the one called Gilda. We listen.

'I don't know this film. *Come si chiama?*' asks Ninuccia.

'*La Festa di Babette*; it's a pretty film, pretty enough but . . .' says Gilda.

'I saw it, too. This cook killed a turtle; after I saw that scene – enough, ' says Paolina.

'Did she cook it over the ashes?' asks Ninuccia.

'I think she made a broth,' Gilda tells her.

'I'll tell you right off, I don't eat such things,' says Paolina.

'Nor do I,' Ninuccia agrees. 'But what else did she serve?'

'Maybe it would please you to eat a quail suffocated inside a thousand-layer pastry coffin,' Paolina says.

'*Davvero schifoso*. Truly disgusting,' Ninuccia says. 'The lowest circle in hell should be reserved for people who play with food.'

Truly disgusting – they are all in agreement and as I listen to them I am sympathetic. Braised quail tucked inside buttery pastry caskets seem a trumpery to them, as it seemed a trumpery to me not so many years ago as I sat at El Bulli wondering why I wasn't in front of some small tottering table in the ancient village of Sarrià hung high in the hills above Barcelona, dragging charred baby leeks, thin as my finger, into a little pot of romesco, rather than staring at a menu that promised Kellogg's paella – Rice Krispies, shrimp heads and vanilla-scented mashed potatoes – or sizzled embryonic eels afloat in espresso foam. The world is rife with the hungry and yet big-boy chefs must play with food. I think about what Ninuccia has just said: *The lowest circle in hell should be reserved for people who play with food.* I would add: especially those who play with food and get paid for it. But is that what these Umbrians are supposing I shall do?

My reverie is broken by Ninuccia, herself, who is asking me, 'So will Thursdays be like in the film? Is that what we can expect?'

'No. Not at all like in the film. I'm not like her. Not so much like Babette. (I was not telling the whole truth here . . . hence, the hesitation, almost the admittance that I am very much like Babette in that I have and I would again spend my last lire to feed you . . . and more . . . one good supper taken together is a symbol of everything that matters in life.) I promise you a good supper. We'll be together. Every week on the same night. Something to count on. Ritual. Ceremony. Continuance. The idea is pure Umbrian. But the food . . . well, the food can't be if I'm cooking it. I don't have your history, your *hand*. But I have *another* history, my own *hand* . . . will you give me a chance?'

The stillness is brief, electric. It's Gilda who interrupts it. 'Why not? It would be, well, it might be *interesting*.'

'Why not? Because things should remain *as they are*.' This is Ninuccia.

'But there is no more *as they are* – *as they are* has become *as they were*. Weren't you listening to Miranda?' Gilda wants to know.

No one speaks. Gilda continues, 'Doesn't anyone recall Tancredi's words to Don Fabrizio? *If you want things to stay the same, everything must change.*'

'And that signifies?' Ninuccia rises, brushes absent crumbs from the table with the side of her hand.

'That the present can't be preserved like a bushel of apricots tumbled into jars and drowned in rum, Ninuccia. That's what it signifies. There's no defending the present against change. Tonight is already part of the past. It's . . .'

'*Calma, calma*, it's not the *Risorgimento* at stake here – it's supper we're talking about.' This is Iacovo, the widower.

'I say Chou should cook. Miranda says Chou should cook.' This from Gilda.

Disarmed, Ninuccia speaks quietly, '*Forse*, perhaps . . .'

'Certainly, she's clever, but . . .' Paolina remains unconvinced.

Arms resting on the shelf of her bosom, her gaze serene, Miranda is an indulgent mother observing her children in fraternal combat. When she speaks, it's to Filiberto. '*Cosa dici?* What do you say?'

As she knew he would, Filiberto has a solution. 'Perhaps Chou could take on a *collaboratrice* each week. A different partner every Thursday. A rotation of the local talent working alongside her. A joining of ways and means. Of histories. A little like Ravel played with four hands instead of two.'

Lanterns along the Montefiascone road spill tarnished yellow light through the single window of the darkened room and we are a tribe in shadow. In a state of Umbrian impasse.

At last, it's Ninuccia who speaks. 'I wonder, Miranda, if you would consider just one more Thursday night before . . . before we begin this . . . this new *regime*. This variation on Ravel.'

Ninuccia stands as she asks this, goes to Miranda, adjusts her towel turban. Filiberto is on his feet, too, gone to rummage the drawers in the armoire. Breaking the candle rule, he lights two more and goes to stir up the fire.

'*One* more?' Miranda's voice seems made of both laughter and tears.

Enlivened by the new light and as much by Ninuccia's apppeal for clemency, everyone's talking again, shouting out dishes like bingo numbers, foods Miranda hasn't lately cooked or ones she's somehow never cooked at all.

'I've yet to say I will. That I will cook for one more Thursday.' Miranda knows the only way to capture their attention is to whisper. The talk ceases. Barely raising her volume, Miranda says, 'Bring me a haunch of young boar by Sunday evening, a litre of decent brandy and a package of syringes.'

'Syringes?' Half seconds separate each one saying the same word.

'You heard me.' Her wistfulness spent, Miranda begins to play with us. The boar season officially underway, she looks first to

Pierangelo, then to Iacovo, both fervent hunters. Their assignment is clear and each mumbles *va bene, va bene*.

'*Sarà fatto,* it shall be done,' Iacovo confirms. 'But why the syringes?'

There is neither a repeat of the question nor one who answers it. No one seems to know.

'Tell them, my little American.' The blue-black eyes hold mine in silent trust that I will understand what she has in mind. Miranda's challenge is waged not to demonstrate my comfort with the most obscure local culinary patrimony but to spur the others' nostalgia for it. The troupe turns to me, still as a Bruegel vignette.

Very quietly, I take up the gauntlet that Miranda has thrown to me.

'To inject the boar with the brandy. Syringe after syringe of brandy until the flesh is drenched, saturated. Rub the haunch with crushed juniper and let it sit for a few days. Some salt. Nothing else. Roasted over olive and grape woods, the natural sugars from the brandy seep out to form a brittle crust, which keeps the flesh lush. Pan juices. No sauce. The French roast *sanglier* in the same way.'

'You were doing just fine until you brought in the French. Remember who taught them to cook,' Miranda is saying to me over a chorus of, '*Certo, certo,* of course, of course . . . Once upon a time, we always roasted boar in that way.'

'But who had brandy?'

'And who had syringes?'

'Grappa. Just make incisions, pour on the grappa and massage the beast. A little more grappa, another massage.' This is Iacovo.

'Brandy is what it wants,' Miranda insists, 'and only by injecting it can the brandy wet the flesh all the way through. You'll have nothing on your plates but the boar, its crust and its juices. Afterward, a few leaves of whatever grasses I can still find in the meadow.'

I listen and marvel yet again at Miranda's understanding of the human condition. This brandy-boar-syringe act she calculated not to *elevate* me from the tribe but to *include* me. She knew that all of them knew what I knew, save two particulars. That *I* knew of the two particulars that they did not was instantly dispersed into their reminiscences. Without causing the barest nick in their Umbrian pride, Miranda *might* have managed to pull my chair a millimetre closer to the Thursday table.

'And before?' Ninuccia wants to know. 'I think we should have nothing more than a simple soup . . .'

'Only a simple soup – our usual refrain . . .' This is Miranda.

'Roasted chestnuts sautéed with wild mushrooms, pureed with bits of butter and a splash of cream.' The boar story has enboldened me, though not enough to look directly at Ninuccia, who is already glaring at me. 'We could mount a little more cream, perfume it with dry Marsala, a spoonful into each bowl. Let the cream melt into the hot velvety stuff. Ninuccia, please, just listen, just try to taste it in your mind before you . . . all the elements are at hand save, maybe, the Marsala . . . I mean, it *is* the right moment for . . .'

Ninuccia's open disdain causes the others to exaggerate their desire for this anything-but-simple soup and Miranda, tilting back again on the hind legs of her chair, is softly laughing.

•

Between the Thursday of her announced withdrawal from the burners and the very next Thursday's farewell feast with the intoxicated boar, the sting of Miranda's news had yet to be soothed. As we sat down together, it was a muted gaiety the tribe mustered: feeble chatter around a table of funeral meats for the sake of the widow. Neither did the cold winey cream meeting the hot faint smokiness of the soup bring forth half a sigh nor the gold char of the boar's crust nor the exquisite drunkenness of its flesh. As though awaiting a dreaded train onto which only one of us would board – the great black thing having just hurtled into its berth – we linger, saying little. I could be the dancing bear who distracts them from their bile but I will not. Grown weary of what seems their selfishness, I just want the evening to end. We'd not yet cleared the table when the candles had spent themselves and it was by the last of the firelight that we rose – scorning Miranda's plea to leave it all to her – and began carrying things behind the bedsheet curtain, excusing ourselves like strangers if we brushed by one another, reached at the same time for the same dish. So much for pulling my chair a millimetre closer to the Thursday table.

'I need to be alone for a while. Some things I want to do without any of you underfoot. Be off, be gone.'

The tribe bid one another *buonanotte* as though it was *addio*.

All the way back into town I repeat and repeat what Andrè Gide taught me so long ago: *If you want to discover new lands, you must consent to stay a very long time at sea.*

•

It is late November – five weeks since the Thursday night of the boar – and Miranda and I are sitting midst the market-day fracas at Bar Duomo with our high-noon white wine.

'They've been calling and stopping by and generally tormenting me, Chou,' she says.

'I know. They've been calling me as well. I'd not expected that. More I'd assumed they would begin arranging things among themselves, hoping I'd set off for Mars or wherever they think I came from. On that last Thursday, I'd felt it was me, the prospect of my becoming more *present,* that had caused them to be so sullen, so . . .'

'How much you have yet to learn about Umbrians. Had they been anything *but* sullen, it would have been an afront to me, a form of disrespect. You saw and felt them to be unsympathetic. Cold. Both of which may or may not have been the case. They were being themselves. They were being Umbrian.'

'Touché.'

'You cannot be Umbrian. Nor must you try. We are all eternally ourselves.'

'Ditto. Touché.'

'Who's been telephoning you?'

'It's mostly Gilda who calls to say that when she passes by the rustico there's no evidence of progress. Paolina calls, too, but just for a greeting. I've begun suggesting to both Gilda and Paolina that we meet at our place until the work is finished in the rustico but they baulk, say no one wants to drive up into town, look for a parking place, share the corso with tourists bemoaning the dearth of "lasagna" on every menu in *centro storico*.'

Miranda laughs her goddess laugh and sips her wine. 'It's true. Country people tend toward listlessness after the day's work and want nothing of town life to interrupt the tranquility of an evening. Most of us make the trek up onto the rock only on market days and then only if we have something to sell. They must be patient, our friends. Either patient or inclined to open their *own* homes for a Thursday night. Every one of them lives within decent striking distance to the others, wouldn't you say? It would be only you who would have to drive a few extra kilometres. I should have thought to raise that possibility when we were all together.'

She cracks a slender *grissino* and dips the piece into her wine, lets it fall delicately into her mouth, chews thoughtfully, shifting her gaze to two men who sit at a table to our right. In their market-day corduroy suits, freshly ironed shirts buttoned to their throats, black wool *coppolas* pulled to their brows, they are farmers whose wives are in the Piazza del Popolo bartering and selling the stuffs they've grown, harvested this morning before dawn and ported up into Orvieto. At last they can sit together to drink and smoke in *santa pace*, sainted peace. One of them holds a *Toscanello* between his lips, puts a match to its tip and, like a fish, makes short, quick puffs to set the grappa-soaked leaves aflame. He puffs, inhales, puffs some more until, at last, its smoke cuts the wine-laden air of the bar. Miranda closes her eyes.

'All the men I've ever loved have smoked *Toscanelli*: my grandfather, my father, who knows how many uncles and cousins, the first boy who kissed me, my husband . . .'

Without deciding to, I interrupt her. I say, 'Barlozzo smoked them. Vanilla-scented.'

She's quiet for a long time, the *Toscanello* smoke having set her dreaming until, the spell broken, she looks at me, says, 'As far as I can recall, this is the first you've spoken of your old duke since . . .'

'Is it? Is it? I never intended to . . . I guess it's only that . . .'

'It's only that you were in love with him and that makes it difficult, makes it . . .'

She cuts short her thought, sips her wine, waits for me to speak. After a while I say, 'I wish you had known Floriana.'

'An artful foil. Deflect me with talk of his lover, will you?'

Let me be, I beg her silently, knowing she won't. At best, she will only shift recourse. If I won't talk, Miranda will. 'I find myself thinking about him,' she says, 'reminded of things he'd say, how he'd lope rather than walk in that right-sided tilt of his, as though Aeolus walked on his left and he wanted nothing to do with the wind. Will you deny it?'

'Deny that I loved Barlozzo? Why would I?'

'That you were *in love* with him.'

'Miranda, please . . .'

'You've not been the same since, when was it? Nearly a year ago by now?'

'In December. It will be a year in late December.'

'Even widows shed their weeds after a year. Umbrian women, if not Sicilian. You two had – what shall I call it? – a kind of delerium of comradeship. Your affinity was complete and often exclusory. Even Fernando was superfluous, any fool could see that. As far as I know, Barlozzo was an anchorite before you came along and . . .'

'You're mistaken. Fernando excluded himself when his concentration wandered elsewhere, knowing he could re-enter our society at will. And as for the anchorite in Barlozzo, it's true that he lived a long time as a recluse but his renaissance began when he and Flori began to spend time together. He loved her, Miranda, how he loved her, had always loved her since they were children.'

I told her that we, Fernando and I, were background music, a fresh audience for his stories, the tales of his beloved patrimony. Consenting to his raging and blustering, his gestures of imperiousness, we knew he was fragile as a beaten child. To me, he was a tall, skinny boy with a small boy's persistent hunger for caress. He could live on filched eggs, mostly raw, and great quantities of dubious red and if his pantry was bare save half a bushel of chestnuts, he'd invite us to dine, roasting the things, splashing them with wine so they'd go soft like pudding inside their shells. We'd salt the first batch and sugar the second. A two-course feast. '*Non omnis moriar* – I will die but not wholly.' He quoted Horace like prayers.

Sotto voce, Miranda says her own Horatian prayer: 'Be wise and strain the wine for life is brief. Prune back hope. Even while we speak, envious time has passed; mistrust tomorrow and seize the day.'

She takes my chin in her hand, looks at me hard and long. 'Better to admit that you were in love with him.'

During these past months I have been writing about our years in San Casciano. About Barlozzo. I think to an early passage in the text:

A man they call Barlozzo appears to be the village chieftan, walking as he does up and down the tables, setting down plates, pouring wine, patting shoulders. Somewhere beyond seventy, Barlozzo is long and lean, his eyes so black they flicker up shards of silver. Gritty, he seems. Mesmeric. I will come to know those eyes, the way they soften to grey in the doom just before a storm, be it an act of God or some more personal tempest. His thick smooth hair is white and blond and announces that he is at once very young and very old. And for as long as I will know him, I will never be certain if time is pulling him backward or beckoning him ahead. A chronicler, a raconteur, a ghost. A *mago* is Barlozzo. He will become my muse, this old man, my *animatore*, the soul of things for me.

Miranda breaks another breadstick in two, wets half in her wine. Holding it near her mouth, she says, 'Whether or not you were in love with him, let him go. It's time to let him go.'

A parting gift, she hands me the wine-soaked piece of breadstick, sips the heel of her wine, kisses the top of my bent head. 'I'll see you later, little one.'

Worse than a Cassandra, my darling Miranda. How does she *see*, how can she know. *Let him go?* Not now. Not yet. I notice the breadstick still in my hand and so eat the limp, wet thing without tasting it. I ask for another glass of wine, move to a table closer to the farmers, all the better to take in the smoke of their *Toscanelli*. I let myself remember him saying:

> I stood up and began buttoning my jacket as he was looking down at some piece of paper, running his finger along a line of numbers and droning about statistics and therapies for multiple metastasis. In a voice louder than I'd meant to use I asked the doctor to tell me, plain and simple, how much time I would have if I just let things be. At first he seemed not to understand. He raised his head, sat back in his chair, stared at me as though wondering who I was. As though he was seeing me for the first time. Not a morbid festering mass of blood and bones but a man. Still a man. He waited a long time before he answered. 'A year. More or less. I'd estimate a year, Signor Barlozzo.'

The old duke had arranged two kitchen chairs under the stand of oaks behind his ruin of a house, his facing into the hot light of a straight-up sun, mine looking at him. Looking at him, I hear him, too, the soft baritone broken by a sigh now and then or a drag on his cigarette. At some point a while ago I'd stopped hearing the words, though. Stopped consenting to them. Silver swam in his great dark eyes and the long taut length of him was slouched, slanted in the chair, his spider legs crossed at the knee. He crushed the stub of a Camel against the green tin of an ashtray decorated with the Martini vermouth label. 'I've never liked vermouth. Just ruins the good clean taste of gin,' he would always say. He lit another cigarette.

No noxious drenches, no carving away at my innards, no withering burns. Nothing. It's not that I shall lie still and make it easy for the old Horseman. I shall fight him to the death, you see, duel with him, give him a fine game and, when I must, I shall surrender to him. But meanwhile I would like nothing better than to live this year in company with you and Fernando. Not in grief, mind you, not in mourning, not with you stepping lightly, pacifying desires and avoiding words and deeds which you deem unseemly. It is not a year in which I shall practise to die but one in which I shall live the rest of my life. Complete with all the sentiments and emotions and frailties and impulses which I suppose are the sum of it. I shall not take on new guises in the hopes of passing on more nobly. What and who I love, and what and who I don't, have been fixed for a while now. And so the categories shall remain. I have no wish to walk along The Great Wall nor to see the sun rise over a pyramid. Above that meadow out there, day breaks red and yellow like the cleaved heart of a peach and, when the ewes have lambed, the spectacle is accompanied by their squealing and baa-ing and it's then that I wish the whole world could be sitting here with me on this hill. I want a year of ordinary days, Chou. October days, November days. Rain in great fat splashes beating tunnels into the earth when it's dry, thunder so fierce it stops your heart, I want to hold the new leaves on the vines in the palm of my hand. I don't want different than what I have now. I don't even want more. I've always thought the gods have been just with me. Always liked my portion of things. I shall receive this last one with open arms.

No, I won't let you go. How I miss you. And, yes, how I love you.

•

Later that same day, Miranda and I meet at the rustico. The once cracked and sagging floor tiles have been torn up to reveal a foundation of packed earth and stones, which Miranda's nephews have covered, in part, with paint-dripped tarps and plastic sheeting and decorated, strategically, with buckets to catch the almost daily autumn rains that seep through the newly completed roof repairs. The cosy wreckage that was the rustico seems a desolate, ravaged place as we high-step through the tiny precinct, intent on conserving a windfall of pears from Ninuccia's trees.

'We'll put everything right, you'll see,' Miranda chirps at me over her shoulder as I go about lighting fires in the hearth and the iron stove.

Having stripe-peeled and poached four bushels of brown-skinned Boscs and bathed them in spiced red, Miranda and I are wiping down one-litre jars of the rubied fruit, stacking them on the shelves along with the fifty or so jars of other fruits and vegetables already saved for winter and spring Thursday suppers. Smoothing her pinafore, patting the pearly sweat from her forehead, she moves from the pantry back into the kitchen, and takes up a cleaver. She says, 'Let's get to the *violenza*.'

In a basket on the work table there are perhaps a dozen heads of garlic, the purple colour of the cloves bright beneath papery skins. Slapping head after head with the flat of the cleaver, she scrapes the smashed, unpeeled cloves into a five-litre jug of new oil in which she'd earlier stuffed leaves of wild sage, wild fennel flowers, rosemary, a fistful of crushed, very hot chillies. She is building one of her famous potions. Violence, she calls it. She uses it to gloss vegetables before tumbling them into the roasting pan, to massage loins of pork and the breasts and thighs of her own fat chickens, to drizzle over burning hot charcoaled beef and veal.

'It's good for everything but lamb and wild birds and the aches and pains of most men; though, more than once, I've rubbed it into a cut or a scrape, disinfecting the wound better than straight alcohol could and leaving a much more pleasing perfume on the skin.'

'The aches and pains of most men? The ones they inflict or the ones they suffer?'

'I guess I was thinking more about the ones they inflict.'

'Is that why you've never married again?'

Anticipating that Miranda would resume her talk of Barlozzo, I am prepared. I play offence. Her eyes cast downward, she tears the leaves off a branch of sage, pushes them through the neck of the bottle. I try again.

'Is it? Is that why you've never married again?'

'Could be.'

'Have you even considered it?'

'Are you about to punish me for my ranting at you about Barlozzo? Is that . . .'

'Punish? Hardly.'

'Good, because . . . because I feel it's my *right*, age has rights, in our case, a kind of *mother's right* . . .'

'Mostly, I saw Barlozzo as my child. Sometimes you see me as *your* child . . . we're all trying to save someone when the most – no, the best – we can do might be to cook a good supper for each other and let life shape itself. I think that you were talking to yourself when you told me to "let him go". I think there's someone you've yet to *let go*. And like a mother, yes, *like a mother*, you don't want what's happened to you to happen to me. But I don't need saving, Miranda, really I don't.'

'Less do I. I'm Umbrian, you'll recall. Umbrian women are as choice of pain as we are of pleasure. Who would Job be without his burden? In any case, I shall answer your question. The truth is that I have considered marrying again. The greater truth is that I never would. It's either too late or not late enough, I can't decide which.'

'But if some day you were to feel it was neither too late nor too soon, which one would you choose? Of all the men you know, if you could choose, which one would it be?'

'None of them.'

'Not even Filiberto?'

'Not even him. I'm still working on the ending of my first marriage.'

'A very long ending.'

Miranda has never spoken more than in passing about her husband. I know that he died young, suddenly. A very long time ago. She sits down, absently wiping down the sides of the oil bottle with a corner of her apron, corking it. She wraps her arms around the great jug, leans her kitchen towel turbaned head against it. As though against a tree. Or the chest of a lover. She looks at me.

'He was a great beast of a man, my husband, kind as a baby deer, worked and laughed and slept and ate and drank passionately. His cousin was my neighbour in Castelpietro and when she married, Nilo came from Grosseto to the wedding. A Tuscan, Nilo Bracciolini was. We were married three months later. Or was it two? The foreman in a brick-making factory in Grosseto, that was Nilo's job and, being such a good one, he wouldn't hear of leaving it to come live in Castelpietro. Nor would I hear of leaving my parents, my sister and her children, my own work, my village. I couldn't imagine crossing that border from Umbria into Toscana, save to visit. But we'd talked of all that before we married. *Ci arrangeremo*, we'd said; we'll arrange things. He'd go off on Monday morning with four days' worth of suppers packed in the boot of his Fiat 600; pots and bowls, a two-kilo loaf. A demijohn when he needed it. Empty pots and bundles of laundry in tow, Nilo would come home early on Friday and I'd be waiting for him. He'd bathe and we'd rest together and then he'd take me to supper at *la Palomba*. Every Friday. I'd go with him to Grosseto once a month, sometimes twice; I'd scour his apartment from floor to ceiling, stock his pantry, do what needed doing. I'd always fill the place with flowers and Nilo liked that. I could never stay more than a night or two because of my own job and so he'd put me on a bus back to Orvieto and from there I'd get myself to Castelpietro. To wait for Friday. For years and years that was our life. A good one. A good life. Nilo held me up like a china doll. Sometimes I still believe that's what he did.'

I'm lost. I stay quiet, waiting for her to show me the way.

'Nilo's dying was made of two swords falling. How was it that a man could go off one Monday morning, big and sweet and crushing my lips with his coffee-wet moustache, telling me he loved me just as he always told me, how could it be that he never came back? That he could be counting stacks of bricks, sending them down a line to be wrapped, readied for shipping, all the while talking to the man working next to him and, in the time it took for that man to turn around and talk to the person next to him on the line, then turn back to Nilo, Nilo was already dead. Slumped in a heap on the spot where he'd been standing and laughing two minutes before. That was sword number one.

'The second sword came after the mass, the funeral mass. The coffin had been carried out to the hearse and I should have followed it but, instead, I'd wanted to stay a while alone. Giorgia wouldn't leave me, though, my sister, Giorgia. Shadowing me, insisting I was too weak to kneel another time. So I just stood there, my back to the altar, facing the main aisle, remembering how I'd minced along its length on my father's arm and in my mother's ivory satin, never minding how the dress strangled me about my bosoms or that it barely reached my ankles rather than sweeping the floor as it was meant to. When I arrived beside him, the first thing Nilo whispered was, *"Amore mio, sei in attesa di un diluvio?* Were you expecting a flood, my love?" That always made me laugh, him saying that, and so I stood there playing the scene over and over, willing it to paint over the fresh red hole where my life once was.

'And then I noticed a child. A small, thin boy striding toward me from the main door of the church. He was pallid, weeping, maybe ten years old, maybe less. Even from a distance his eyes shackled mine. I waited for him. When we were toe to toe, I thought I must be dreaming, for it was Nilo. There before me was my husband as a boy. Skin so white I could see his veins, deep black pools, the eyes. Even his mouth, the point of his chin, it was Nilo. I stayed silent and the boy, save trying to stave his weeping, he was quiet, too. And then I felt it, like something falling away. From my eyes, from my throat, my body, some kind of veneer shattering. Glass, ice. Something that had been gently suffocating me for so long that I'd learned to breathe through it. All of it gone. I knew it before he told me. Sober as Abraham, that little boy, I knew it was true before he could say it: *Sono figlio di Nilo.* I am Nilo's son.

'I think the boy neither expected me to speak nor wished me to, it being enough for him to say the words aloud. Out of the dark, revealed. By then it was I who was keeping Giorgia upright, bending to soothe her, telling her I was fine, and when I looked back at the boy, there stood behind him a girl. *Another one,* I thought. *Two children. Jesus help me.* The girl stepped closer. "*Io sono l'altra.* I'm the other one," she said. "Of course you are," I whispered. White-skinned, red-haired, just like the boy. But not like the boy. Not like Nilo. In the yellow light of the church she might have been a statue, sculpted, serene. "*Io sono l'altra,*" she said again. "*L'altra,* the other one," she repeated and, though I tried to make her eyes slide off mine, she held them there until she was sure I'd understood. *The other woman.* The second sword. I never said a word.

'There was nothing to do but take her by the hand, the boy with my other hand, walk down the aisle and out the door, down the steps where all the mourners were lined up on either side, waiting to console the widow. *We were both widows,* I kept thinking that. We just kept walking. I could hear Giorgia muttering behind me. Someone folded us into the long black funeral car, smelling of lilies. Even now, lilies bring me to a faint, a frenzy. I don't recall much after that. The boy's weeping, I remember that. And that we never did let go of one another's hands all morning long. The girl, she never cried or spoke; taut as a palace guard, she stayed. They let go first, mother and son, they let go of my hands when it was over. Half a nod, they turned, began walking away. I called after them, they who'd become my comfort, if you can believe that. In the arc of an hour, they'd gone from being the embodiment of my mortification to becoming, somehow, just *mine.* How strange. How . . .'

'Not strange. Not for you. Not strange at all.'

'Perhaps not. We tried to be a kind of family but that failed. Instead we slipped into twice- or thrice-yearly visits made more of duty than pleasure. I tried then to forge a friendship with them. I had more than they did, more than I needed. As soon as it was comfortable for the tenants to vacate it, I signed over the deed to Nilo's family property up here in Umbria. It was the place where we'd planned to retire some day. A fine stretch of land, a small house, in Civitella del Lago. They moved there, mother and son, and she worked in the village. I think it might have been two, maybe three years later when she sold everything. They went back to Grosseto. Nilo's son is married, I think it was four or five years ago. The friendship didn't work, either. After all this time, I'm still not certain if it was more her pain or mine that kept us from it. I expect one day that he'll come to see me, Nilo's son. That he'll bring his children. Another grandmother, I would like to be that for them. I wait for it but I would never ask for it. I do think that Nilo must have spoken well and often to his son of me, maybe not as his wife but as a good person. A good woman, something of the sort. Wishful thinking? Is my notion made of only that?

'Nilo's betrayal did not leave me in despair. I never sat and rocked, imagining him kissing her or tangling his legs around hers in the candlelight, his feeling her belly when the baby quickened, I never did. All of that belonged to him and to her. It wasn't the betrayal but Nilo's treachery in not owning up to it. The dupe. That's what left me stammering, inarticulate. It left me defenceless. And profiting from my teetering state, fear took over. Set up to stay. I was and remain victorious over despair, but fear is still with me. I cover it up with my prancing and joking, with my cooking. Once again, to answer your question, I would choose none of them.'

'But you and Filiberto . . .'

'Filiberto and I. An unlived love. Which is not the same as love denied or undeclared. It's a love with distance between the lovers. A mostly private, mostly silent love, which – by its nature – avoids every kind of injury. Not even love can staunch a wound, Chou. Or if it can, while it's doing its work on the old wound, the new love is equally busy wounding one in another place. If not in the same place.'

Miranda smiles, looks up at me as if for sympathy, for accord but, so lost am I in my own story of wounds, both vintage and of recent harvest, I say nothing. She squints her eyes then, as though the old light by which she tries to look at the past has grown dim. When she looks at me again, she returns to the discourse about her shepherd lover.

'So, yes, Filiberto and I . . . there is this distance between us. As though there was a stand of ancient elms we must traverse in order to get to one another. And so we wander through the trees and that's enough for us and has been for twenty years. It's enough that I feel wiser and lovelier when he's near, which doesn't mean I can't manage when he's not. It's Filiberto I run to on the morning when I see the olives have budded. I need to tell him about beautiful things. Him, exactly him. One must put a face to love. One must know who to run to.'

'Quaint. Charming enough. Perhaps even *ideal*. But . . .'

'Not *real*?' Miranda smiles.

'It would be like living on sweets. I would miss the salt. Half a love.'

'The good half,' she tells me.

'You said it: *I'm still working on the ending of my first marriage.* Not a stand of fine old elms, it's Nilo who is the distance between you and Filiberto.'

'And what if he is?'

'Then he is. I just think it's good that you *know* it's Nilo and not the trees.'

'Doesn't change anything, does it? What name I give it?'

'No. No, it doesn't change. But don't you wonder if . . .'

'I thought we were telling truths here. Hard ones. Or are we only telling mine?'

I stay quiet.

'Fine. Then I'll tell one of yours. The old duke was *your unlived love.*'

'Not a truth of mine. A detour from yours.'

For all this time that we've been talking, I've been settled on the edge of the work table while Miranda has been sitting on a stool in front of it, every now and then wiping down the great jug of *violenza* with a damp cloth, polishing it with a corner of her apron, wiping it down again. She rises now, lifts the jug, walks to the armoire with it, sets it on an empty shelf. As though she spots an errant smudge, she rubs the jug again with her apron, slams her palm down on the already tight cork. She closes the armoire doors and, still facing them, she says, 'What are you reaching for, Chou? I think it's guilt you want to know about, isn't it? You want to know if I once thought or still think that I failed Nilo somehow and thus sent him racing off for succour somewhere else . . . Do I wonder if he'd have gone to her if I hadn't chosen to stay in Castelpietro? Would he have wanted her if I'd been better or kinder or more beautiful? If I'd been a more faithful panderer?'

'Panderer?'

'*Si, ruffiana*. Panderer. Men need a daily dose of fawning. As we would coax a contrary child with bread and sugar so must men be coaxed. We must enoble them. The most gentle critique is censure to a man. He retreats. Even when he fights back, he is retreating, saving up small, sharp pieces of his displeasure, a bag of sticks and stones for whenever he might feel strong enough to fight. Maybe I allowed Nilo's bag to get too full and, rather than heaving stones at me, he left. Essentially, he did *leave* me. With neither the will nor the talent to pander, I made the fatal error of being sincere. I was indeed guilty. Guilty even though I knew that fable, what's it called? The one in which the courtiers compliment the king on his new suit while he prances naked before them. Those people knew he needed the compliment more than he needed the truth. What's that story called?'

'"The Emperor's New Clothes" in English. I don't know the title in Italian. Virginia Woolf said it better, though. Do you know of Virginia Woolf?'

'Do I know of *la lupacchiotta*? That's what Signora Giacomini called Virginia. The she-wolf.'

'Who is Signora Giacomini?'

'Was. The matriarch of the clan Giacomini– four generations of them all living in the same palazzo. It's where I was cook and housekeeper until I married Nilo. *La signora* loved English novels – in translation, of course – and she being nearly blind when I was there, it fell to me to read aloud to her after lunch. The she-wolf was her favourite and she knew by heart every line of two or three of her books so that when I'd try to skip a page or even a phrase, she'd reach out to pinch my arm, keen and mumble until I'd go back to where I'd left off. It was her lullabye, my reading, the only way she could have her afternoon sleep. Yes, I know about Virginia.'

'Sotto voce,' I quote 'Women have served all these centuries as looking glasses possessing the magic and delicious power of reflecting the figure of a man at twice his natural size.'

'*Non capisco*. What did the she-wolf say?'

'From *A Room of One's Own*: Women have served all these . . .'

'Never mind. The last thing I need right now is a dose of pontification from *la lupacchiotta*. She's a big stick that women use to beat men over the head with, and I say there's nothing wrong with men that isn't likewise wrong with us.'

I know her dethroning of Woolf is burlesque but still it irks me and I let her know by refusing to parry. Miranda rises, comes to me, takes my face in her hands, shakes it back and forth as she might to a loved child. In a tired, gravelly whisper, she says, 'We were talking about Nilo Bracciolini and Miranda Filippeschi and I could give a damn at this moment about Virginia Woolf.'

'Fair enough,' I concede and she returns to her chair.

'It wasn't our living apart four days a week. I've never believed it was that which provoked Nilo's betrayal. Out of sight, out of mind signifies something less than love. Our story was likely finished long before he ever held the other one in his arms. Our story ended when we struck a truce, when we stopped trying to finesse one another, when we quit the game of convincing and beguiling. Beware of tolerance between lovers. We are obliging only of those we don't love. The more obliging we are, the less we love the one obliged. Love and tolerance are antagonists. No, they are mortal enemies. Nilo and I, at some point in time, we became *tolerant* of one another. Believing we'd earned it, I saw nothing of peril in the long, unbroken peace we lived and I called it happiness. I named it happiness, the good-natured dance we did, *adagio, adagio*, around the carcass of a long-dead love.'

She stands upright, unties her kitchen-towel turban, rewraps it around her braids, pats it into place, goes then to fetch two baskets from where they hang by the back door, slips them over one arm. She tells me she's going to see what vegetables the others have left in the shed. Weary of groping in that darkish past, I think it's the present Miranda's gone to retrieve as much as the vegetables. No sooner out the door, she comes back in.

'In case you're also wondering if I miss him, I will tell you that I don't. I don't miss Nilo, not he, himself.' She heads out the door, turns back once again. 'Ah, but how I long for the man I thought he was.'

For the man I thought he was. I don't know how much time passes before I hear her shouting, half laughing, from the shed. 'Come and help me with the wine, will you, Chou?'

Some of the mischief back in her gaze, she nods to a demijohn and we begin rolling it the few metres between the shed and the back door into the kitchen.

'And as for *la lupacchiotta*, the she-wolf, everything I've read of hers sounds as though her nostrils quiver when she speaks. *Puzzo sotto il naso* – a stink under the nose.'

Seeking relief in sarcasm, Miranda is pleased with her lampoon and begins to launch another one, but I'm already telling her about the time I tried to speak of Proust to Barlozzo.

'All I did was to ask him if he'd ever read Proust,' I tell Miranda as we position the barrel near the supper table, both of us already laughing.

'And he said, "For pity's sake, an epicene Frenchman rhapsodising over a cake damped in tea, no less. At the least he might have poured himself a thimbleful of *vin santo*. I can't imagine what he might have written had there been a tin of cornmeal biscotti thick with pine nuts and white raisins near to hand . . . Better yet, spaghetti carbonara, the pancetta crisp, a whole hill of pecorino on top, a lovely glass of red . . . I could understand a man getting misty over the taste of that."'

Miranda laughs with only half a heart, the rest of her lingering among the ancient elms with Nilo and the costumeless emperor. Perhaps she's still in the church with *l'altra*. I feel desolate with wanting to bring Miranda back. I try another dose of folly. I tell her about little Biagio. My darling Biagio, an eighty-something farmer from western Tuscany who has long been my friend. Another in the anti-Proust league, he'd start ranting and snorting every time I'd paraphrase Proustian text about twilight: *When the trees are black and the sky is still light . . .*

'Look, Biagio, it's Proust light,' I'd tell him.

'Who the hell is Proust?'

'You know very well who is Proust.'

'And what did he know about light? My grandfather would call all of us out into the vineyard just before twilight. He'd already be there, the legs of his wooden chair stuck into the earth between the vines, his head thrown back, studying the sky. He said he could smell the twilight before it fell. I wonder if Proust ever smelled the twilight. Every damn farmer who's ever ploughed a field at sunset could have told you more and told you better than a body who sat squinting at things from a window.'

'End of that discussion,' I say, knowing it's the end of another one. We are quiet too long before we remember to laugh. But our laughter now has no music and so dies quickly, the foolish repartee impotent against the past where Miranda's eyes still search. She adjusts her headdress, pinches her upper lip between thumb and forefinger, tilts her head to look at me.

'Life's a bungled hobble over thin ice, my love.'

'Always thin, the ice?'

'Mostly thin. Such a foolish sight we must be from some other vantage than our own as we leap, floe to floe, our gathered trifles – mostly worldly – weighing us down and causing much of the bungling.'

As though she can see herself now – a lifetime of leaping, gathering, bungling – Miranda's laugh is raucous, contagious and then my own parade of storms and passions marches before me and, through the strange broken old place on the verges of the Montefiescone Road, my laughing echoes hers.

At last, gasping for air, Miranda says, 'I say we should heed Orazio and prune back hopes for anything more than tonight's supper. And you?'

She's on her feet and out the door to the gravel drive before I can shout, 'Where are you going?'

'To light the lantern. Miranda's back in business for the evening and my truckers need to know. And to hell with the buckets and the rodent holes and will you please go to see what creatures might be hanging in the cheese hut and bring them here so we can get to work? But first, go to Bazzica and use the phone, get Fernando here.'

'We'd already agreed that he would be here at seven so . . .'

'Wonderful. And Filiberto . . . He'll see the lantern lit and come to find out why, but you must still go to Bazzica to telephone Ninuccia. Tell her to bring her supper here and to call the others. They'll all know what to do. '*Vai, vai,* go, go,' she says, first hugging me close then heaving me away as she begins to topple down the tables stacked up along the walls by the nephews. Flapping her great lovely form about the place, she stops only to press the hem of her apron to the weepy midnight blue of her eyes, pulls down another table and another one, lining them up, wiping them down with a kitchen towel dipped in a rainwater bucket and I think that Miranda-of-the-Bosoms, goddess of Buonrespiro, is a queen bee in connubial frenzy. She stops in mid flight, looks at me, 'How I miss him, Chou. I miss Filiberto who is real and I am decidedly not longing for the man I thought was Nilo and I'm thinking that the ice is good and hard this evening and that I'm hungry in my belly and my soul and how dearly I wish Orazio was here. And Barlozzo. Tell Ninuccia to bring a pack of *Toscanelli.*'

'Is that all?'

'*Per ora*, for now.'

PART II

NINUCCIA

'AFTER ALL, I'LL BE SEVENTY-SIX IN FEBRUARY, GOOD ENOUGH reason for me to stay out of the trees, wouldn't you say?'

It's a late afternoon in the first week of December and, having neither seen nor heard from her in a few days, I've telephoned Miranda, asked her if she would join us – the Thursday tribe – tomorrow morning while we work at harvesting olives on a farm belonging to Ninuccia's cousins.

'I wasn't suggesting that you pick but just that you be there with us. We've missed you during these days of the *raccolta* . . . and besides, what has your being seventy-six to do with anything. You've been seventy-six for as long as I've known you.'

'Have I? And for how long has that been?'

'Six years.'

'Do I understand that you are accusing me of approaching my eighty-second birthday?'

'Based on what you, yourself, have told me of your anagraphic history, I am only suggesting that . . .'

'You needn't bother accusing or *suggesting* since it's my life and I like being seventy-six and so I'll just carry on being seventy-six until I feel like being seventy-five. Besides, no one has yet to take me even for sixty-six. Not to my face.'

'All I was trying to tell you is that this is the first year we haven't harvested together in one grove or another . . .'

'Have you been working with Ninuccia?'

'She's been picking in the northern groves with family members while I've been working in the more southern territory with Gilda and a group of Moldavans from Porano. The harvest is just about finished and that's why I wanted you to come tomorrow. The only trees left to strip are the ones on the farthest southern corner below where we've been working, not more than a day's work if some of the others come to help us. Maybe Ninuccia.'

'Good. I've been hoping that you two would spend some time together, get to know one another. Have you decided who'll be your first Thursday partner?'

'Not really. It's not as though any one of them is waving her arms in longing to get into the kitchen with me. I'm not so certain this "cooperative effort" is going to be . . .'

'*Zitta*. Hush. I, myself, I'd begin with Ninuccia.'

'What makes you think she . . .'

'I just do. She's a lovely creature, Ninuccia.'

'Lovely, yes, even though she's the self-appointed president of the International Society for the Supression of Savage Customs.'

'Did you just make that up?'

'No. Thomas Hardy, I think it was.'

'A friend of yours?'

'Not exactly.'

'Well, the title would suit our Ninuccia. Her traditionalism is religious, result, in part, I think, of her long sojourn in the south. Pierangelo is Calabrian, you know, and when they first were married she lived with him down there in some mountain village on the edge of the world. Ninuccia and her stories.'

'More a despot than a storyteller . . .'

'*Appunto*. Exactly. I've always known her family. I remember her as a girl. Hardworking as a mule, a big lumbering gawky sort of girl. Loveable. Her parents delighted in her, despaired for her. No one came to court Ninuccia until Pierangelo. The just-wed girl who set off for Calabria with her love returned a few years later still in Ninuccia's form, the same only in her form, her spirit having been transformed. Dour, withdrawn, save when she was pontificating. From then until now, when she does speak of her life in the south, it's always of the isolation, the beauty of the place. Almost never about people save her mother-in-law whom, it would seem, she adored. How ever it was that they lived up there in those mountains, whatever it was that happened there, it was what shaped Ninuccia.'

'And what shaped her belongs to her. Why would you need to know more?'

'Not a *need*. Her severe facade, such a heavy shield. I think she might long to lay it down once in a while. You know she's fond of you.'

'No. I don't know that and less do I *seek* her fondness . . . Why must you *invent* these . . .'

'Talk to her, Chou.'

'Talk to her about what? I have a hard time getting beyond *buonasera* with her. All we have in common are you and Thursdays. I . . .'

'Why is it that of all the men and women who have been my friends and confidantes and enemies and lovers for these past seventy-some years, why do you suppose it was to you, only you, to whom I've talked to more honestly than I could even to myself? Even to my agonising self, alone in the dark, wishing away thousands of nights?'

I am an uneasy repository for the private truths of others, my own being unwieldly as they are. And yet, more here in Italy than in the other places where I've lived, I have often become the safe one. I am outside the clan and thus outside the clan's judgement. The eternal stranger, a fresh white page. Talking to me is talking to the wind, to the wall. No matter how long I stay, I will always be just passing through. I think that's it. Why else it may or may not be that I am often appointed custodian of another's emotional archives is too elusive for my grasp. *Antonia, Tosca, Floriana, Barlozzo.* Fernando says it's because when someone speaks, I am rapt. No interjections, no comparisons to events or sentiments of my own. As though I am empty, ready and waiting to be filled up with what they long to tell. And everyone longs to tell. Miranda has been talking while I have been wandering in my thoughts and, returning to her, I hear, 'And while you're at it, suggest a Thursday night to celebrate the new oil.'

'While I'm *at what?*'

'Talking to Ninuccia. The new oil. The new wine. Pasta cooked in wine, sauced with oil and cracked pepper and a few gratings of pecorino and then we could . . .'

'So much for permitting me to compose menus. Has there been such great progress on the work in the rustico over the past few weeks or are you ready for another supper among the buckets . . .'

'I was thinking we might use the old mill in Castelpietro where the olives are pressed. The floor is packed earth and the walls are bare stone but there are tables and chairs, a good-enough five-burner gas range bought from a restaurant in Montefiascone years ago. Plenty of pots and pans and the hearth is wonderful: big enough to roast an elk. We would pay Settimio for the wood we burned and . . . Do you know him, Settimio?'

'The mill caretaker. I don't really know him but . . .'

'He'd be thrilled enough to let us use the place. More would he be to sit down to supper with us.'

'Would you speak to him then?'

'Yes, yes. I'll stop by the mill. It'll be grand, Chou. Why didn't I think of this before?'

•

A day later on a morning smelling of snow, there are four of us hitched up in the glittery ruckus of the leaves of ancient trees dripping with purply black fruit. Ninuccia, Gilda, Paolina and I are harvesting together, picking the olives by hand. Picking them one by one. Wrapped in kerchiefs and shawls, a layer of woollies, one of skirt, one of apron poufed out from under two of sweater, we are a sturdy breed of sylph. Shouting to one another across the winds, our collective mood is jubilant on this last morning of the *raccolta* with only twenty or so of the eight hundred-tree grove left to pick. I think how I'll miss sitting up here in the high perch of one tree or another. I look at my old hands, the half-numbed fingers sticking out from cut-off gloves, plucking at the fruit, stripping the limbs and branches, guiding the olives into the basket strapped around my waist. As we finish a tree, climb down the homemade wooden ladders to dump our baskets into the sacks waiting below, we spar over which of the remaining trees 'belongs' to whom.

Each year I wonder if it will be the last one when we pick by hand in this ancient way, since almost every farmer – save those who tend a grove only for the family table – now uses machines that shake the trees until the fruit falls into nets spread on the ground below them, a violent method which bruises the fruit and risks the purity of the oil. The word that's been buzzing about during our work these past days is that Ninuccia's cousins are selling this grove to a consortium. If that's so, the fruit from future harvests of these eight hundred trees will be tossed together with that from groves all over the region and from other regions as well, the mass shipped to a central location to be pressed in a stainless-steel factory and then passed off as prestigious extra-virgin oil. Traditional life is vanishing.

At least this harvest – these olives – are being poured into endless fifty-kilo sacks and loaded onto the beds of old trucks and carted to a stone barn situated just outside the village of Castelpietro. Stacked up by the mill door, the sacks will be carried inside by local boys who, all in good time, hurl the fruit into the crusher to be pummelled and split between great slabs of travertine by the force of a velvet-eyed she-ass harnessed by a rope: a ritual perhaps 4000 years old in these Umbrian hills. Elders of the family will stand guard over the process, all the while crooning to and praising the fat little beast as she plods her circuit. They stop her course often, petting her while she rests and eats and drinks. Miranda is right. The *raccolta* deserves to be celebrated.

With her usual ease Miranda had arranged for our use of the mill for a Thursday night .Next Thursday night to be exact. Three days hence. She had also spoken with Ninuccia. This morning, while I was layering on my clothes and preparing to get to work, Ninuccia came to me, started in naming dishes her family had always cooked for the harvest, rattled off what there was waiting to be picked from her garden, what herbs and vegetables were already strung and set to dry in her attic.

'Of course it's yours to decide . . . the menu, I mean. But listen, when we've finished with the harvesting this morning let's go to the mill and talk a bit. I'll tell Gilda and Paolina to come, too, and we can make a lunch of wine and bread and oil. Also, I left a pot of beans there on my way here this morning, nourishment for my cousins, the old ones who stay at the mill all day long.'

'I'll telephone Miranda.'

'If I know her, she'll be there before us. But surely, call her. *Va bene?*'

'*Va benissimo.*'

●

It is nearly one o'clock when we four climb down from the last trees and – chilled and starving and triumphant – make our way up onto the bed of an old blue truck to collapse among the sacks of olives. Laughing and shouting and wishing we had wine to warm us, we are a quartet of Cleopatras being carted ceremonially through the grove to the mill by a handsome young charioteer called Gianmario.

One of the cousins is toasting bread in the hearth, smearing it with the new oil, thick as honey and green as jade. Jugs of wine and a collection of tumblers are set out on a long wooden table where Ninuccia's beans wait in a deep, black-speckled terracotta pot. Half-dried figs threaded on butcher's twine hang from iron hooks on the stone wall behind the table and Gilda takes down a string, pulls the still plump fruit free and begins slicing it thickly, pressing the pieces onto the hot oiled bread and offering the trenchers to the old cousins, to us. To the she-ass. It is the first time I'd ever eaten figs on bread. How delicious but how strange I thought until I thought again, of Fig Newtons and then of raisin bread and then of my favourite biscuits, the ones stuffed with dried apricots. Dried fruit and something bread-like or cake-like to embrace it. Breaking through my Fig Newton reverie, one of the cousins announces, *'E arrivata la Miranda.'*

Miranda has arrived. Am I mistaken or did he take off his cap, smooth his hair, place it back with a certain precision? Miranda-of-the-Bosoms – at seventy-six plus six – can still make the little boys cry. Sure enough the thrum of her *ape* – a three-wheeled, two-seat truck with a miniscule flatbed and tiny motor that sounds like a buzzing bee – sputters to silence and, in two beats, she shambles through the door, unwrapping her shawls, begins ladling out the beans and their good-smelling winey broth, refilling tumblers with the brawny teeth-staining red, asking after each of us, greeting the cousins and the she-ass. She takes a small piece of untoasted bread, holds it under the spout where the crushed, but not yet pressed, olives are sliding out in a dense, creamy paste. Letting a few drops of it fall onto the bread, she bites into it.

Glorioso, she says and the cousins pat one another on the back as though they, instead of the rain and the sun and the wind and the hundred-year-old lymph coursing through the trees, had made the olives good.

Sitting herself down at the table with us, she reaches for the bottle of oil, pours out a few drops onto the fleshy part of her palm just below the thumb and sucks at the oil, rolling her eyes in delight.

'The only way to taste new oil,' she says, laughing and smacking her lips. 'There's a pepper mill around here somewhere if anyone wants it for the figs. Am I to understand that this little convention is going about the work of resuming Thursday suppers?'

'I think it will be,' I tell her. 'It was warmth and wine and food we were after first, though. I was just about to . . .'

Having helped herself to the beans, Miranda interrupts, 'The oregano is good in the beans. Just enough. *Brava,*' she says glancing at Ninuccia and nodding her head, her mouth turned down in a gesture of admiration. Shifting her gaze then to me, she asks, 'So what will you cook, Chou?'

'To begin, *crostate di olivada*' – free-form rounds of cornmeal pastry folded and pleated over part of the olive pesto. A lattice work of pastry over the middle. We would use the new oil in the pastry and also in the *olivada*. 'I think it's good to use what's left of last year's olives – the ones we brined and dried. And, in the same dish, to use the new oil. You know, old and new. Round.'

'Chou must always have a story with her bread,' Miranda says. '*Bene, d'accordo*. Good, I agree. And then?'

'I would cook pasta in *novello* – *in the new wine*.'

'An ancient method.' This is Gilda.

'Right,' I say, relieved not to have been countered. 'It's the only way dried pasta was cooked for centuries . . . boiling it in water is a relatively novel notion. From the middle of the ninteenth century, I think.'

Apart from Gilda, who is nodding her assent, the others swivel their heads in concert, looking to Miranda to dash this blasphemy. But she sits quietly, her silence a consent.

I wait a few beats before saying, 'The method is almost the same as for risotto. A little new oil warmed in the pot with a minced onion, the raw pasta is then tossed about to coat it well, kept moving in the hot oil until it takes on a golden crust . . .'

'Like the *tostatura* for rice?' wonders Paolina, her shock softened by the comfort of something familiar.

'Exactly. Then – also like for risotto – begin adding the wine in small doses, stirring the pasta until the wine is absorbed. Add more wine, let the pasta drink it in. Add more. Small doses. In about twelve minutes the pasta becomes rosy, perfectly al dente and all plumped with the wine. In this case the only sauce would

be a bit more oil, some pepper and . . .' Here I falter, not quite
ready to tell them how I'll finish the dish. I'm grateful when
Miranda steps in.

'*E poi*, and then? What will be next?'

'Loins of caramelised pork braised in more *novello* with . . .'
I hesitate again before saying, 'with prunes and cloves and
cinnamon and . . .'

I look to Ninuccia, see her perplexity. *This strange American;
prunes with her pork?* But it's Paolina who saves me, she having
sifted through childhood to find a memory.

'I remember that my mother would make a braise of pork
with dried prunes. And spices, too. Cinnamon. Surely she used
cinnamon. But I don't know if she cooked it in wine or broth. It
must have been wine . . .'

Now it's Ninuccia who recalls: 'I remember a neighbour
woman who came to help each December when we slaughtered
a pig. She was from Lubriano, or maybe it was Bagnoregio, but
anyhow she would make a kind of sausage with trimmings and
prunes and spices, shape the paste into ovals and fry them dark
and crisp. We'd stand by the stove, my cousins and I, wait for
her to stuff one or two between thin slices of bread. We'd grab
them and run away fast as we could, out of the house and up into
the woods, clutching the hot little parcels tight to our chests as
though someone would try to steal them. How good they were.
I don't know why we always ran up into the woods with them
rather than just inhale them on the spot. I wonder. I hadn't
thought about that in forty years.'

I watch Miranda watching the others, listening to them, and I think she is content for this small exchange of memory and nostalgia. Miranda, too, *must always have a story with her bread.*

'And then don't you think we should have something with chestnuts?' I ask. 'Fried chestnut-flour cakes with raisins. And chestnuts cooked in spiced wine. The tastes of these are like a reprise of the pork . . . continuation. In fact, the little cakes and the drunken chestnuts could be served *with* the pork. It would all work together.'

'*Adesso, io ho fame.* Now I'm hungry,' says Ninuccia.

'*Anch'io.* Me, too,' says an old cousin who'd seated himself, prick-eared, at the end of the table with his tumbler and a pitcher of wine, intent on our homey discourse. Miranda shoos him away and, as he moves back toward his watch over the grinding stones, he turns around and says, '*A Natale ci sposeremo.* At Christmas, we'll be married.'

'*Scemo, cretino.*' She calls him a fool, a cretin, her blush belying her pleasure.

Everyone putters about clearing the table and washing up, each one saying what she'll bring along to the mill later that evening or in the morning to contribute to the supper. I'm about to leave, too, when Ninuccia says, 'Wait a bit, won't you? *Faccio un caffè,*' she says, riffling through a cupboard drawer for the parts to a Bialetti.

I'm tired and want mostly to get home to Fernando and to a bath and a rest, to think about our own Thursday supper. But having found all the pieces to the little pot, she's already packed it tightly with ground espresso, set it on the flame. I sit down again, take off my shawl and wonder – has she waited until now to tell me her impressions of the dishes I talked about? I am thinking that I do like this Ninuccia. And that maybe I do *seek* her friendship. Or is it Miranda's powers of suggestion at work?

An elbow on the table, I rest my chin in the hollow of my hand and watch her fussing about the cups and searching for sugar. A great mass of bound Titian hair, her skin is pale and freckled, the congregation of spots, heavy on her cheeks and across her nose, makes a coppery mask under eyes grey and soft as pussywillow; she might be an Irishwoman as soon as an Umbrian one. She is sixty-six, so she said not long ago, though she looks to be far younger, her small breasts high and proud under her sweater, her hips wide, muscular, hers is a body shaped by a life of physical labours. Pouring out the coffee, she sings softly in a minor key, the words in a dialect I don't understand. She sits down across from me.

'Did you know that I lived in Calabria when Pierangelo and I were first married?'

I nod, yes, but I don't speak.

'Have you been there? Oh, I don't mean to the beaches or . . .'

'I've been in the mountains.'

'Ah, well, then you know a bit how *different* it can be . . . there from here. Another country. Another world. It's not as though I'd come from a wealthy home but, whatever we might have done without, our table was always full. Full enough. What I'm trying to say is that how I lived down there with Pierangelo and his mother and the others in that mountain village, well, that time left its mark. Not a scar, mind you, but an impact, still fresh. It shows in almost everything I do but, especially, it shows in how I cook. We Umbrians are mostly frugal, restrained – unlike the Emilians and the Lombards, for instance, or the Sicilians when they've the means to embroider. But it has become my nature to be . . . Spartan. I guess that's the word. So I hope you'll understand if I ask . . . don't you think your menu is . . . well, let's say that if the Sumptuary laws were still . . .' She laughs rather than finishes her query. I am smiling, thinking how she is hardly the first person to accuse me of culinary lavishness. Ninuccia continues, '*Una bontá, sicuramente*, very good certainly but, Thursday suppers have always been, well, less themed, less formal, less complicated. *Cosa c'é, c'é.* You know, "What there is, there is". That was my mother-in-law's daily expression. Thrice daily. She could make supper out of sticks. I wonder if, in her whole life, she'd ever sat down to a supper like you've described.'

'She, your mother-in-law, is she . . .'

'She died a long time ago. When Pierangelo and I decided to move back up here to work my father's farm, we begged her, begged and beseeched her to come with us but . . . Her home had a floor just like this one.' Looking down, she pounds the toe of her boot onto the packed dirt. 'Being poor in Calabria is akin to misery.' Raising her eyes back to mine, she says, 'She was very tall, dark-skinned, night-black eyes, so black they looked silver. Not big, her eyes, but long like wide slits of light in the smooth darkness of her face. Cosima, she was called.'

'You are very much describing your husband. His eyes are . . .'

'They are. Just like hers. Pierangelo Santacaterina. Such a name. Eleven syllables. I loved him instantly.'

'Calabria, Umbria, how did you find one another?'

'I was nearing twenty-five, a perilous age to be still a virgin since, back then, it was somewhere shy of thirty when *una ragazza singola,* an unmarried girl, was edged over into the rank of *la zitella,* an old maid. Not only had I yet to live a love story but, worse, I'd yet to dream one. I was too happy, too full being my parents' child, my brother's sister, my larger family's *preferita,* their favourite.

'Though I didn't understand it then, my father worked toward this extended "adolescence" of mine. Subtly, he schemed to insure it: "The world is evil. Stay at home as long as you can." He kept me tethered tight as a wayward goat but most fathers did in those days. Sometimes in their own interest, I admit. My father, though, he was gentle and proper as he was devoted.

'He drove me to school in the *ape* and either he or my brother was there to fetch me when class ended. No matter where I went, someone from the family always went with me. As I think about it, they needn't have bothered so much about me. I was plain and timid and awkward, a trio of barriers potent as black plague when it came to keeping the boys away. And by some standards, we were poor – that might have been the cherry. But I didn't mind much. I was a *pataciona,* a big potato, mature in body, a little girl in spirit. I really don't recall suffering for this sentimental exclusion by my peers. I do, however, remember that my maternal grandmother could make me cry.

'Before every meal for the two summer months when she stayed with us, she would take the day's *pagnotta* and go to sit in her chair by the spent hearth. Tucking the great loaf neatly under her chins, resting it like a violin on the shelf of her bosom, she'd slice at the bread in the exuberant sawing motions of capriccio – always toward her – the pieces falling into a basket she held tight between her knees. As though the feat itself were not enough of a spectacle, she also talked to me while she sawed: how to fix my hair or my dress, when to wear the gold hoop earrings, when to wear the ones with little red stones. Was I washing my face with olive oil twice a week? The times I hated most, though, were when she would pull a length of butcher's twine from her pocket, turn me to face the wall, stretch the string taut against my backside then hold out the length of it for me to see, tsk, tsking, saying, "And this is only half the circumference of those prosperous hips of yours, *amore mio.*" That damn piece of string haunted me. She'd pull it out once a week and put me through the same agony. She'd always end the event by saying, "Ninuccia, Ninuccia . . . all that white meat of yours." Anyway, after what she'd sliced of the *pagnotta* for breakfast and lunch, there wasn't so much left of the two-kilo loaf by suppertime. Still she sawed and still she talked until the heel of it hit the basket. She'd always close her performance with the same line: "It wants a rather particular sort to court a girl like you."

'It was she, this grandmother of mine, who made me feel odd and strange and unworthy. I might have borne those sensations for always save that, one afternoon, Pierangelo Santacaterina stopped by.'

All this while as she was speaking, Ninuccia gazed up and down and beyond where we sat. Everywhere but at me. As though I was in a room nearby, the door ajar – clandestine, mute – she wanted me to *hear* her story rather than tell it to me. Neither a question nor an affirmation, she would suffer no hindrance to memory's course. Ninuccia's was a soliloquy.

'I'd been weeding in the *orto*, barefoot, bent to the earth, skirt kilted to my hips, fairly blind from the sun. My first glimpse of him was upside down, between my legs. He scared me so I screeched and nearly fell over trying to right myself. Shading my eyes with both hands, I tried to see him, and asked: "*Chi desidera? Who do you desire?*" He laughed and shook his head and laughed again, finally saying he had an appointment with my father. I think I gestured to the house, "*Si accomodi.* Be comfortable." I remember sliding my kerchief from my head, letting my hair down, wiping my face with that sweat-soaked thing, stumbling a few times before getting my feet to move in synchrony so I could run off toward the field where my father was working.

But how did this Calabrian find his way to us? you must be wondering. Essentially it was via the clans. *'Ndrangheta.* The Calabrian mafia. That is, the Calabrian mafia in its most delicate incarnation. As so many men – and boys, too – were and are wont to do in those parts, Pierangelo made his living doing the clans' bidding. You see, a few days before Pierangelo's appearance on the farm my father had been refused a loan at the *Cassa di Risparmio* in Orvieto. Bankers are often as diffident to modest desires as they are malleable to excessive ones. Pierangelo was entrenched in an unofficial partnership with the very banker who refused my father. This banker would purposefully decline requests for relatively small short-term loans and then send his "partner" – in the guise of an independent estimator – to view the needy person's property or land or machinery, and, after lengthy deliberation, agree to lend the funds, if at a somewhat higher rate of interest than the bank's. Distilled, Pierangelo and the banker were in league with a band of *truffatori* – swindlers, thieves, forgers, usurers. Having first put the banker in place, Pierangelo's clan then sent him north to have a go at the Umbrian pigeons set up by the banker. That's how Pierangelo Santacaterina came to Umbria. And for some mystical reason, which I have yet to comprehend, he wanted me: me, *la pataciona*.

'After that first sighting – Pierangelo of me and I of him – the business of the loan turned to figment, pretext for his further visits to my father. I would pass through the *salotto* as they sat with their grappa and their discourse and station myself – skirt fanned, legs crossed in feint nonchalance – on the veranda to await his arrivals and departures. Much later would my father tell me that, on his second visit, Pierangelo Santacaterina asked him for my hand. Dismissing ritual queries and a decorous phase of observation, my father surrendered to the sufficiency of his instinct and to, what he perceived to be, the will of the Fates. My father told Pierangelo Santacaterina that he believed I was already his.

'When he began to court me and spend Sundays at our place, everyone was all a titter. "*Ninuccia ha un ragazzo. E che ragazzo, mamma mia.*" As handsome as he is now, when he was twenty-five, he could stop your breath. Even my grandmother loved him. She began the butcher-string business with him, too, measuring not his backside but his shoulders and, as dismayed as she was with my measurement, that's how thrilled she was with his. She took to measuring me with one string, he with another. Then she'd stretch the two strings, one against the other, demonstrating that they were just about equal: the breadth of Pierangelo's shoulders and that of my backside. Ach. But I was speaking of Cosima, wasn't I?

'Pierangelo spoke often and lovingly of his mother. "She and home are the same thing for me. Now you and she are my home." I'd never met Cosima until Pierangelo and I – married two days before in the town hall in Orvieto – made our way, in his heroic nineteen-year-old white Cinquecento, up into the isolation of the Aspromonte.

'*Aspromonte*, bitter mountain. My husband had, at length and most candidly, spoken of the village where he was born and had always lived, enumerating on the fingers of both his hands the perils, the hardships, the dissimilarities between the modest idyll of my Umbrian life and the one I would meet in Acquapendente di Sopra, a village of sixty-three souls, "if no one's died or been born since Christmas when I was last there". Sixty-three souls, some of them damned, he said. Shaking my head, muffling his warning speeches with my hand or my mouth, all I wanted was him. But he would persist: "Many of the men stay down in the seaside villages to fish, selling their catch to the restaurants, only wandering back up to the mountains once a week for conjugal visits, to leave a wad of bills, often thin. When called upon they perform simple favours for the clans. Or more complex ones, as I did with the banker. But that's over now. I'll invent something else. No, of course not. Nothing dangerous. Nothing at all that's dangerous." As we withdrew that afternoon further into the wilderness, I began to feel a kind of qualm, mild enough at first before building to a tease, to a menace and causing my chatter to sound tinny, far away. Someone else's noise. I would look at my husband who looked only ahead, the muscles in his face rippling under flesh gone white. *Nothing dangerous. Nothing at all that's dangerous.*

'Hung from a mountain spur two thousand metres above the sea, the village seemed a pile of Iron Age stones relieved here and there by a ruin from the epochs of the Greeks and the Romans. Though people were about the narrow lanes in front of and between the houses, so pure was the silence that I'd thought to have lost the capacity to hear. Later Pierangelo would explain to me that it wasn't silence I heard but the great, incessant noise of streams and torrents and waterfalls that surrounded the place. *Aquapendente*, falling waters. It was the raucous crashing of water that I took for silence.

'Pierangelo stopped the auto in a curve of the unpaved road in front of a long, narrow stone building that would have seemed abandoned were it not for wisps of woodsmoke rising from four chimneys and window curtains of bright-coloured cloth swelling in the breeze. Four separate dwellings were suggested by as many wooden doors, one of them opened to reveal a room not two metres high, a bed and a chair filling its whole space. A small flock of scraggy, brownish sheep were being rallied through the lanes by two despotic dogs and I remember waiting until the parade passed before opening the auto door. And then I saw Cosima. She'd come, unnoticed by me, to within a metre or so of us and there she stood, arms crossed over her chest, weeping and smiling. In a shapeless black dress and men's shoes too large, she was a romantic figure, a kind of timid enchantress from whom someone had stolen her real clothes. I waited for Pierangelo to go to her but he sat quietly in his seat. I stepped out and Cosima stepped closer – another kind of love at first sight. Gathering me to her, saying a few words of welcome, our sympathies were immediate, reciprocal, tender. All that I loved about my husband was *authenticated* in her. His cautionary tales he needn't have told but rather he should have trusted his mother to be also mine, and to know that both would be my shelter.

'Cosima's house was the most spacious of the four in the low stone dwelling with its blue shale roof and paint-peeled doors. The walls she whitewashed every Easter and Christmas and the packed-earth floor had so long been swept and trod upon that it had the texture and the sheen of stone. In the sitting room there were white-painted iron sconces on the walls, only occasionally stuck with light bulbs, hand-hewn chairs also painted white, a kind of sofa strewn in a length of salvaged boat sail from the seaside markets and a woodpile laid neat and even. In the kitchen there were four more chairs about a small square wooden table scrubbed nearly to splintering and a pile of plates in a basket by the hearth. Three pots hung from the stones above the hearth shelf, though two were for show since Cosima always reached for the same one no matter what she was about to cook. In the sleeping room there was a small white bed and a trunk larger than it on which stood two tall silver candlesticks, almost garish in that setting, about which she never spoke. Only a sheaf of evergreen or a bottle stuck with wildflowers intruded upon the shades of white in Cosima's house and the dark figure of her moving about against the pale light there made a *quadro vivente*, primitive, calming.

'The sail-clothed sofa became Cosima's bed and there was never a word of bickering among us about her will to relinquish the sleeping room: "The sofa had been Pierangelo's and now it will be mine. The bed had been mine and now it will be yours." Cosima had a wondrous way of weeding her discourse, plunging as she did to the marrow of a thing. And her talk reflected her resolve, her ideas slow-ripening as mountain fruit. She seemed free of dilemma. Hers was a road straight, cleared of obstacles, immutable. Divine in its way. Even her wrath she managed with serenity. No bile, no hackles, never demurring from her path, she could unburden rage as genteelly as she could embrace peace. "Lament is futile. Scorn makes bitterness. Vendetta soothes," she would say.

'Pierangelo soon slipped back into the life he'd led before his sojourn to Umbria. Before us. Setting out with his former mates to fish for tuna, he'd stay away for three or four days, return for one or two, before going off again. I knew it wasn't always to the sea where Pierangelo went. Normal as raising sheep or fishing the seas, working a job now and then for the clans. "We all do it. Nothing dangerous. I told you, nothing dangerous at all."

'Meanwhile I learned more about my mother-in-law. Unsought, unacknowledged by her, Cosima had long ago been assigned to the province of myth by the women of Acquapendente di Sopra, she having ministered to two generations of them since she was in her early adolescence. In her men's black shoes and her shapeless black dress, loping over the fields or between the lanes, she'd be bent on birthing babies, washing the dead, keeping vigil over the sick. Pulling an anise cake from her basket, the perfumed thing still warm from her hearth, she could light up gloom by walking through the door. But her more constant sympathies Cosima reserved for the seven women who lived within her nearest reach in the three houses attached to hers.

'Save when they slept or on the occasions when their husbands or sons were at home, the seven and Cosima were together. In summer they cooked in the spare kitchen of the deconsecrated church's cellar where it was cool. In winter when the cellar was cheered only by a small hearth by which hermit monks once warmed themselves, they cooked together there as well, neither knowing how to nor desiring to live separately from one another. Bringing shaped and risen loaves covered with cloths to the communal oven, which sat in a clearing of oak scrub just outside the village, they'd settle themselves on stones or among the weeds with their knitting while their bread baked. On Mondays, they mounted their washing in baskets on their heads and walked to one or another of the nearby streams, whichever one was rushing good and fast. At noon they ate bread and cheese from their pockets and, at sunset, laid supper on a table in the front lane when it was fair or piled together in one of their houses or back in the church cellar when it was cold. The table cleared away, their kitchen chairs in a half circle in the lane, they'd once again pick up their needles and yarn and talk and work and sing. *Santo cielo,* sainted heaven, how they could sing. Not an alto among them, they raised their seven soprano voices in a blaze of plainsong or chanted and keened as women before them had chanted and keened in those mountains for thousands of years, their sounds visceral, their pitch mesmeric, orgasmic, sweetening, finally, almost to a whisper.

'And so I went about my days as they did theirs, blithe as well-loved children. Their almost breezy sanguinuity sprang, it seemed, from their abiding concern for one another, each one trusting the others to be thinking of her while she was thinking of them. Though those who were widows – Cosima and two others – were pensioned by the State and the others supported, more or less, by their husbands, their economic lives were mostly operated collectively. Whoever had, shared. Cosima was their purser. They worked an *orto*, kept hens and raised rabbits, and bartered lamb and cheese from the shepherds. They decided upon things by "committee": who was to get her boots repaired, her knives sharpened, her teeth fixed, how much wood was to be cut, which mattresses were to be restuffed. What they didn't grow in their *orto* or forage in the meadows and the woods, they bought from the *fruttivendolo ambulante,* the travelling fruit and vegetable wagon, on Saturday. And to supplement mean times – their own or, more often, those of their neighbours – they sold their handiwork: prized by the fancy women of Reggio and Catanzaro were the table covers and bedspreads of vast dimension and heirloom design, which were crocheted by the women of Acquapendente di Sopra from white cotton string, tea-dyed to a pallid amber brown. And what they didn't knit or sew, they would fetch in the markets, riding down the mountain to Reggio in the Thursday or the Saturday bus several times a year. You will recall that it was 1969 when I arrived in Acquapendente di Sopra. That these women lived then in that cloistered self-sufficiency seems an imponderable truth. Having so little, they were free to have everything.'

•

Never asking me if I'd wanted another caffè, Ninuccia has been up and down, slapping the wet grains from the Bialetti into the sink, rinsing all its parts, spooning out more ground espresso, packing it into place, filling the pot with water. Never breaking the stride of her story, she lights the burner, sits down. We avoid one another's gaze. I don't want to hear more of this story. I don't want this Cosima to be relegated to fable. I want to know her. I am wishing that I *was* her. At the least, I want to be there with her, with all of them. I belong there. I'm certain of this. How can it be that I am feeling the loss of a woman I never knew, would never know? I think of their soprano voices in the evening, under the mountains.

My throat tightens, tears threaten. I think how absurd is this response of mine to the women of Acquapendente di Sopra. I will drink this fresh caffè and then explain to Ninuccia that I really must go. First I will steer our talk to the present. To the less remote past.

'I never knew it was you who began the Thursday Night Suppers. I mean, with Miranda.'

'Those Marvellous Thursday Nights, that's what Cosima called them. Yes, yes, it was me who carried the idea home to Miranda years ago when I returned from Calabria. Missing life with

Cosima and the women as I did, I'd hoped to feed my nostalgia for those nights in the mountains by raising up some kinship here in Umbria. Of course, it was not at all the same. I should never have expected it to be. What they had and who they were in Calabria and what we have and who we are here . . . was *unequal*. Discordant. How could I expect to satisfy them with what had delighted Cosima's tribe?'

'I would cook a pot of beans, not so different from that one over there, and call it Thursday Night Supper. There were more of us back then, sometimes as many as twenty squeezed into the rustico. I'd ladle out beans or some thick soup of barley and spelt scented with whatever herbs were near. Bread, wine. Of course, there was always cheese. Once I made *la polenta in catene* – cornmeal in chains – thin cornmeal mixed with stewed white beans spooned into deep bowls over bread. Filiberto called it war food. He remembered his father hanging a sardine from a string tied to the light above the kitchen table; the oil dripping from the little fish was the only condiment for his family's nightly polenta during the meanest years. His father never changed the sardine for another until only bones swung from the string.

'"We'd cut a piece of the flat, yellow pudding, swipe it across the sardine, trying to wet it with the little fish's salty oil," Filiberto told us. "There was watered wine until that ran out. Nothing of bread."

'Filiberto's stories led to Miranda's,' Ninuccia says.

'Not only at your table,' she said, trying for Miranda's voice. My family fared better than most of our ilk, I having begun working as maid and kitchen apprentice for the Giacomini when I was sixteen. I'm not telling you that their stores allowed the usual five-course lunch and the thick soups and cheeses and dry sausages and six or seven *conserva di frutta*, which composed their light supper of an evening. Deep pockets, the black market, they 'arranged' things. Everyday Cook sent me home with almost enough to feed my family. Six of us and my mother – my father already gone by that time. Cook and also Signora Giacomini, I think, knew I supplemented their gifts with my own mild thieving – mostly soap and flour. A kilo of flour consoled my mother. Soap, too. At least her children would be clean, would have bread. My brothers were apprentices of a sort, too, running and fetching for the Partigiani even though the youngest was ten when things went bad. Sometimes one of them would come home with a sack of eggs, as many as five or six, and I think it was those eggs that saved us as much as anything. I've always thought it was the eggs. I took to bringing Giorgia, then nine or ten, with me to the Giacomini each morning, knowing that Cook would sit her down, fill a bowl with some sort of pap – sometimes a piece of bread with sugar. Can you imagine sugar during the war? The grace of the Giacomini gave way, though, when I trooped in with two cousins, the daughters of my mother's sister, who was faring less well than we. They were kind about drawing the line but draw it they did. Years afterward I remember my aunt telling how they survived for weeks and months on a prized two-kilo tin of salted Spanish anchovies. I remember that tin – wedged between the more usual goods – in the kitchen armoire. It had been there for years, maybe as many as ten, as though my aunt knew to save it. Red and blue and *foreign*-looking. Sometimes I would pull it forward on the shelf, finger all the writing on it that I couldn't read. A gift from someone who'd travelled to Spain. I don't remember who. When there was nothing left but sacks of polenta, my aunt opened the tin, her two tiny girls standing on chairs to watch her. The story goes that, without bothering to rinse away their preserving salt, she mashed a few of the fish to a paste, mixed in whatever broth she'd brewed that morning from wild herbs and then spread the mess thinly over their nightly polenta.

"'Ninuccia's polenta is hardly war food," Miranda told Filiberto that evening, mortifying him as much with her gaze as with her words. It was the first time I'd ever heard her speak with pure contempt. Not the last, though. I think it was when she told us that story of the anchovies that I knew I loved Miranda. I think it was that night. In any case, Filiberto sought immediate reparation by rising from his place, coming to me, taking both my hands, kissing the palms. Once back in his chair, he looked at Miranda. After a moment or two he said:

Winter was the worst: being hungry and being cold, too. We had snow one year, an unusual amount. Surely it was the first snow of my own young life. Exciting as it was, it faded soon enough to tedium. We'd just kneel in front of the window watching it fall. One morning, a hungry morning, my father wrapped us in some sort of shawl or blanket, brought us to the door, opening it to a moaning wind. He said, 'Look out there, do you see it? Do you see all that bread under the snow? Can't you see it? Close your eyes, imagine all that germination going on deep under the insulating snow. When it melts, even though the earth will still be brown and bare, there'll be bright shoots sticking their heads straight up to the sun. Acres of young wheat. Loaves and loaves of good crusty bread.' Of course it was a lie. Sometimes all we have are lies.

'We others were not old enough to remember the war, some of us not yet born. We listened to the polenta stories and the bread-growing-under-the-snow as to fables but when the solemn moment passed the tribe sat, forks pointing north, waiting for what would next be brought to table. The first of my suppers were not a successs.

'But Miranda had understood what I'd had in mind to make of Thursday nights and so she began to help me, to choose and cook dishes that, though they resonated less abundant times, had some chance at pleasing.

'One time we begged lambs' innards from the butcher who bought stock from Filiberto, and brought them back to the rustico almost still pulsing. We set pancetta and salt pork to melt over a quiet flame with rosemary, onion, garlic and peperoncino and gilded it all until the smell it sent up set our mouths to watering. Meanwhile we chopped the innards almost to a pulp and added them to the pot, marrying them to the hot, perfumed fat. A little sea salt, a litre of red, tomato conserve, all of it distilling down to a delectable mash to spread on thick slabs of roasted bread.

Miranda called it *soffritto di agnello,* said it was a piquant second
cousin to the traditional Roman dish *coratella* (lamb innards
stewed in white wine with fennel and sage) and even closer kin
to the *lampredotto* of the Tuscans (veal stomach stewed with
tomato, onion, celery and spooned onto trenchers of crusty bread).
Il soffritto won a restrained sort of applause but, as before, the
group sniffed about for what would come next and then next
after that.

'Once Miranda and I bartered with the Catanzarese in the
market: eight dozen baby artichokes for two rounds of Filiberto's
pecorino. The colour of violets and tiny as a baby's fist, 20
centimetres of leafy stem. All we did was light the wood oven,
peel the stems, cut them in two and let them sit in lemon water
for half an hour. Into three oiled terracotta dishes, we laid them
down in a single layer, poured in white wine – only about half
an inch – then dusted them with sea salt and bread crumbs, gave
them a good dose of oil and let them roast slowly until their
chokeless hearts were soft. Then we heaved on fistful of grated
pecorino, poured on another thread of oil and slid the dishes back
into the oven until the cheese went bronze. The group poked at
the tiny little crisped things, spooned one or two out to taste, all
the while mumbling that no decent artichoke was roasted but
braised in white wine with lemon and mint, this latter another
dish that the Umbrians borrow from the Roman canons. Eight
people devoured ninety-six artichokes, slid bread in the juices
of the terracotta dish closest to them, moved brazenly to polish
juices in the further territory of the other dishes. *"Buoni, buoni
davvero, ma adesso?* Good, very good, but now?"

'"*Le frittate di bruscandoli,* wild asparagus omelettes," I told them, proud as if the dishes I carried from behind the bedsheet curtain were set with truffle-stuffed songbirds. I was so excited to tell them about the gifts from the gods Miranda and I had found on the far hillside behind the sheepfold, a great patch of the skinny brown twig-like things, which make only a fleeting spring appearance but almost never in any but sparse quantity. A savour to which no cultivated asparagus could ever aspire, they taste like roasted hazelnuts. Delicate . . .'

•

'You mean, *luppoli,* hops. *Bruscandoli* are wild hops and not asparagus at all but there is great controversy among the cognoscenti over this distinction. I would wait for them every May to arrive by boat from the island of Sant'Erasmo to the Rialto. For risotto. However many the foragers would bring to the markets, the chefs from Harry's Bar always got most of the bounty. But I managed. I'd begin my haunting of the marketeers for them around Easter time. I . . .'

Ninuccia will not tolerate interruption. This one of mine was made of words she hadn't heard. Before I finish speaking, she proceeds: 'As you know, Miranda had – long before this beginning of the Thursday Nights – begun to offer supper three or four evenings a week to the truckers and the nearby farm families. And it was that uniquely Miranda sort of supper that they all expected on Thursday nights. The group wholly embraced the idea of sitting down to supper together in the rustico every Thursday but how and what I longed to feed them, they did not embrace at all.'

Having been looking down at her hands or perusing the room while she spoke, Ninuccia takes a breath, looks at me.

'A grand part of why I bewailed the thought of you in the rustico kitchen was raised up from the unhealed part of my old resentment at having failed to please the others. If I couldn't, how could you? Of all people, why should it be a stranger who would cook for us? I remain distrustful, I want you to know that. Wary. I'm wary still but less so for two reasons: I know that Miranda will be hovering and that one of us will always be there to keep you in line, save you from committing foolishness. As I said, I wanted you to know all that.'

'Good.' I smile at her. Having expected something of defence from me, she waits, lifts her gaze to mine before looking down again at her hands, perusing the room.

'In any case, I stopped bringing my pots of soup or beans and Miranda pushed her sack of polenta to the back of the armoire. Every Tuesday we all brought what we had to her and every Thursday Miranda cooked for us.'

'Every Thursday until . . .'

'Until now. But how far I've wandered. From Cosima. From the mountains.'

'You must be tired and . . .'

'No, no. Not at all, not tired,' she says, raising a hand to cover her smile, an uncommonly girlish gesture for Ninuccia. 'The truth is that I never wander very far from her. From Cosima. From the mountains. Never very far. I still compare them, you know. The Thursday Nights there, ours here. A foolish exercise. *Quei Meravigliosi Giovedì Sera*. Those Marvellous Thursday Nights with

Cosima. Though the theme was the same as every other night
– *cosa c'è, c'è*– what there is, there is – little fistful of hoarded
things would appear on the Thursday work tables. Cosima and
the others would take stock and get to work. A favourite dish
was one of long, slender sweet green capsicums stuffed with old
bread softened in white wine, dried olives, raisins, pine nuts,
capers, pecorino, bits of lamb if they had it, an egg, maybe two,
and handfuls of wild greens if it was spring. Laid on a grate high
over the slow fire they took turns roasting them, painting them
with oil, gently turning them until they blistered, plumped, a tin
underneath to catch their juices. There'd be a sauce ready to pour
over the hot things, a smash of garlic, oil, lots of onion shaved
thin, red wine vinegar added to the hot juices in the tin. How
good they were. And we drank wine on Thursdays, shunning
the water pitcher.

'Cosima always baked her *anisella*. With a quarter-litre jar and
a screw top in her pocket, she'd walk the two kilometres or so
through the woods to the *bottiglieria*, the tiny wine dispensary,
to fetch a dose of anisette. Eggs, oil, sugar, flour and anise seeds
toasted in a hot pan, she'd pour the batter into a round tin, large
and shallow, cover it with a pot lid, reversed and filled with hot
embers, and settle the whole into the white hot ash of her hearth.

'On Thursday Nights the women dressed as they might for
mass had there been a priest to celebrate it. And if there *had*
been a priest, I'd have wondered at the women's will to share
their pagan affinities for an hour with he and Mother Church.
The old goddesses were their confidantes, their undisputed
authorities and, being so familiar with them, they'd call upon

Hera and Hestia, Aphrodite, Artemis and Demeter, as they would neighbours from a village down the mountain. They knew too much, the women of Acquapendente di Sopra. They knew that the clans and the Church and the State were as united a family as the Father, Son and Holy Ghost. But there I go again, wandering.

'In any case, the women's toilettes were enhanced on Thursdays, all of them primping in their way, patting *Borotalco* from a green and gold tin over freshly bathed bodies, braiding hair or twisting it into intricate knots, festooning themselves with bits of matriarchal jewels and a change of dress. The eldest was forty-eight, the youngest perhaps forty and it was she who, with a sharpened wedge of wood burnt to charcoal, would, always on a Thursday, draw black lines along the slant of her eyelids and I swear those two lines changed how she moved, how she spoke and smiled.

'Oh, yes, does it surprise you how young they all were? Had you been conjuring a bevy of ancients? And have you been wondering about their children?

'Well, those who'd mothered sons had seen them off to their labours by then, down the mountain or to a marriage with a girl from the cities, while their daughters had, likewise, followed their husbands' paths. Just as I'd done. For some, visits to or from their children were rare enough. Life in the mountains is often lived in epochs – clearly marked – one ending, the next beginning, in a succession natural as the seasons, children yearning sometimes to forget from whence they came, their parents, having loved them well, trusting their babies to the Fates, to the old goddesses. Now, all that about children, that wasn't what you'd call meandering, was it? Maybe just a little.'

•

By now I am captive to Ninuccia. I know nothing of the present. How long have we been sitting here at the long wooden table in the mill? Someone has lit candles in the lanterns, which hang from iron hooks here and there about the place. I know that Ninuccia has placed a string of those half-dried figs near to my hand, that she has pushed toward me the roasted bread that one of the cousins brought to the table. From the tail of my eye, I am aware of men and women who come and go, lugging sacks of olives, carrying away wooden boxes filled with two-litre bottles of new oil. I hear the sound of stones crushing the fruit, the gentle brays of the velvet-eyed she-ass. Ninuccia stops only to eat a fig.

•

'Cosima. Cosima wore the same dress every Thursday. The colour was of a kind of pewter iridescence that shimmered gold when she moved in it, the heavy silk falling like warmed metal and sheathing the long, skinny frame of her. Her husband had brought it home on the night of her twenty-first birthday. She said she knew it had been thieved, that dress – a spoil from some larger plundering. She said she'd been sure his treachery was greater than that which would yield the humble haul of a pewter-coloured dress.

'On a January dawn less than a month later, while she was still abed with two-year-old Pierangelo asleep beside her, Cosima heard the dull thud her husband's corpse made as it smite the lane outside the cottage door. She'd always expected it, she knew, she said. She pulled at the bed cover, wadded it up her arms and, barefoot, went to him, covering him, swaddling him, dragging and pushing and pulling him into the house. Not meaning to, she said, she lay down on top of him and rocked and wept until she noticed that Pierangelo, also rocking and weeping, had lain down next to her, next to his father. In that truculent way of hers, Cosima told me this and then never spoke of it again. When once I asked Pierangelo to tell me of his father's death, he looked at me, held my gaze so fast and hard it frightened me. When he looked away, he said, "I don't know. No one ever knows."

'When Cosima wore the dress on Thursday nights, she'd always say how she preferred her black one, that any other one felt like someone else's. Her heart-shaped lips compressed, nearly stretched into a smile, she'd touch the bodice, pat her hands cautiously here and there about the dress and wonder aloud if it truly *had* once been someone else's. And if it had, she wondered, too, who was that someone else? What was she like? And what had her husband known of her?

'One evening while we sat out in the lane, she pulled the dress from her work sack, proceeded to cut off the sleeves, frayed and split as they were. Piecing together the remnants into one long length, she wrapped it about her head, securing the ends under her braids. She looked up at me, the metallic glint of the headdress dancing in her eyes like moonshine and, on the next Thursday when she wore it with the dress, I thought, at last, that Cosima had the right clothes for an enchantress. She never wore any other shoes, though, than the too-large black men's oxfords or, in winter,

Pierangelo's discarded hunting boots. Had she manoeuvred things in another way, Cosima might have had more – more clothes, more comforts. Once when I asked her, "Wouldn't you like to have . . ." it was the only time I saw her veer toward anger. "*Non hai capito niente. L'abbondanza é pericolosa.* You've understood nothing. Abundance is perilous."

'Were any of the men at home on a Thursday, they would sit and eat and drink with us, having first made their own extraordinary ablutions for the event. White shirts, starched, ironed, buttoned to the neck, jeans or black trousers tucked into boots and, smelling of bergamot and red wine, their skins dark and luminous in the candlelight, they were knights errant, intriguing, erotic, fresh from battle, more lovers than husbands. As I was living it, that *divided* life seemed a noble one, unmuddied as it was by the niggling hostilities and household tyrannies of an everyday life. When we were together, we seemed new and, I think, exotic to one another. Every time was the first time. When we were apart, well, that's how it was. Men left to their machinations and their swaggering. To their whoring. Maybe to their whoring. Women – loosed from the quotidian needs and wants of a domesticated man – could tend to one another, to their babies, to *themselves* and their own *modo d'essere*, their own way of being. To their own swagger and lust, I don't know. I shall admit that for all these years since we returned to Orvieto I've adored that every-evening moment when I lay down with Pierangelo, limbs tangled, his breath even on my cheek. Still, there was something about that other way of being a couple, that other reality, which was good.

'Thursday Nights notwithstanding, I need not tell you that storms shook the lives of the women of Acquapendente di Sopra. No, I needn't tell you that. But it was Cosima who kept things apace. Boiling up the mess of life until it came out right, she could lull an anguish, knead a rogue terror into calm, stir beans and potatoes into a feast, she could do that. All this sway of hers, though, was wider than over the seven women. You see, Cosima had a niece.

•

'Sitting not a hundred metres from Cosima's place, Sofia lived in the *borghetto*, a group of cottages clustered on a rise and surrounded by tilled fields and sheepfolds, all of it the property of Sofia's husband's family. The daughter and only child of Cosima's younger brother, Sofia had been orphaned when she was eleven years old. That would have been seventeen years before my time in Acquapendente di Sopra. Sofia was twenty-eight when I met her. Having in some manner displeased the clans, Sofia's parents – Cosima's brother and his wife – had also been dispatched in ritual fashion: he heaved into the lane, throat slit, castrated, his severed member placed in his mouth to stifle his final scream; the corpse of his wife strewn, nude and raped, in a ditch in the nearby woods. Cosima took Sofia to live with her and Pierangelo and there Sofia remained until her marriage to Lamberto – eldest son of the "richest" family in the village – when she went to live with him in the *borghetto*.

Lamberto, too, did the clans' bidding. It wasn't that the malevolence of the clans was less than brazenly clear to him – or to the other men, for that matter – rather it was that each man thought himself to be above or beyond that brazen malevolence. In the way that the rest of us believe dying happens to others, each man in the village took a turn believing that his rapport with the clans would end in riches and glory. Never in a stifled scream. Never him.

'As did the other men, Lamberto lived a once-in-a-while life in the village, spending more of his time soldiering for the clans. This despite his relative familial wealth. This despite his undisguised love for Sofia and the twin daughters who'd been born to them only days after my arrival in Acquapendente di Sopra. Surrounded, coddled – perhaps suffocated – as she and her baby daughters were by the women in Lamberto's extended family, Sofia only infrequently visited her aunt Cosima. When she did wander down the rise and through the woods to us, each of her fat cherubs tucked into her own sack, the sacks criss-crossed upon Sofia's chest, Cosima's mood was festal. But as much as Cosima would dandle and coo to the baby girls, it was Sofia upon whom her gaze lingered, Cosima never having, I think, outlived the time when Sofia was her own baby girl.

'But even greater than first-blood kinship, there was another connection between Cosima and Sofia. That Cosima's husband and Sofia's father – who was, you'll recall, Cosima's brother – had been entrenched in the higher echelons of the clans, that their murders both bore the grotesque clan shibboleth, this was the crucial tie that bound Cosima and Sofia. And when one of Lamberto's sisters came screaming to our door so early one morning that the light was still grey, Cosima, bent to the fire toasting bread while I was seeing to the coffee, took her shawl from a hook near the hearth and walked behind the woman to the *borghetto*. I walked behind Cosima.

'It was December. Someone, one of the shepherds I think, had carried Lamberto's body into an outbuilding under the main house, thinking to wait until Sofia had been told before bringing him upstairs. Cosima set to work, sending me to fetch oil, to ask for the finest sheets in the house. Candles, incense. Cosima decided that Sofia would never see her husband until she had prepared him, washed him like a newborn, swaddled him in scented linens so that only his head was free, the cloth cunningly wrapped to cover his garrotted throat, and the other indignities that had been perpetrated upon him. She lit six candles around the wooden table where he lay. Then she called for Sofia.

'Having left Sofia to be alone with Lamberto, Cosima soon joined me outdoors, gestured for me to follow along a beaten path to a shed of sorts, which housed a stove, a stone sink, a work table already laid with baskets of eggs, vegetables, meats, oil, wine, a bin of flour, other things she'd asked to be brought to her. From the rafters of the shed, haunches of prosciutto were aging and, hung by their feet from a wire strung along one wall, freshly killed pheasants and guinea hens twisted in the breezes seeping through the cracks of the rough wooden walls. There was an electric light bulb in a wire frame above the work table. Patting the surface of the table with one hand, Cosima said, "This is where they butcher pigs. By the smell in the air, I'd say they slaughtered one a few days ago. Maybe yesterday." Walking about the room, inspecting the pans and cooking pots, shuffling through them until she found what she needed, she sniffed the air. "*C'è una puzza*. There's a stink." She walked along the wire where the birds were hung, sniffing and inspecting, finding nothing amiss until, toward the end of the wire, she discovered the cause of the stink.

"'Pig testicles. As I said, they must have slaughtered yesterday. These are fresh off the beast and need to be hung for a day or so to release the poison. Then a saltwater bath, a scrubbing, another day under salt, a bath in white wine and herbs. A long procedure. Polluted things. Worth the work, though. Delicious in a *soffritto*. Untreated, they are deadlier than an amanita. Once we get onions and garlic moving in a pan, we'll hardly notice the hideous things," she said, already ripping skins from onions.

'Leaving the women of Lamberto's family to their mourning, Cosima would prepare the vigil supper for that evening. For a long time I don't think she said a word save to direct me to the next job and the next one after that. At one point, though, and without raising her head from her task, she said, "The one who murdered him will come to offer condolences to Sofia this evening. All part of the clans' love of spectacle. They always send the assassin to visit the widow. A mass card, an envelope filled with lira. He will take Sofia's hand in both of his. Perhaps he will weep. And then he will sit down to supper."

'Her face was contorted as she spoke, her breath coming in gasps as though she'd been running, her smooth, dark skin leeched to white. I knew my telling her to sit a while would fall on deaf ears and so I stayed quiet at my work, only looking at her from the tail of my eye. Trying to breathe for her. After a while I remember asking her if we would stay to serve and she said we wouldn't. We'd tell the maids what was what. She could trust them to the job. And then we'd go home.

'When there seemed nothing left for me to do, I went to the stove where Cosima was still at work. "What is it that you're preparing?"

'"*Un soffritto*. Pancetta, lard, rosemary, garlic, onions, peperoncini, red wine, tomatoes. Spooned over bread, a little antipasto."

'"And in that other pan?" I pointed to a small battered saucepan on the back burner.

'"More of the same. A bit of flesh in this one."

'"What sort?"

'"*Cosa c'era, c'era.* What there was, there was."

'Covering the small battered saucepan with a soup plate, carrying it in both hands, she left the shed. She was gone for a long time; it seemed long. When she returned, her face was almost hers again. She went to the sink, scrubbed her hands, digging under her nails with a brush, letting water run and run over them. Drying them on an apron hung by the door, she reached for her shawl.

'"*Andiamo, tesoro.* Let's go, my darling."

'We walked out into the December afternoon, already dark, down the hill, back through the woods. Cosima held my hand. Having no need for words, we were free to listen to the shuddering of the pines as the wind rose. We both loved that sound, waited for it of an evening. As we walked I thought I was hardly certain of what Cosima did or didn't do or meant to do back there in the grim little shed. If she wanted me to know, she would tell me. I would never ask her.

'When we were back inside Cosima's house she crouched to mend the fire, poked at it absently. Suddenly she stood. From the wood pile she lifted two logs, foisted them down from on high, bashing the embers as I saw her do to the head of a viper with a stone one day in the woods. Striking match after match, throwing down faggots of kindling still tied in their ropes, she willed the blaze to leap and rage, and it obeyed. Arms crossed upon her chest, she bent her body over the fire, pressed her forehead against the mantle shelf and wept. When she stood straight again, she held her hands above the flames for a while, taunting the fire to lick them. She dared the flames, dancing her hands lower, lower still, raising them only just in time.

'Without turning to me, she said, "*Maligno* – fiend. Only vengeance can hinder a fiend. Tomorrow I will ride the bus to Reggio. I will go to offer condolences to his widow. Do you remember, *tesoro*? The assassin always visits the widow. Will you come with me, *tesoro mio*?"

•

Rising from her chair, her palms still flat on the table, Ninuccia looked at me from the still-faraway place where she'd been. Arranging her mouth in a smile then, she walked around the table to where I sat, cupped my face in her hands, moved it gently, side to side. An apologetic caress. Buttoning her sweater, she said, 'They were patient with her, the clans, their *admiration* for her courage keeping them at bay for years. Patient but not forgetful, they took Cosima one evening a few months after we'd come back to live up here. *Sparita*. Disappeared. A respectful end, to disappear.'

•

I don't remember driving home from the mill that evening. The first thing I do recall is seeing Fernando standing at the entrance to *la Porta Romana*, the Roman gate, as I drove through it. Ninuccia had called him, told him when I'd left her so he might anticipate my arrival back into town.

I stop the auto, push the window button. Resting his arms on the edge of the open window and the closed car door, he leans in to kiss me. He kisses me hard.

'I'm sorry I didn't . . . I never thought to . . .'

'You aren't going to tell me that you've been picking olives by the light of the moon, are you?'

'No. I'm not going to tell you that. I . . .'

'Miranda came by about seven, just about the time I was beginning to wonder about you. She told me she'd left you with Ninuccia, said I shouldn't worry. Miranda-style, she marched right in, looked about for something to cook for my supper. I told her to wash her face and fix her hair, that I'd take her to Eliano for lamb ribs, *scottadito*. I gave her your white shawl and we sat for a while downstairs and smoked cigars. And drank Campari. We waited until nine, just in case you might come home in time to go with us. I'd left you a note. When we walked into the darkened salon after eleven and knew you still hadn't come, I stood out on the balcony, willing you to appear around the corner of the *vicolo*. I heard Miranda chuckling behind me saying that all was happening just as she knew it would. Whatever that meant. I wouldn't let her drive home so late. She's asleep in the downstairs bedroom.'

All of this he has recounted from his position of leaning into the open window. Now he opens the door, pulls me out and upright. He holds me as though I'd been gone for years. Or is it me holding him that way?

'Calabria. She was telling me about the place where she lived. About the people . . . Fernando, I want us to go back again to those villages in the mountains, I . . .'

'She could have driven you down there for all the time she spent telling you about it. Jesus. And don't give me those eyes. Get inside. You can tell me all about it tomorrow. But whatever it is that you tell me, whatever it was that bewitched you tonight, we are not moving to Calabria.'

He sits in the driver's seat, and guns the still-running car before taking it out of neutral. I get in on the passenger side, and tell him, 'I'm not ready to go home. I have things I want to tell you now, things I want to think about. I wish I were a soprano.'

'*Cosa?* What?'

'I wish I were a soprano. I wish I could sing plainsong. I wish I knew how to . . .'

'Is this about Calabria? Do I understand that you wish you were a Calabrian soprano?' He tries for mirth but exasperation shows through. I can hardly blame him.

'I'm sorry, I know you're tired and . . .'

'I've missed you. It's only that. Every evening counts. I hate to miss one with you.'

'Is that how you felt when I'd stay up half the night talking to B.?'

'How did we get from Calabria and plainsong to B.?'

'Something Miranda said to me not long ago. Did B. and I make you feel *excluded*? Did you ever think that I was . . . that I was in love with him?'

'No, to the first. No, to the second. Almost, no. You were enchanted by him, he by you. A state that sometimes can exceed being *in love*. I never imagined you running off with him or . . . *I* loved him.'

'I know.'

'Would it hurt if I told you that he and I were closer than were the two of you?'

'No. I think that's true, enchantment being a barrier of sorts to love.'

'*Brava*. Can we stop driving now? I know nothing about plainsong and I find your small raspy voice sensual.'

We park the car in Piazza Ipollito Scalza, climb the stairs at 34 to find Miranda building a midnight fire.

'I couldn't sleep. Are either of you hungry?'

'No,' we tell her in quiet unison.

'Now that both of you are here, I *can* sleep,' Fernando tells us. 'Don't either of you depart for Calabria until I awake.' Fernando embraces Miranda. Then, the blueberry eyes admonishing, to me he says, '*A presto, amore mio*. Soon, my love.'

I urge Miranda back to bed. I go into the little red room where I work, search for a copy of a book I wrote in 1999. I find the chapter on Calabria:

> . . . a region of loose precincts, mostly uninterrupted and surely untamed by time, nearly all of her is of mountains, the villages that bestride them, fortressed one from another, unsavvy to any but its own rites and rituals, its own dialect. Hers is a legacy of brigands. Of brigantesse. After the unification of Italy in 1861 and Rome's decree against latifondismo – the holding of great parcels of land by a handful of citizens – the south was politically, spiritually abandoned. No enforcement, no intervention came from the new governors and an even more base epoch of serfdom, of insufficiency ensued. Unlike in other southern regions where the poor simply died of hunger or ran away from it, the Calabresi hoisted up their own impassioned service of justice. 'Ndrangheta it's called. Having perfected if not refined its manners over the years, still 'ndrangheta ministers power over Calabria . . .

•

I have quietly opened the door to our bedroom thinking that, though only ten minutes had passed since he went upstairs, Fernando would be asleep. I'm not quite through the door when, up from the dark, he says, 'What is it, what is it that draws you so *compulsively* to . . . ?'

'To whom? To what?'

'To the *primitive*.' He whispers this.

Throwing off my clothes, I settle myself next to him. I whisper, too. 'Are you saying that Miranda is *primitive*? She or the others or . . .'

'No. Yes. In a way she is, they are: their glaring forthrightness, their uncluttered wisdom. Their communalism.'

'Do you think it's not good that these things *draw* me to them?'

'No. Not at all. But sometimes I wonder how, when you . . . when you began to desire to live the lives of your heroines. Now it's Ninuccia.'

'Not Ninuccia. Her mother-in-law. Cosima was her name.'

'Cosima. Now it's Cosima. In Sicily it was Tosca . . .'

'And when I was young I wanted to be Anna Karenina and Emma Bovary, neither of whom one could term *primitive* . . . Maybe when I lived in California I had a too-choking dose of ladies-who-lunch. I was thought *primitive* by their measure.'

'What I'm trying to say is that you don't have to live in the Aspromonte or keep goats or sing plainsong all the better to emulate these women you admire. *You already are who they are.* You have their defiance. That may be the pith. *Defiance.* Wandering about in another *mise*, with another past, with other gifts than theirs, still, you are *of them*. Don't you know that yet? It's what B. saw, it's what fascinated him. I can still hear his laugh that morning when he found you on the terrace in jeans and sandals with fourteen-centimetre heels. Already having lit the bread oven, skinned and fried a rabbit, you were slapping three kilos of bread dough on the table with the force of a Fury. You were wearing some sort of *unlikely* shirt. What was it?'

'I don't remember.'

'You remember everything. It was a kind of . . .'

'A brown taffeta bustier. And B. had done most of the skinning before he left the beast – headless, slit and deprived of its pluck – the day before. And I wore those sandals maybe twice in all the time we lived in San Casciano. You hate it when I wear workboots, think it odd when I wear shoes with high heels, but when I wear boots you ask whatever happened to all those beautiful shoes . . .'

'You see? Defiance. For you there are only two kinds of footwear.'

'Was it my *primitiveness* that drew you to me?'

'I didn't know it then, but, yes. I think it was. Most notably, the defiance part.'

•

'*Pronto.*' I fumble for the bedside telephone and my just-awakened voice is tentative, frightened. I think it's the middle of the night.

'Chou, *buongiorno*. Don't tell me you're still abed?'

'Ninuccia. *Buongiorno.* I . . . we . . .'

'Will you meet me at the mill in an hour? I think we should give that pasta a trial before tomorrow night. The wine and oil are there and I'll bring pasta. Just the two of us, though I'll tell Miranda and . . .'

'Yes, yes, of course, Miranda . . . Why don't you leave that to me . . . you see, she's here. I mean I think she's here . . .'

I call down the stairs to Miranda but there is no answer. I bathe, dress, leave Fernando to his sleeping. A dark blue paper-wrapped box tied in silver string waits on the kitchen table. Miranda has left croissants from Scarponi, prepared the Bialetti for the flame. *A più tardi*, later, she's scrawled with a fountain pen on a piece of paper towel, the ink having seeped through to the tablecloth. Having no clock in the house nor watches for our wrists, we tell time mostly by the bells and those of the Duomo are now announcing a quarter to eleven. I call Miranda and tell her what Ninuccia has asked.

'I'll come back into town so you can leave the car for Fernando. Twenty minutes. Be downstairs.'

As I do so often, I pray to the gods, should I someday reach Miranda's age, that I shall be like her.

Leaving things as Miranda has arranged them, I write a note to Fernando inviting him to join Ninuccia and Miranda and I at the mill at about one. I take a half-kilo pat of local butter and a stem of ginger from the fridge, and wrap them in a kitchen towel. From the spices in the armoire, I take a piece of cinnamon bark and a glass tube of Madagascar cloves, tuck everything into an old Dean & DeLuca canvas sack. I have a quick espresso at Bar Duomo, run the few metres to i Swizzeri to buy chocolate: 200 grams of Lindt, 99 per cent cacao, into the sack. Time for another espresso before the goddess of Buonrespiro sputters to a stop in front of San Giuseppe.

'This is a good sign, I hope you realise that,' she says.

Luminous this morning, her braids just done and pinned into an extra-high crown, Miranda wears a navy faille dress, which she usually saves for evening, and, I think, a delicate smudge of rouge across her cheekbones.

'This is not a lack of trust on Ninuccia's part. It's curiousity. It's . . .'

The bells of San Bartolomeo begin ringing high noon as we enter Castelpietro – the town entire sitting on a single curve of the road – and, by the time we're already through the place, the bells have yet to get to nine. A few minutes later when we walk into the mill, Paolina and Gilda, Settimio (the mill caretaker), four men whom I've never seen before, Ninuccia and at least five of her cousins are all busy at one thing or another: laying a cloth on the long wooden table, taking this morning's loaves from their brown paper sacks, setting down platters of Settimio's house made *sulame*, filling wine jugs, carrying a pasta-cauldron full of water, placing it on the flame, dragging in more olives, carrying out more boxes of two-litre and five-litre bottles of new oil. Two of the cousins are at the work of brushing down the she-ass and feeding her.

Greetings and small talk are cut short when Ninuccia says, 'Okay, Chou, take over.'

I add my shawl and hat to the others already hanging by the door, wash my hands at the sink which must once have been a baptismal font. The challenge begins.

'Let's gather together everything I'll need,' I say.

Ninuccia moves a bowl of dried pasta closer to the stove.

Tre kili di penne rigate,' she tells me, arms crossed upon her chest.

Nearly seven pounds of penne. Seven pounds. It's only then that I understand that Ninuccia's aforementioned intimate lunch among three or four of us has grown into a *festa* for maybe twenty. Hence the enormous cauldron on the flame. 'I'll need sea salt, four litres of red, a pepper grinder, a mortar and pestle.

I've brought the . . . the other things I'll need.' I'm not yet ready to speak of cloves and ginger and chocolate. I am less ready to speak of butter here in the birthing room of Umbria's finest oil.

'I'm right behind you, Chou. Give me a job.' This is Gilda.

Having found the mortar and pestle with Settimio's help, Paolina brings it to me.

'*Allora*, Paolina, fifteen cloves pounded with this piece of cinnamon bark,' I tell her, taking the spices from my sack. Paolina sets to work and several of the others, already mystified, gather closer in.

'Gilda, please peel this ginger, then chop and smash it to a paste.'

'*Questo é zenzero?*'

'That's *real* ginger. What you call ginger in dialect is actually *peperoncino.*'

'*Non ho capito.*'

I repeat, '*Per voi, zenzero vuol dire peperoncino.* For you, *zenzero* means peperoncino. Ginger, it's called in English.' Miranda rescues. 'Geen-jer. A pretty word. Geen-jer,' she repeats and some of the others take up the chant. One of the cousins tells the she-ass about geen-jer.

'*L'acqua bolle,*' shouts Ninuccia and, after heaving in four good fistful of coarse sea salt, I throw in the pasta, stir it with a metre-long olivewood spoon.

Gilda brings a ricketty metal stool over to the stove and tells me 'You're too small to work with that monster of a pot.'

'Three minutes. Only three minutes, Ninuccia, and then drain it,' I tell her.

'I? You drain it.' She knows I won't be able to lift that cauldron by myself but Paolina is right there.

'I'll watch the time, and in exactly two and a half minutes, Gilda and I will drain it.'

I pour three litres of red into a pot and heat it over a low flame. In a smaller pot, I heat another litre of red and, girding myself for scorn, add half the butter I've brought, about 250 grams. No one comments. No one, at least not close enough so that I hear. I ask Miranda to grind pepper with a heavy hand into the butter-wine mixture, to keep the flame only high enough to melt the butter.

'I must have a pan large enough in which to toss all the pasta,' I say perhaps a bit too loudly.

I'm assured there isn't such a thing there and so I'll use the cauldron again, once the pasta is drained. Now everyone but the she-ass has gathered in. The unabashed scrutiny both rattles and exhilarates me.

Without my asking them to, Paolina and Gilda drain the pasta at the three-minute mark, leaving it slightly wet, just as it should be. I take up the empty cauldron, add the litre of oil, the other half of the butter and set it on a medium flame.

'I'll need the ginger now . . . and the pounded cinnamon and cloves.'

'Geen-jer *pronto*.' Gilda brings the ginger on the blade of her knife and Paolina hands me the mortar. I scrape in the ginger and dump the spices into the hot fats, let the mass warm and send up opulent, spicy steam. People begin to sniff, to move closer yet to the stove. Into the cauldron then with the barely cooked pasta. With the olivewood spoon, I begin rolling the pasta about

in the perfumed fats. In my mind, I thank Gilda for thinking
of the stool. My arm aches as I try to get to the bottom of the
seven pounds of pasta. Dig, turn, dig, turn. I switch hands but
my right one is too weak and so take the spoon back into my left,
supporting it at the elbow with my right. I raise the flame then,
allow the pasta to take on some colour, some crust. I move it all
again, leave it to colour a bit more. Now, two large ladlesful at
a time, I begin dosing the pasta with the three litres of warmed
wine. I can tell even now that I'll need at least another litre.
Paolina is close enough for me to ask her to pour more wine into
the pot so it will warm with what's already there. As the pasta
drinks in the wine, I add more. Ninuccia has handed out tumblers
and Miranda has gone around with the wine pitchers. The pasta
drinks, the crowd drinks and takes turns tearing at the loaves on
the table. They plunder Settimio's *salame*. Fernando arrives and
gets to the work of heating the dishes by the fire before bringing
them, stacked and warmed, to the table near the stove.

'Why didn't you wake me?' he says, massaging my shoulders.
'Good thing about your shoes,' he says close to my ear.

'What about them?'

'The heels. Can't be much over ten centimetres. Perfect for a
stint on a stool at the stove in an olive mill.'

Turning to him, I try for a glare but begin to laugh, and take
time to kiss the tips of my fingers, flinging them toward Paolina
and Gilda who stand guard nearby. I turn back to the dosing of
the pasta until it reaches the desired still-toothy texture, add the
litre of wine, which I'd warmed with butter and pepper. I call
for another large wooden spoon and with both in my hands I

begin to toss and toss, glossing every piece of pasta, which, by now, has taken on the colour of old Bordeaux – amaranthine with a golden rim. I know why Paolina and Gilda don't offer to spell me in this last step of the process.

'*A tavola, a tavola.* To the table, to the table,' Miranda claps her hands and it's Ninuccia and Gilda who hold out the deep warmed plates into which I ladle the pasta – twenty-two plates to be precise. It's Paolina who carries the plates to the table, four at a time, two plates resting on each of her inner arms. As she takes the last four plates, I take a small, sharp knife from a drawer, unwrap my 99 per cent chocolate and, one by one, I stop by each place, shaving the chocolate over the hot, hot pasta so that it melts on contact. I think most of the people don't know it's chocolate but perhaps some strange truffle or a sort of exotic cheese. Miranda sees what I'm doing, asks Settimio for his clasp-knife and, cracking off a large piece of the chocolate in my hand for herself, begins on the other side of the table. Finally Miranda and I sit in front of our own plates, she shaving chocolate over mine, I over hers. No one speaks. The soft noises of slurping, chomping, of grinding mandibles and clacking dentures fill the room. Then a voice.

'*E favolosa, questa pasta.*' I don't know the name of this man who names the pasta fabulous, still I want to kiss him. Instead, Miranda gets up, does just that. They are asking for more but there is none. I drink deeply of my wine, watch Ninuccia watching me.

Sated, everyone seems content to sit a while. Very softly then, as though only to herself, Ninuccia begins to sing. Not sing, really, but chant in what must be the minor-key wail of the women in the mountains. Never before have I heard these sounds from an Umbrian yet others join her, only two, maybe three. I try to echo the sounds Ninuccia makes. I realise this is what the others are also doing. Now there are more of us. Ninuccia always leading, her eyes closed, her voice grows stronger and so do ours. The men begin to sing. Fernando is singing and I'm singing and weeping and Miranda is weeping. I think to Cosima in her Thursday Night dress: shimmering like gold when she moved in it . . . to her tribe chanting and keening, their sounds visceral, their pitch mesmeric, orgasmic, sweetening, finally, almost to a whisper.

Ninuccia's voice goes silent and the others, perhaps a note or two later, quieten, too. I feel Ninuccia looking at me again and raise my head to see it's so. What is it in those great grey eyes? She knows I've been thinking of Cosima. Is there also some small apology in that gaze? For having set me up for this impromptu lunch for two to which she'd invited twenty? A test?

Still no one has moved from the table. Communion has been taken but the mass has not ended. Why have they sung someone else's song, these Umbrians who are mostly very old? As though water and mountains and time have never separated one tribe from another.

It's Settimio who speaks first. 'That . . . that song with no words, it was the one my mother sang to us. Four of us. One bed, my mother rocking in her chair, I swear it was that song she sang.'

A murmur of compliance. An aunt, a mother, another mother, also they sang that song. It can't be so, not that very song, and yet Ninuccia's voice has comforted them as did long-ago voices raised in the melancholoy of a lullabye, a night song, a sonata in B flat minor. In the mountains, in Cosima's mountains, the chanting was another kind of comfort, the sound of the tribe's own angelus signalling rebellion. A prelude to vendetta.

'Shall we make a pact, here and now? Every year when the wine and the oil are new, we'll meet at this same table for this same meal?' This is Ninuccia.

Miranda looks at me and I know she is telling me, *Do you understand? This is how it happens . . . The way rituals are born.* As Fernando said I was, Miranda is also telling me, *you are of us.*

One of Ninuccia's cousins, a woman with the same Titian hair as hers, asks the man who sits across from her, 'Enrico, didn't you like the pasta? Why aren't you happy?'

'*Certo, certo*, certainly I liked it. And of course I'm happy.'

'Then why aren't you crying?'

PART III

PAOLINA

Grapes

IT IS LATE IN OCTOBER OF 2006, TWO YEARS AFTER Miranda's fraudulently professed withdrawal from Thursday Night cooking. Not only has Miranda been constantly at the Thursday burners, but all four of we others have been there with her. Ten-handed Ravel we've been playing. We spar and tiff, we quarrel and laugh and sometimes we sing.

Having chipped at icons early on in our sessions together, we began to allow nostalgia a grander role in what we cooked, honouring traditions but divining them down to more familial ways. One of the women might say, 'I know that *agnello stufato*, braised lamb, is made without tomatoes but my grandmother used tomatoes. Let's use tomatoes.' And so we used tomatoes with the lamb or beat up a frying batter with white wine rather than beer or left a suckling lamb to braise overnight in nothing but butter and sea salt in a terracotta pot – its lid sealed shut with a paste of flour and water – in the waning heat of the wood oven. We began to expand the Thursday Night repertoire of dishes and stories by retreating even farther back into the women's individual and collective pasts.

I've always thought it was Miranda's brandy-drenched boar that emboldened them.

As for their resistance to *l'Americana*, it abides. As I knew it would. That long-ago day at the mill, my standing on a stool to stir three kilos of wine-plumped pasta in that witch's cauldron, shifted me into their folkloric history if not their unguarded confidence about things culinary. Trust in that camp having never been the animus of my desire to be among them, I am not troubled by the continuing absence of it. It is only Ninuccia's sometimes acidic expressions of resistance – as much to me as to how I think and work with food – that burn. *Pazienza*. Patience.

I have learned to quench all reference to the gastronomy of France, my own first and eternal love. All Gallic regions and their glories are begrudged; carrots, onions and celery sautéed in butter – butter, by now, a pardoned sacrilege – I call *soffrito*, never breathing, *mirepoix*. If I crust beef in the fat from crisped pancetta with shallots and wild thyme, braise it in red wine, add the dried zest of an orange and Niçoise olives – the olives contraband along with wines and cheeses, Armagnac and Alsatian framboise carried home from visits over the border into the territory of the profane – I say *da medioevo*, from the medieval, and they are appeased as they would never be should I have called it what it is: a little stew from Provence.

Far more than the small French dalliances that I have enacted upon them have they enriched me. From study and research and observation during my journalist life, I'd learned of Umbria's culinary traditions, mine a scholarly knowledge, only somewhat fortified, tested in my early Orvieto years by listening to Miranda, chopping and stirring for her. Never once in these two years having written a recipe or even a method, the women *talk* to me, *show* me as did their mothers and grandmothers to them. Or, in Miranda's case, as did the ancient and revered cook to the noble family for whom she began to work when she was sixteen. When they battle among themselves about which reading of a dish is the *authentic* one, I step aside. I follow the consensus.

The composition of Thursday suppers they have, for all this time, left to me. I write the menus and all of us cook. They have grown to like and expect the *filo conduttore* approach to all the parts of a supper, the conducting thread technique in which Miranda believed but often failed to execute. I can do it well, string the dishes together – *antipasto* through *dolce* – with the barely discernable, subtle, or bold use of a single herb, a spice, a fruit, the dishes building in intensity as wines should, were we ever to drink any but our own local red. This I do while respecting their rules and that pleases them. It has sometimes become their game at table to identify the supper's *filo conduttore*.

And when I cook a dish alone and perpetrate some exotic fillip, they accept it as a specimen from the old tomes. Or pretend to. By now Filiberto has begun to say, at first taste, *da medioevo*, thus avoiding further comment from the tribe. Still, when I work at the dishes that belong to them, they watch me, if with a guise of nonchalance. *No matter how long I stay, I will always be just passing through.*

We grow and forage and barter just as Miranda had always done. We save bits and pieces of one supper and build upon them for the next. Our needs having outgrown the garden outside the rustico – a plot too sheltered by a stand of old oaks – a half hectare of fine black earth we've rented from a farmer outside Porano, the village that sits, as the crow flies, two kilometres across a valley from Orvieto. We have planted an *orto* on this land, which we and our men tend and harvest. And it's there, right at the edge of the *orto*, where, sometimes in late spring and summer and into early autumn, we set up for Thursday suppers. Everyone who has an auto carts up to the site one or two tables from the rustico, a bench or some excuse for a chair. And our bread and wine. We shell just-picked peas or marbled red beans or skinned favas directly into a pot of water boiling upon a tripod fire and roast sausages and bulbs of fennel or tiny eggplant or just-dug baby onions or fat bull's-eye tomatoes over the white-hot ash of another fire, which Filiberto has set in a pit he'd dug and lined with river stones.

As the light pales to lilac, we begin pouring out one another's wine, take up our chairs and turn them to the improbable beauty of the town, which has sat upon its great volcanic plateau since Iron Age Villanovan tribes settled there a thousand years before Christ. Barely breathing, no one speaks. Perched on the edge of her chair, inclining herself toward the sun, her hands flat upon her aproned thighs, Miranda closes her eyes. All the better to feel the light. She waits. A low-slung breeze thrums the sheets of metal that protect the woodpile behind us, makes a wind harp of them, and she waits half a beat longer, taunting Apollo, her eyes wide open now, goading him on his way through reddish clouds thin as tulle. And then she whispers, '*Ecco la torta,* behold the cake.'

Ornamented, bejewelled, its scars and sins blurred, Orvieto at sunset is a glittering wedding cake awaiting a bride, the long train of her silver-mesh dress scraping across the old stones. Gold-rose gleams splash upon the gothic face of the Duomo di Santa Maria Assunta, dazzling the red-roofed *palazzi* that enfold her, lighting up the meadows flung out over the green silk valley below the town, spangling wild iris tangled in the high grasses and yellow corn strutting across the fields. And the vines, everywhere the vines.

The torches we've pummelled into the earth we light now, take our places at the strange many-clothed, many-levelled table, take one another's hand, the breeze trembling the flames of the torches, making the wind harp moan. We say, '*Vivi per sempre.* Live forever.'

Unlike Thursdays in the rustico where the dishes are brought out one by one, here we take our supper as we will, all the pans and bowls within reach upon the table. Helping one another to each thing, one tears at the bread, passes the piece to the one nearest, then passes on the loaf so that the next one can do the same. Tear, pass, pass.

Tourists who drive by on the road to and from Porano often stop, sometimes to a screeching halt. Tumbling out of their autos, cameras at the ready, they fix the scene as they would a monument, a vista. Standing in a row gaping at what must seem a spectral pageant, they say nothing. Nor, often, do we. When Italians, local or not, stop to look, they shout from their windows, '*Siete pronti per un macchiaiolo* or *siete proprio Felliniani.* You are ready to be painted. You are Fellini characters.' If one of Miranda's truckers passes by, he whistles, takes both hands off the steering wheel, blows kisses to her, yells 'Amore mio' into the darkening.

Stars and moon and the light of the torches rouse discourse at the table by the *orto* unlike the one under the slouching beams of the rustico. Out here our talk tends to mystery.

'*Voi credete nel malocchio?* Do you believe in the evil eye?' This is Ninuccia, her enquiry meant for all of us.

'Not at all,' Filiberto answers her.

'Nor do I,' says Iacovo, standing up to take a turn pouring our wine. 'But it's power is absolute.'

'*It does not exist but it's power is absolute.* Both are true. What is not made of at least two truths?' Adjusting her braids, Miranda looks around the table. One hunger sated, now she has appetite for provocation.

'Have you been victim of the evil eye?' This is Paolina asking Miranda.

But Ninuccia, Pierangelo and Iacovo speak at once and so Miranda does not answer Paolina, waits while the three tell of instances, undisputed they say, of tragedies caused by the power of the evil eye. Injuries, reverses of fortune, malaise, unexplained deaths, a well gone dry in a biblical rainstorm. Ninuccia is naming upon her fingers the races in which some form of the evil eye is believed, practised, respected: Greeks, Arabs, Spaniards, Jews, Russians, Turks among them. Save Miranda, Paolina, Fernando and I, the others have joined in to agree or dispute. Paolina tries repeatedly to be heard but it's only when Miranda calls forcefully for *santa calma,* holy calm, that the others turn to her and wait for her to speak.

'How many of you wear or carry the little horn?' Paolina asks, pulling a chain out from under her black T-shirt as she speaks. A tiny gold horn hangs from it. Amulets in the shape of a horn are believed to stave off the evil eye.

Pierangelo takes a five centimetre-long red ceramic horn from his pocket and lays it on the table. Reaching under her sweater into the space between her breasts, Ninuccia pulls out her own red horn and holds it in her open palm. Miranda works her hand to the same place on her own body and holds up a tiny golden ring encircled with six horns. One by one, everyone owns up. Only Fernando and I are wandering through life without protection from the evil eye.

Everyone laughs at Paolina's cunning, some saying that carrying the horn is tradition more than belief, others likening it to wearing a crucifix or a blessed medal. The horn *and* a crucifix together, a double buttress. Paolina insists that some seminary students she once knew carried horns in the pockets of their soutanes. Filiberto says that old Don Piervito still does. Even those insisting that the evil eye does not exist say, 'Why take a chance?'

'Miranda, have you been the object of *malocchio*?' Once again, this is Paolina.

'My darling girl, I don't think I really know. I carry the horns because my mother did and, I suppose, everyone I've ever known did, does. I have never felt menaced by a person or an event. Certainly not by something that felt like *stregoneria*, witchcraft. Destiny has had her way with me but that's another thing. Or is it?'

'I think there is *only* destiny.' I say this more to myself than to the others.

'Witchcraft is primordial. Witches who harm, witches who heal,' says Pierangelo, son of the south, son of Cosima.

'Very little call for witches these days, white or black, at least as far as I know,' Miranda tells him.

'The call is still very much present. Secrecy, covertness more finely honed. How *appalled* you would be, Miranda . . .' Pierangelo goes quiet, picks up his amulet, holds it in his hand for a moment, returns it to his pocket.

'Are we talking about the devil?' This is the first time that Fernando speaks.

'Does such a force exist?' Miranda asks, looking up and around the table.

'I don't think we've established that, but . . .' Filiberto says before Paolina speaks over him.

'Are we all part devil? I mean, isn't there some impulse to vendetta lurking in each of us? Even the most innocent sort? If there is an innocent sort . . .'

'I think we've shifted now from vendetta to pure fiendishness. The evil eye and the devil are not related,' says Fernando.

'So you are all in accord: *il diavolo* exists,' Miranda says, the barest hint of question in the last three words.

'Miranda, not even of you could I believe such ingenuousness? Think back to the gods and their various authorities, savage and benign . . .' Pierangelo is prepared to proceed but an imperious Miranda flutters the back of her hand in dismissal.

'Mythology.'

'Yes, myth . . . myth drawn from reality. From the forces of nature but also from human actions witnessed, lived . . .' Pierangelo tries again. 'Maybe those who have more lately prac- tised depravity will someday be relegated to myth. A god called Hitler in league with the one called Lucifer . . .' Filiberto is bent on taking us back to less incendiary ground. The others mutter, feud sotto voce until there is quiet again.

Without deciding I will, I say aloud what I'm thinking. 'Destiny. Rife with charm and cruelty, if in unequal portions, there is only destiny. It's another word for God, for fate. Maybe it's another word for devil. The stones are thrown before we hit the light and what we do with the choices we're allowed, now and then, might cause destiny to rethrow a stone or two. Apart from that . . .'

'Chou, *sei noiosa stasera*, you are annoying this evening,' Miranda tells me in the tone of a weary mother. 'Why do you insist on piling every human mystery into destiny's arms? Try this one. Was Jesus God, incarnate?'

Sotto voce murmurings begin again.

'I don't know. I know He existed, that He wandered the earth, spoke of sublime ethics, which must have been the last thoughts on the minds of the Romans and even the Jews, ethics that most of us have yet to pursue. Was he the son of God? I don't know. How could I know that when I don't know who is God? Jesus is a figure I can *conceive*. God is . . . less *substantial* in my mind.'

'Less *substantial*, yes, of course, so why not just add Him to Destiny's already heavy load?' Miranda shakes me between her teeth and I lose my way. I look at her but she doesn't look at me. The wind harp whines.

'Nor do I know who Jesus was,' she says, the despot in her spent. 'Maybe he was the son of the Hebrew God who created the universe, the God who has always been and will always be, whether or not He be *substantial* in our minds. Maybe Jesus was just a lovely Jewish boy, born of a mother prone to visions. Maybe the Nazarene carpenter – humble, submissive – absolved the beautiful Maria of her annunciation story and married her anyway. Loved her baby boy as his own.' As she says this, she turns to me, gently sets me down, almost unharmed.

'A universal God, his son, the prophets, the teachers, the miracle workers, witches, the devil, all of them newcomers if one thinks to the legions of dieties who managed us in antiquity. A god for every need. A goddess. Far fewer unanswerable questions back then. We knew what was what, who was who, where to go and what to do, what would happen should we stray,' Paolina says.

'Back to mythology, is it? I thought you'd lived long enough among the Jesuits to . . .' Miranda girds for one more round but Paolina is faster.

'Miranda, everything we think we know may well be *myth*.'

'*Già*. Indeed.' Miranda consents.

'*I Moirai*, the Fates, they were at work even before the gods,' Ninuccia says and she – along with Paolina – begins to tell the story, the two spelling one another, line after line.

'Clotho, Lachesis, Atropos.'

'To gods and mortals, they give each one a portion of good and evil.'

'Clotho spins the thread of life.'

'Lachesis decides the length of the thread.'

'It's Atropos who cuts the thread.'

I love this myth and want a part in its telling but gather the sense to stay silent. Conjuring them as grisly ancients, hearing the story of the goddesses frightened me more than any gory fairytale when I was six or maybe seven; Clotho bending over her wheel spinning life-threads, Lachesis scrutinising a just-birthed baby, awarding it the length of it's life-thread, and the dread Atropos brandishing scissors like a battle axe. Herself a grisly ancient, it was a Sister called Odile who instructed us in Mythology and it was only *after* she'd read to us of the goddesses that she passed about a print of three diaphanously-upholstered seraphs, explaining that mythology was story-telling rather than truth, that we need only be good girls, good little convent girls.

'You use the present tense,' Miranda notes, her gaze shifting from Ninuccia to Paolina. 'Who's to say they're not still at their jobs?' I ask her.

'Which brings us neatly back to destiny,' she says, smiling and saying *l'Americana* just above a whisper. 'I'm not sure if it's the smoking torches or the beauty of all this, the goodness of our sitting up here under the stars and beside our pretty beans winding up those stakes. No, I'm not sure if it's smoke or beauty that's stinging my eyes, causing me to weep a little and my heart to break. I'd like to think that if Jesus happened upon us just now, we'd make room for him at the table. He'd rest a while with us, I suspect, he still loving bread and wine as he once did. In any case, shall we drink to the dullness of Atropos's scissors?'

•

It is the last Thursday in this October. Fernando has left me here at the rustico while he heads to San Casciano to hunt *galletti*, wild mushrooms, with old friends from our life there, Stefania and Marco. It was Stefania who telephoned last evening, predicting a night of soft rain and saying, 'Let's hunt wild mushrooms tomorrow morning.'

Some seasons rare others profuse, *i galletti* – little hens – are *chanterelle* in France. I tell Stefania that I won't be able to come but Fernando promises to be there by seven.

'It will be too late. Come to sleep here and we can begin at sunrise,' she cajoles, reminds me it's been weeks since we've visited, promises Marco's luscious *galetti* sauce for the *pici*, thick ropes of pasta that he and Grazia, one of their cooks, will roll one by one. I love my friends, I love *galetti*, I love Marco's cooking but nothing, no one, seduces me from Thursday Nights.

Since we have only one auto, Fernando will leave me at the rustico on his way to San Casciano, hours in advance of my usual time to begin cooking.

'They'll have been in the woods for hours by the time you arrive,' I tell Fernando as we drive up to the rustico. He'd asked Stefania to wake us at five and, though she did, we chose to stay longer in bed.

'I know where to find them,' he tells me.

'I know, too. In the bar, sipping grappa and telling *galetti* stories.'

'More likely they'll have taken a flask with them. I'll stay for lunch but I'll be back here long before supper. With two kilos of *galetti* for the tribe.'

'Such a greedy forager. Half a kilo would do.'

I watch him manoeuvre the old BMW back onto the Montefiescone road and almost begin to wave him back. I've never been alone in the rustico for more than an hour or so but this morning the tiny woodsmoked refuge is all mine. I open the never-locked door, touch things here and there as I walk through, crouch to shovel ashes from the hearth, push aside the bedsheet curtain, carry the full pail out to the ash barrel behind the rustico. On the work table Miranda has made a still-life of the clements of supper: masses of gnarled rosemary branches; long, leafy arms of wine grapes freshly cut from the vines; a great pyramid of green and black figs layered with their leaves; a sack of red and brown-skinned pears; and paper packets and tiny cloth bags of spices. A haunch of her home-cured prosciutto hangs above the table and a demijohn of new wine sits by the door.

Only Paolina and I will be cooking for tonight, others still involved in some stage of the *vendemmia*, the harvesting of the grapes. Fernando and I have been cutting grapes these last six mornings with Ninuccia and Pierangelo and their small army of workers, while Miranda and neighbouring farm wives went about the task of feeding all of us. Miranda will be there with them again today. Perhaps Gilda will decide to join Paolina and I. One never knows about Gilda.

I don't expect Paolina until eleven or so. I look about for something to do, take up cloths and set about cleaning the already clean tables and benches and chairs. A futile task, I sweep the floor, still a mosaic of broken, half-sunken terracotta tiles, scraps of linoleum, lengths of wood fitted in here and there like puzzle pieces. That famous truckload of antique tiles with which Miranda's nephews were, two years ago, to have laid a new floor in the rustico, they sold at a grandiose price to an outlander whose villa they were restructuring. Thanks to the nephews, though, the beams slouch less and in places where the stones of the walls had shifted, they've stuccoed, and washed the patches with a sponge in a tint more rose than apricot.

Miranda conceded to a length of ruined water-green brocade, which Paolina, Gilda and I found on the Neopolitan's used-clothing table in the market one Saturday. Gilda clutched the stuff, burnt to crumbling rags along its hem, against her chest: 'An enraged man must have heaved a lit candelabra across the room, smashing the window, setting afire the curtains while a woman screamed and wept. We have to have this.'

When Paolina asked its price, the Neopolitan gently took it from Gilda, folded it carefully as he would the shroud of Turin. 'I think you must be right. About the man and the candelabra and the woman. I'm sure of it,' he told her, handing it to her with his compliments.

An Umbrian merchant would never have fallen so utterly for Gilda's figment. Neopolitans, as intrinsically susceptible to romance as they are to villainy, might well have lifted her purse with one hand while offering the brocade with the other. The piece falls now from the iron hook where we once hung herbs to dry, and is draped over the top and down one side of the single window, as though it's always been there.

I feel at odds with this uncommon, undesigned time. I walk about, look again at the work table, adjust things that don't need adjusting. I go outside, open the bread oven, give it a good sweeping, take logs from Iacovo's wood pile, place them in a square, add kindling on top, another layer of wood, more kindling, a third layer of wood, more kindling in the centre. I light a faggot of twigs and throw them, flaming, into the centre of the square. A single match does it. No bellows, no fanning. I pull the iron door almost closed, and go back inside to get the woodstove started. A surprise for Paolina, I will make a small batch of *tortucce* for our lunch. No room on the work table, I take up the oilcloth on the supper table, scoop out flour straight onto the scrubbed wood, build up the sides to make a well, pour in yeast softened in warmed white wine, sea salt, a piece of butter from my private stash in the cheese hut, a few drops of oil, crushed fennel seeds. The mass feels good under my hands and I knead it with a rhythmic thud. Waves slapping on sand. Miranda says kneading bread is like a Gregorian chant, both taking on the cadence of the kneader's or chanter's heartbeat. I desire to believe this, so I do. Into a bowl, covered with a kitchen towel, I set the dough on a chair pulled close to the warming stove. I pour oil into a pot but won't begin to warm it until Paolina is here.

I go out to the sheepfold wall where I've left my sack, pull out a hard folder papered in a scene from *Benozzo Gozzoli*, take it back inside and, onto the place I scrubbed after mixing the dough, I dump out sundry sizes and types of paper held together in a corner by the two-tears-and-a-fold method. I will work. The book about Tuscany already published, the finished narrative recounting our early days in Orvieto well into the production process, it's a Sicilian story that I shall work on now, the events of three weeks spent in the mountains there during the first summer of our marriage while we were still living in Venice. Scarce useful material in the fat pile, words and half sentences scribbled mostly on bar napkins and ripped-off edges of the thick brown paper of caffè-table covers and fancy pastry-box wrappings. Never having ceased to relive them, I hardly need notes to restore me to those days. To those people. For these past twelve years since that summer, I've never stopped writing the story, jealously guarding it in its own separate cache in my mind, all the while working on other books. I pick up the pieces, stuff them back into the folder, knowing that all I really need now is time to let the story write itself. How strange to think that what has been part of me for so long – faces and voices and words, neroli riding every breeze, the crisp just-fried shell of a *cannolo* under my teeth, the cut of one woman's eyes, the scent of lavender in still-wet hair, the stomp of horses' hooves below my window at sunrise – all of it to become pages in a book. We all die a little when something finishes. It's how we use up our time. How we use up the thread that Lachesis bequeathes us. Beautiful or painful, we die a little from every ending.

I place two chairs face to face in front of the spent hearth, sit, stretch my legs out straight as the space will allow. This won't do. There's just enough wood in the hearth basket to make a fire. My third fire of the morning, I feel a primeval rush watching the flames take hold and crackle with the first match. I look at my strong, small hands, which are older than I am, my nails hard and short and filed square. How many hundreds of years ago was it?

The era of my silk-wrapped California nails. I make a pillow of my jacket, lie on the least rugged space of the floor and I sleep.

An auto careening off the Montefiescone road onto the gravel outside wakes me. Paolina.

'*Mi dispiace tanto*, I'm so sorry you've been waiting . . . I was with the Dutch in Bolsena . . .'

Having flung open the door before she'd come to a full stop, Paolina shouts her apology, exits from her old black Mini, legs first; a long stretch of skinny jeans before her black mud-caked boots crunch down on the stones. Unfolding the rest of her to reveal her signature black T-shirt, a pashmina – also black – hanging from one shoulder, a canvas sack hung from the other. We embrace and I smell sun and olive oil and woodsmoke on her skin. As is mine today, Paolina's hair is unbound and we laugh at the similarities of our long, curly manes. Leaning back a bit, she spreads her fingers and runs them through my tangles, tells me, 'Yours is worse than mine. I left my clip in Bolsena. What's your excuse?'

'Don't have one. I'll get some elastics from my purse.'

Piling up our hair, washing our hands, our alliance is easy. Over these past two years, Paolina and I and Miranda have been the Thursday constants, with Gilda and Ninuccia joining us often enough. We walk about the work table and I watch Paolina tenderly touching things, standing back to look at the whole, then moving closer again. She has grown up and spent all her life among this bounty, and still the beauty of it amazes her. To be able to be *amazed* by the familiar is the one incontestable gift that we five women share. So has pronounced Miranda over and over again.

'I'd rather paint this than cook it,' she says.

'We can save pieces of everything and lay the supper table just like this one.'

'Yes, that's what we'll do. I'm starving, always starving after I finish a lesson.'

She begins to unpack her sack. She looks up at me, starts to say something but stops, turns the words into a smile. Paolina seems otherwise engrossed today, gentle, sweet but far away. Secretive. Happily so. I will not ask what causes this other spirit. She will tell me if she chooses.

'What did you manage to teach your two Dutchmen this morning?' I ask her, lighting the flame under the oil. She looks at me as I do this and yet doesn't seem to see me or the pot or the flame beneath it.

She says, 'We're still at the beginning – fresh pasta and potato gnocchi. They always want to make the same things and so that's what we do. *Sono pignoli*. They are perfectionists. We used thirty-six eggs this morning since they're expecting twenty-two for dinner. I warned them I wouldn't be back to serve or wash up. *Siete per conto vostro*, you're on your own, I told them.'

Paolina is a cooking teacher whose students are mostly German and Dutch tourists who rent the same countryside villas near the lake of Bolsena year after year. She is legendary among them and I sense it's the wistful beauty of her as much as her talent that intrigues them. Paolina is docile by nature, shy, hesitant, yet what she says is often *pungente*, piercing. Though one wouldn't flinch to hear that she was ten years younger, Paolina is sixty.

'I made dough to fry. For our lunch,' I tell her. 'A few *tortucce*, a sliver of prosciutto, some wine.'

'Perfect. But first a pair of *bruschette*. An Umbrian woman must have her *bruschette* . . .'

From the half loaf she's carried in her sack, she cuts four thin slices, shakes the ash from the grate and sets the bread over the fire.

'Bread before bread?'

'Why not?'

'And there will be two more breads at supper tonight.'

'Lovely.'

Atkins rolling about in his tomb flashes in my mind. As do our guests, mostly those from America, whose organisms rebel at wheat, all glutenous foods. The culprits are pesticides. Good clean wheat nourished most of the world for millenia. Here the greatest compliment one person can pay another is to say, *lei è buono come pane*, she's good as bread. Even the word companion, when divined down from the Latin, signifies *the one with whom I take my bread*. So, yes, bread before bread. As long as it's made from honest, unmanipulated wheat.

I watch Paolina slitting the skins of two figs from the pile on the work table then spreading the red flesh of them onto the hot bread. She drizzles on some oil, a few turns of the pepper mill. Beckoning me to the fire, she is arranging the four beautiful *bruschette* on the tin that Miranda uses to catch drippings from meat as it cooks over the embers.

'You know, Miranda never cleans this old tin. Just swipes it with a piece of soft bread and . . .'

'I know. And, if you're anywhere near, she tears the bread in half and . . .'

'Ah, so you *do* know. It must be suffused with twenty years' worth of flavours from herbs and flesh and wood and I always use it when I come here, even if it's only – like today – as a tray. Here, rub the *bruschetta* across the bottom of the tin before you take it.'

I go to see about the oil, pinch off a tiny piece of dough, drop it into the pot and watch as it turns deep gold in a few seconds. Ready. I stretch to thinness two small nuggets of dough and slip them into the hot oil. Immediately they blister, begin dancing about. 'Paolina, will you slice the prosciutto?'

More proficient even than Miranda at the job, Paolina works a knife, saw fashion, across the haunch, lays the ruffles of almost transparent ham over the luscious hot little breads, letting it melt into them. We don't bother with plates or even to sit but eat out of hand, taking time only to open the spigot on the wine barrel, to fill two tumblers. Now we are ready to begin.

We need workspace and so defile Miranda's still-life, moving it in diminutive form to the supper table. Paolina holds a chair while I slip the crotch of a sheaf of grapes over a beam. We like the look of this and so hang three others in the same way so that the grape leaves nearly touch the table, as though we'd set up among the vines.

Stripping the pointy little rosemary leaves from their branches, chopping them with a rocking motion of her knife directly on the wooden work table, Paolina mixes the dough for fig *schiacciate*: flatbreads of yeast softened in warm red wine, flour, a little sugar, sea salt, oil. Working part of the rosemary into the dough, she sets it to rise beside the woodstove, then places the remaining rosemary in the hearth basket, scent for the fire during supper. Meanwhile I put together the dough for the wine bread, which wants a slow four-hour rise and so I carry it out to the coolness of the cheese hut. We talk about timing, calculate when the wine bread will go into and be ready to come out of the oven, agree that we won't bake the *schiacciate* until after the pears are done. I stripe-peel and core some of both the brown and red-skinned ones, cut a thin slice from their bottoms, leave their stems intact and sit them to rest in a bath of red wine warmed with butter. Once the wine breads are baked, I'll wrap a spiral of pancetta around the pears, slide them into the oven, roast them to softness but not to collapse and the pancetta to an almost-charred crispness. The red wine and buttery juice from the pears will have formed a fine sauce with which I'll glaze them while they're still hot.

The menu for tonight is simple, a good part of it already prepared. We'll start with the roasted pears and a round of Filiberto's new pecorino, still creamy after only a few weeks of aging. Then the *schiacciate*, Paolina's rosemary-scented dough stretched flat, laid with halved figs still in their skins, more rosemary on top, a good dose of oil in the hollows formed by a final knuckling of the dough. The juices from the figs will caramelise in the oven's fierce heat and, as we we did with the *tortucce*, we'll lay the hot flatbreads with prosciutto. As the tribe is vanquishing those, harvest sausages will be already crisping over the hearth fire. Made of coarsely ground pork (three parts lean, one part fat) dried grapes from last year's harvest saved precisely for this purpose, as well as new grapes, seeded and peeled, new red wine, wild fennel flowers, sea salt and coarse-ground pepper, I mixed it at home on Tuesday morning, left it for a day to age in the fridge. It was Mocetti, our faithful butcher, who stuffed the winey, grape-studded mass into casings, tying the fat rope with thick string at short intervals. Yesterday Fernando and I hung the sausages from hooks in the cheese hut. Another day for the flavours to mingle. Once roasted, we'll sit the plump, juice-dripping things on a puree of potatoes cooked in red wine rather than water and pounded to smoothness with oil. We'll pass the *vendemmia* bread hand to hand. In final praise to the harvest, our *dolce* will be a cake made with wine grapes, if in yet another form. It was Ninuccia who, earlier in the week, cooked four or five kilos of new grapes in a copper, tin-lined pot over embers for a day and a night, the fruit slowly, very slowly, giving up its juices then reabsorbing them to form a dense compost. Once filtered, the compost becomes *il mosto*, a precious condiment used in both sweet and savoury harvest dishes. Ninuccia handed me a litre jar of *mosto* a few days ago, instructing from across her shoulder as she was doing something else: 'More sugar than flour, wine, no more than two eggs, salt and olive oil, 300 grams of *mosto*. It you make it tonight, it will be just right for Thursday.' My first *torta di mosto* waits in Miranda's armoire, safe under a yellow bowl. Yes, every single dish made with wine.

The rustico heady as a wine cellar, dough under our nails, flour everywhere on our clothes, our hair mostly unbound again, we are giddy girls playing house. Paolina says, 'We're dangerous together, you and I. We could let the bread burn while we dream. When we talk I feel soothed. And when we're quiet, as we are today, I feel *soothed*. Does that make sense? Maybe that's the wrong word. Perhaps it's that I feel *understood* . . . revealed without my having to work at explaining.'

Remembering Ninuccia's *mosto*, I think Paolina's words are pure and dense as wine cooked to syrup. Silent as she is, an uncommon *allegria* flits about her this afternoon.

'To understand and to be understood . . .' I say.

'Yes, yes. It's exactly that. With Niccolò I have always had that '

Niccolò. Nearly every time that Paolina and I have cooked together, she has been accompanied by a man – *bello come il sole,* beautiful as the sun, Miranda says of him – the same man who accompanies her sometimes to Thursday Nights. An arresting figure in English tweeds and paisley foulards, he might be an aging actor come to live out his dotage in the countryside and yet he is a gentleman farmer. And, as it's said here of people who love the table, he is *una forchetta d'oro*, a golden fork. He walks with a cane but also with a swagger, this Niccolò.

'I was going to ask you why he didn't come with you today . . .'

'He's up at Castello della Sala observing the harvest or surely he would be here, if only to tell us what we're doing wrong. My darling Niccolò.'

Paolina touches her suddenly flushed face, and says something about the woodstove and the fire. 'Shall we go for a walk?'

We wander out into the afternoon. Under the ripe five o'clock sun, the air is as gold as Orvieto wine and we walk a while in the meadow. We sit then among the weeds on the edge of

Miranda's *oliveto* to face a long stand of slender young trees, their branches drooping nearly to the ground with still-green fruit, the leaves hissing, quivering like the silvered net skirts of a hundred ballerinas. From the pocket of her jeans, Paolina pulls out a small metal box fitted with tobacco, rolling papers and matches. Using her thigh as a workspace, she expertly rolls a thin cigarette, hands it to me, rolls another, lights mine with a tiny wooden match, which the Italians call *svedesi*. She lights her cigarette from mine and we lean back, each with an arm under her head, watching the trees and the light. We smoke the cigarettes halfway then snuff them on a stone. Paolina puts the dead ends into her metal box.

Looking up at the sky, she says, 'I'm sixty, Chou, and last evening I had my first proposal of marriage.'

I look over at her but she keeps her gaze upward. I sit up, ask, 'One of the Dutch?'

'Not one of the Dutch.'

'Not one of the Dutch,' I repeat inanely.

'I'm . . . I'm trying to tell you . . . He's seventy-eight years old. He's . . . he's been my cavalier since I was . . .'

'Niccolò?'

'Himself.'

Seventy-eight. A Sean Connery seventy-eight, I say to myself; this Niccolò wants only a kilt and a burr. Miranda calls him *un vecchio querce*, an old oak. 'So many males, but how few men,' Miranda says whenever Niccolò is near.

I'm imagining Niccolò in a kilt while Paolina is saying, 'I understand that there's a practical side to his offer. I do not delude myself into thinking he's been moved by . . . you know, by romantic notions. Long ago he named me executrix of his estate but I think, well, perhaps *he* thinks that my sons and I will be more protected if he and I marry. I think that's it. A part of it.'

'Surely not the all of it. Even given the multiple and sinuous interpretations of Italian law, he can arrange things as he pleases. Why do you think it's so strange that he wants to marry you?'

'If you knew Niccolò you would not ask that. I can't tell this to Miranda, less to Ninuccia, maybe I could to Gilda. Not to my sons.'

To my sons. Paolina speaks often of her four sons but never of their father. If I'd thought about it at all over the years, I suppose I'd assumed she'd long been widowed or divorced. But she has just said, *my first proposal* . . .

'Will you accept him?'

'How archaic you are, Chou. *Accept.*' She looks at me and smiles, looks away. 'I truly don't know. There is something of the ludicrous about the idea. Maybe of the ridiculous. But, well, if you knew about the past . . .'

An auto crunching on the gravel distracts us and we look to our left.

'This will be Niccolò,' Paolina says. 'I knew he wouldn't resist coming to check on us.'

'*Dove sei?* Where are you?' It's Fernando who calls out.

'In the *oliveto*,' Paolina shouts. Was it disappointment flickering her eyes?

One of Stefania's baskets piled in *galetti* riding on his arm, Fernando comes to offer us his treasure. We smell and touch and properly admire the flat-capped ochre-coloured beauties. My image of Niccolò in a kilt lingers. Back in the kitchen, it lingers while I wipe the *galetti* with a damp cloth, trim and slice them, then heave them into a pan with more butter than oil, the fats scented in garlic and parsley. It's lingering still as I shake the pan, flipping the mushrooms rather than stirring them, rubbing flakes of sea salt over them, shaking and flipping with more constancy than is necessary. Now I work on hearing a voice with an Italianate burr. I add white wine, leave the *galetti* to their drinking. A last shake, a last fistful of *gremolata* – raw garlic and parsley – to refresh the soft buttery things. I cover the pan.

I understand that Paolina, had she wished to talk more to me of private things, would find a way for us to stay apart from Fernando. Rather she seems intent on his uninterrupted presence, even asking him if he would mind working on scraping and cleaning an old wooden shutter, which has leant against a wall in the cheese hut for as long as any of us can remember.

'Because of the open slats, it would make a perfect cooling rack for bread,' she tells him, going to fetch it, setting it outside the door.

All three of us work on the shutter and when it's scraped and scrubbed, Paolina opens wide the kitchen window, and lays it over the sill. Later we set the breads to cool on it, the water-green brocade their frame. The washing up done, table set, sausages readied for the fire, I tell Paolina and Fernando that I will go home to bathe and change, leave what's left to be done to them but Paolina, too, says she will go home for a bit. We both kiss Fernando, find our sacks. '*Io raccomando*,' Paolina tells him, trying for Miranda's goddess voice. 'Take care of things.'

At first I think Paolina plans to come home with me so that we can talk but she settles herself in the Mini, waits for me to drive out first. '*A più tardi*' is all she says.

•

Knowing I'll only be a few minutes, I leave the auto, illegally, just down from Bar Duomo. Is that Gilda waving from a front row table?

'I've been waitiing for you . . . I, I knew, I mean, you usually come home to change before . . .' Whisky-coloured eyes peering out from under the brim of her fedora, Gilda looks tired.

'Yes, yes, come up with me . . . Are you all right?'

'Fine, fine, but . . . Nothing really, I . . . Could you please lend me twenty euros? It's my foolish car, the gas guage never tells the truth and . . .'

'Of course, but where *is* your car?'

'Just down the hill, in Sferracavallo. Outside the village. It gave out in a safe place, almost safe. I don't know anyone down there, and, well, I thought I had a bill tucked away, actually I knew I didn't have anything tucked away but . . .'

'Gilli, it's nothing, everybody runs out of gas. Come up with me. Relax while I get ready. There's a gas can in the boot of my car, we'll get it filled and . . .'

'Would you mind paying for my espresso? I felt uncomfortable just sitting there without ordering anything.'

I call to Yari who is standing at the door to the bar, '*Ciao bellissimo. Stai bene?* Are you well? Gilli's caffé is on my bill. *A domani.* Until tomorrow.'

Gilda and I race up the twenty-eight stairs to our apartment and, once inside, up the other two flights from the *salone* to the bedroom. I pull Fernando's favourite of my winter dresses from the armoire and nudge Gilda aside from where she stands in front of my dresser mirror trying on hats. I take fresh lingerie, tell her it's cognac in the tiny perfume bottle on the table near my bed, should she like a sip. She's talking to me while I'm in the shower but her voice is only noise. I dress, turn my head upside down, comb my hair with my fingers. I can't find the boots I want and then notice that Gilda is wearing them.

'Look, they fit me perfectly. As I was saying before, don't, please don't tell Miranda about any of this.'

I find other boots, pull a grey wool basque down to my eyebrows. 'Ready?'

'You do promise, don't you? About Miranda.'

'Gilda, it's hardly criminal to run out of gas, it's ... Why are you always so cautious of Miranda's ...'

Sitting on my bed, she takes off her fedora, sets my small black velvet hat with a veil in its place, this one revealing more of her hair. Of the palest ash brown lit with thick chunks of blonde and shorn just below her jaw, it caresses the sharp bones of her cheeks and chin. Her whisky gaze is almost always bemused, already engaged, as though all that Gilda can see lies on the other side of a window pane. She gets up, looks at herself in the mirror, adjusts the hat, pulls at the veil until it touches her cheeks, turns to me and says, 'It's only to deflect her angst. For Miranda, I have never grown up from the fifteen-year-old stray I was when she first saw me. I am the daughter she never had. And maybe she is the only mother I have ever really known. Perforce our connection is *byzantine*, made of entangled complications.'

'That's an oxymoron.'

'Which is also *byzantine*.'

'I see.' I don't see at all. 'But still, running out of gas . . .'

'But I've run out of money as well, I mean, not exactly run out of it but . . . There was this man, a boy really, maybe eighteen, maybe less. It was a market day, a Saturday. A few weeks ago. It was raining, that soft-hearted autumn rain, light but enduring. Well, he was standing on the corner of *via del Duomo* and the *corso*, you know, right in front of the bank. Paganini. Number Five. Of course he would be playing Number Five. A child-sized umbrella he'd rigged upon one shoulder to protect the violin and the side of his face, which caressed it while the rain fell freely on the other side. How he played, Chou. I couldn't move, stood in the doorway to the pharmacy. No hat on the stones in front of him, no open violin case, he just played. As I said, it was a Saturday, the first one of the month. The day when Bernandino pays me, usually in five one-hundred-euro bills. That morning he'd given me one of those purple ones. At first I didn't know what it was. A five-hundred-euro note, I'd never seen one before. It was there in my jacket pocket. Without taking it out, I folded it twice, made it very small, walked over to the boy, and slipped it into his pocket, on the dry side of his jacket. I kissed the wet side of his face and then I ran. I've managed wonderfully through the month. I mean, what do I need of money when you really think about it? I have no rent to pay, I lunch with the other staff at Bernandino every day, I have my garden, my faithful Miranda and her baskets. Iacovo brings me wood, he's always brought me wood . . .'

I don't tell her that it's been years since Fernando has consented to my carrying about our money for the day since, no matter how much or how little the sum, it would always be gone before the day was. So many musicians, singers, Nigerian boys selling socks. And what about the kids who work in the caffés and are never tipped save by strangers, mostly American. I don't tell her any of that, though I envy her having had that five-hundred-euro note to give away. There is something I can tell her, though.

'My son was born to Paganini's Fifth. On my little tape player. Itzhak Perlman. I wish I'd been with you that day in the rain. I wish you'd been with me when Erich was born.'

Sitting on the bed in the little black hat, she stays quiet for a long time. Until the memory that plays behind the whisky eyes is finished.

'Never tell this to Miranda. Never,' she says.

'Never.'

'I'll be paid on Saturday and so . . .'

'You might tell Bernandino that you prefer smaller bills. Just in case.'

In less than twenty minutes of our racing here and there, Gilda's auto roars to life.

'Will you wait here, let me get a head start? If we arrive at the same time, she'll know something's amiss. Please.' Still wearing the hat with the veil, though I don't think she is aware of it, she hugs me. And while I wait on the curve of Sferracavallo, I think of my son who was born to Paganini, his great dark eyes wide open as though he'd been listening.

I arrive at the rustico just before nine to find some of the tribe standing near or sitting on the sheepfold wall, tumblers of wine in hand, Miranda castigating Gilda's hat, Paolina insisting it suits her perfectly. Heedless of both, Gilda's gone dreamy about the gibbous moon and the first of the stars tangled in the tresses of the pines, while Niccolò, Fernando, Iacovo and Filiberto smoke the *Toscanelli* Miranda has passed among them. Fernando comes to kiss me as does Gilda, as though she and I haven't seen one another since last week. Gilda whispers, 'How I wish you could have heard him, Chou.' I take the wine Paolina pours for me and look hard first at her, then at Niccolò, searching for some evidence of the Dulcinea effect, a sign that she has thrown him a rose. I ask after Ninuccia and Pierangelo.

'They finished the harvest this morning and so stayed on the farm to celebrate with the others. I wanted all of them here but Ninuccia, being more rational than impetuous, muttered about loaves and fishes and tucked me into the *ape*,' Miranda tells me.

Hungry but loath to go indoors, we drink our wine. Miranda comes closer to where Gilda and I stand, sniffs the air.

'Chou, have you given up Opium for *eau di benzina*, the scent of gasoline? Gilli seems to be wearing the same. I shall not ask what the two of you have lately undertaken. Gilli, would you please go inside to turn the sausages?'

I go inside, too. Behind the bedsheet curtain, I begin spooning the *galetti* into small bowls or cups, whatever I can find. Gilda comes to help, placing the *galetti* on a tray with forks and three of the flatbreads. We all sit, take one another's hand, thank the gods for another harvest. Miranda picks up one of the breads, tears a piece – pushing an extra fig onto it – passes it about and we begin this candlelit Thursday night at the oil-clothed table under the grape leaves, the rustico window open to the moon still rising above the Montefiascone road.

Her hat still in place, Gilda and I serve the supper while Miranda frets over Paolina, saying she looks feverish.

'Fernando, change places with Paolina, will you? Her back should be to the fire.'

As we carry out the dishes, Gilda tells me she, too, notices something is amiss with Paolina.

'Not fever, though, is it?'

'Not fever,' I say without looking at her.

'Probably those damn Dutch torturing her twice a week with those endless gnocchi.'

'Could be the damn Dutch.'

The tribe goes quiet over the pears, sheening ruby red from the wine. Just right with Filiberto's new pecorino, they say. Chatter ceases again when Gilda puts down the sausages in Miranda's old metal pan. I go around the table with the bowl of mashed wine-cooked potatoes and the colour of them raises suspicion until the taste of them pleases. Crumbs are the only evidence of the kilo round of *vendemmia* bread, still warm from the oven when we tore into its crust, hard and nearly black from rye and buckwheat flours. It's Niccolò who suggests that we return outdoors for a breath of air, rest a bit before the *dolce*.

'Rest? I think we should dance,' Miranda says, all of us rising, she leading us out into the darkness. 'It's been so long since we've danced . . . How long has it been?'

'A week. Last Thursday up near the *orto*,' Filiberto reminds her, but she's rooting about in her sweater pocket among the herbs and weeds for The Gypsy Kings. She can't see the buttons on her tiny machine and so hands it to me to put into action. A shepherd, a Venetian, Iacovo the farmer and Sean Connery assemble and, as is the rural Umbrian way for men to dance, they stand in a circle, hold one another's elbows and, as though they hear another kind of music, stamp their feet and kick their legs, move in some aboriginal *tarantella*, as much Russian and Greek as Italian. We women pair off and trot about on the gravel, our arms moving like the blades of a windmill and I see the scene as from a distance and I think *how lovely this is, how unbearably lovely.* Long before the tape ends, we stop, gather closer together and I am certain this is the moment when Niccolò will make his announcement. Rather it's he who rounds up the tribe and guides us back to the table.

La torta al mosto is rich, properly underbaked so it's as much pudding as cake. Slicing skinny pieces, I am named a miser and so I cut again. I try to count up the litres of wine with which we have made this supper and those we've drunk with it. I stop counting, let my thoughts wander back to the boy with the violin. To my son and Paganini. To Niccolò in the kilt. Neither he nor Paolina, save her flush, has exhibited any but the most usual behaviour. It's Miranda who insists that Paolina leave her auto at the rustico, allow Niccolò to drive her home.

'Stay abed tomorrow. I'll stop by and . . .'

'*Mirandina*, I'm quite well and . . .'

Paolina never uses the tender diminutive of Miranda's name as do we others. Miranda takes note, says nothing more. Gilda begins to gather the last of the dishes from the table but Miranda waves her back into her chair, scans the table, pausing to stare at each of us until she turns back to Gilda whose hand she has taken into hers. Laughing, Miranda makes glittering slits of her blue-black eyes.

'In the first half of your life, you have the face with which you were born; in the second half you have the face you've merited. I think that's it. It occurs to me, maybe not often enough, that you are a fine-looking tribe. How many things do I save to tell you? Things I've always wanted you to know. Why do I count on your already knowing them? I should remember to *say* the words. Those words. *Quanto vi voglio bene, ragazzi*. How much I love you.'

We stay quiet until I – mostly because my throat's too tight to let out a word – softly, slowly pound my hands upon the table. One by one, two by two, the others take up the ritual demonstration of honour.

Still plaintive, Miranda speaks over the commotion, 'So you think it's Athropos who decides? I mean, about when our time's up? When to cut the thread?' Her gaze far away, her voice is very small.

'*Amore mio*, please, enough for tonight.' Filiberto beseeches her with not quite feigned dismay.

'Oh, I don't intend to get back to God and the *sublime ethics* of Jesus or witchcraft, though I will say that over these past few days I've wondered about old Giuseppe and what became of him while Mary was off ascending and being assumed. History's made mostly of empty spaces. In any case, I've had to rethink my image of Death after being reminded of those three women who sit somewhere spinning and snipping and ... I've always thought of death as The Horseman. My father used to call him that: *quel Cavaliere Nero*, that black Horseman. Intimately and often, my father spoke of him. A long-time nemesis who lived just over the hill. I have always feared a man on a black horse.'

'In *Il Gattopardo*, Don Fabrizio saw Death as a handsome woman in a brown travelling suit. She came to sit by his bed in the hotel, do you remember?' I say this but do not say that I fear a woman in a brown suit.

'With her sitting beside him, Fabrizio told himself he'd lived the sum of three happy weeks in his life. By which, I suppose, he meant he was tranquil about leaving with her.' Paolina says this with spare conviction.

'A few perfect days. I've had a whole handful of them, more than most, I think. No one has a right to more. Most days are made of something less than and something more than *happiness*.' Miranda's voice is a whisper.

'*Già*, indeed.' The tribe is in harmony.

A pair of candles he'd taken earlier from the armoire and tucked in his jacket pocket for just this moment, Fernando lights them now as the others burn away. Filiberto takes up his mandolin and tonight his hoarse whispery voice lulls Miranda. Her snoring a whistle, faint, steady, she sleeps as we do the washing up, smother the ashes, gather our things. *Buonanotte.*

Filiberto helps Miranda into his truck and I watch them, wonder about them. Does he stay with her in her house in Castelpietro? Does she stay with him in his house, which sits beyond the farthest meadow off the Montefiescone road? Once a *fenile*, a stone hay barn, it's where he makes cheese, births lambs and tends the ailing ones, where he shears sheep, where he cooks and washes and eats and sleeps. Maybe the goddess of Buonrespiro is right: maybe the good half of a love is enough.

As we drive home, I wonder if the boy with the violin will pass through Orvieto again. I am happy that Gilda has so gracefully snitched the black velvet hat. Will Paolina marry Niccolò?

Late on Friday morning, Paolina calls: 'The rustico wants a good cleaning. We were all so tired last night, I don't even remember if we scrubbed the pots. Shall we take care of things together? Maybe tomorrow? Niccolò and his mates from San Severo are going to Rome on the 11:05. Did Fernando tell you that he'd invited him to go along? Pierangelo as well. Armando al Pantheon for lunch, a walk in the Villa Borghese, back to the train. They'll be home in time to take you and Ninuccia and I for *aperitivi* and then to la Palomba for supper.'

'Fernando is, at this moment, upstairs trying on jackets he hasn't worn since Venice. He's so pleased . . .'

'You know he'd asked Niccolò if you and I and Ninuccia might go along but Niccolò wouldn't have it. Just as well. Tomorrow, at about eleven.'

•

On Saturday I leave Fernando at the train station, arrive at the rustico just before eleven-thirty to find Paolina on her knees scrubbing the floor.

'It was a ruse. Asking you to help me. All of it done in less than an hour. I haven't lit the stove or the hearth fire. It's so warm today . . .'

'Come with me then, we'll finish that later. I didn't bring anything for breakfast. Or lunch. Emergency Venchi 85 per cent cacao, three bars in the glove box.'

'We may need it.'

We take up our places prone among the weeds on the edge of Miranda's *oliveto* and smoke Paolina's hand-rolled cigarettes.

'Do you want to know if I've *accepted* him?'

'I suppose I do. Yes, I do.'

'I'll wait to tell you. I'll wait until I've told you other things.'

•

Why can't she just say, I did or I didn't? Yes or no? I wonder as I look at Paolina who seems concentrated on her cigarette, taking it out of her mouth after each inhalation, holding it first close up, then farther away, pondering it as though the 'other things' she wishes to tell me were written on its thin white paper. It's only after she bashes the last millimetre of it on a stone and drops the spent end of it in her metal box that Paolina begins.

'Like a keening wraith, I roved about the rooms of the house where I was born, opening and slapping shut the doors, thinking if I opened them once again, he would be there. She would.'

As she lifts her gaze from a place somewhere in the weeds a streak of sunlight flickers across her eyes, illuminating the tears she'd thought to hide. She sits up, fiddles with a boot buckle. I sit up, caress her arm sooner than speak. After a while, it's she who does.

'*Sto bene*. I'm fine. Only, only a moment. I'm fine.'

Paolina tells me that she, an only child of only children, was not quite eighteen when the young black-bearded man who was her father died while ploughing the dark red earth of a tobacco field. On a Saturday it was when Paolina's father died, a week to the day after her mother – ill and choosing not to linger – had hurried herself away.

'Until almost the end of her days, my mother still ran my bath in the evening, woke me in the morning with a *buongiorno principessa* in falsetto, setting down on my bedside table a tray with a china pot of caffé latte and two croissants fat with marzipan, crusted with roasted almonds and still warm from the pasticceria. *Amore mio, come hai dormito?* My love, how did you sleep?

'Though my father's was a more reticent love, together their devotion commanded me, their authority so congenial I was breathless to resist. Mine had been a life measured out in the melodious two-note chime of meekness and reward. I was their *good girl.* And then they were gone. No matter how many times I opened and shut the doors, I was alone. Save for 'uncle' Niccolò.

'Tall, broad, mercurial as a god was Niccolò back then. Like chunks of sky were his eyes and I loved the smell of his tweeds, smoked as they were in the burley ash of the Brebbia he held between his teeth even as he spoke. Even as he sucked and chewed on the little red pastilles flavoured with *ratanhia root* which he'd pinch from a silver matchbox tucked in the pocket of his vest. As though a companion shade swung a thurible in his wake, when Niccolò went away, the smell of him faded slow as incense. My father's patron, my mother's paladin, our personal banker, oftentimes our chef, Niccolò had been – for as long as I could remember – the perpetrator of small ecstacies, mostly gastronomic. And as my parents commanded me, just as benignly and consummately did Niccolò command them.

'As Niccolò's *fattore di fiducia* – trusted foreman – it was my father who kept in efficient production the small empire that composed his friend's legacy: wheat fields and sheepfolds, plantations of tobacco and sunflowers, groves of olives and vineyards. With my father taking care of things for him, Niccolò was free to indulge his passions for the markets and the caffés and the *trattorie.* For his paramours. Back then, though, I'd known nothing of *paramours.*

'Unexpected, unannounced, Niccolò was wont to tramp through the front hall and into our dining room of an evening just as we were sitting down to supper. He being our Elijah, my mother would set a place for him at every meal. Sometimes he'd just pull up his chair and make himself at home, grinning and rubbing together his hands as my mother helped him to the food, my father to the wine. But on other evenings he'd march in and begin snatching up plates and glasses, corking wine, wrapping the bread in a napkin. *"Andiamo. Let's go."*

"'Let's go? Where?" My mother would shout, throwing up her hands, while my father – his acquiesence to Niccolò a matter of routine – simply rose from his chair, went to turn off the oven and then to find his jacket.

'Once I remember Niccolò pulling a corked, dark glass bottle from his coat pocket, *'Ecco,* behold, oil just pressed, just robbed from my own mill. Tomorrow is soon enough for *pastasciutta.* I booked Roncalli. *Forza, forza,* I've left the auto running . . .

"'It's an hour to Foligno, Niccolò," my mother whined.

"'What do you care? I've *salame* in the other pocket and wine in the boot."

"'But why? Everything is here and . . ."

"'Because there will never be another Friday evening at eight o'clock on November 29, 1959. That's why. *Forza."*

'My mother would strip off her pinafore, run to get her good shoes, lean over the sideboard checking herself in the mirror above it while she kicked off her slippers and slid into the suede pumps she wore to church. The points of her cheeks gone red like rosehips, she'd press her hands to her hair, deepening the already deep blonde waves of it while Niccolò stood there holding out her coat, telling her she would have made Botticelli crazy. Cinderella wrenched from her hearth was my mother, tantalised by a fleshly prince bent on a 10-centimetre Chianina beef steak barely warmed over an olivewood fire. I remember wishing Niccolò would hold out my coat for me. Wishing my own cheeks would go red as rosehips. And wishing my mother was like other mothers.

'Niccolò would bury Norcia truffles in a sack of rice and place it, like an icon, on a shelf in the kitchen. He'd turn back to us, to my mother and me, and say, 'The rice will be properly perfumed by Tuesday. I'll bring everything else. Everything. Your job is to set the table and to be beautiful. *Basta.*'

'He always looked at my mother when he said the part about being beautiful.

'In the post basket hung on the front door, he'd leave a branch of peach blossom or one of tiny pomegranates, their broken skins bleeding juice the colour of Spanish wine. A just-slaughtered and dressed suckling lamb hung around his neck like a scarf, a haunch of deer in a sack slung over his shoulder, under his arm, a brown satin box with glacéed chestnuts nestling in the folds of its black velvet lining, it was Niccolò's doing that by the time I was ten or so – and he was twenty-something – it was already difficult for me to separate one appetite from another. One hunger from another. I loved to eat. I loved *zio* Niccolò.

'As I've said, I was just shy of eighteen when my parents died and in the early days of grieving, Niccolò was my refuge. Burrowing my face into the man-smelling tweed of his coat, his great brown hands caressing my hair, I waited for him to tilt my chin up to him, to press his lips to my forehead. When he moved his hands from my hair to my breasts, I looked straight at him, into his eyes like chunks of sky. I wept and I smiled. I remember looking behind him, as though to make sure she wasn't there. My mother with the rosehip cheeks and the Botticelli face, a strap of her sundress slipping down over the white marble of her shoulder, little beads of sweat glossing her upper lip as she rolled the *umbricelli* – one by one – across the wooden board while Niccolò sat watching her. No, she wasn't there. My rival was no more. Thin solace for the loss of a mother was my victory. Bitter recompense, I thought, pushing my face deeper into Niccolò's chest, trying not to ask myself if losing her was precisely what I'd longed for.

'He would cook for me every day, Niccolò would. I remember most a soup he'd make. He'd sit me down at the kitchen table, slide a small glass of white wine across the oilcloth to me.

'"*Allora. Guardami bene.* Watch me carefully." He'd skin and slice a pair of onions faster than the butter could melt in the sauté pan he'd placed on the burner behind him.

'"*Sempre una fiamma bassa per la minestra.* Always a low flame for soup." He'd leave the onions to melt into the butter while he gathered up the rest of what he needed: yesterday's bread, some milk, a few branches of dried wild thyme, the bottle of white wine. When the onions were soft and gold, he'd rub some rough salt between his hands and then sprinkle the onions with flour; he'd slip the thyme leaves off their branches and crush them between his fingertips over the pan. The stems in his shirt pocket to use later in the hearth. He'd give the mass a good stir, letting the flour and the butter bubble away for a minute; some milk, then some wine. I think about a cup of each. Maybe more wine than milk. When the soup had just begun to thicken, he'd take it from the flame, cover it, let the thyme do its work while he toasted thin slices of the old bread, brushed them with butter, laid them in two wide shallow bowls. He'd sit with me then and we'd drink another glass of wine. He would never set our places directly on the oilcloth even if we were sitting down only to soup or cheese and bread. He'd take out one of the fine embroidered cloths from the armoire, spread it smooth, knot the napkins on one end and, flicking his wrist, shake each one before laying it down, aligning the knot perfectly with the silverware. He'd light a candle even at noon. I think he made the wild thyme soup for me nearly every day for the first month or so. "*Curativo*," he would say. "Healing."

•

He must have known before I did that I was with child because when, all breathless and bridal, I ran to open the door to him one morning after I'd seen *Dottoressa* Ottaviano, Niccolò sat me down at the kitchen table and immediately began speaking of the *aspetto pratico*, the practical aspect, of our situation.

'"But Niccolò, there's time for all of that. Now we must celebrate, think about the wedding, about our child, about . . ."

'"*Tesoro mio, ti voglio tanto bene ma io non mi sposerò mai. Mai.* My darling, I love you but I will never marry. Never. Oh, it's not that I don't like weddings. I would have been a bridegroom a hundred times over by now as long as I could have avoided being a husband. I will hold financial responsibility, be a figure in the child's life, sustain both of you in every way save that of living together as a family. We can even have a wedding if you want. But no marriage."

'He rose then, washed his hands at the kitchen sink. Pontius Pilate with a pipe. Taking a clean towel from the drawer in the cupboard, he slowly dried his hands. He began looking through the onions in the basket on the work table.

"'I'll do the shopping," he said, buttoning his jacket.

'Heeding the old impulse to meekness, I sat quietly. When he returned sometime later, his market bag full, he found me where he'd left me. As though the news might be balm, he said he'd been to consult his attorney. Across the shiny red and yellow cloth on the table, Niccolò spread bank books, lists of goods and chattels, a copy of his testament. The pipe tight between his teeth, he droned out numbers while I unpacked the market bag, moving his papers to make room for white-skinned potatoes and tight little heads of red lettuce, two of purple garlic, the dried stems of them knotted together like castanets. I kept picking up each thing as though weighing it, then putting it down. I never said a word. He relit his pipe, signifying that his presentation was complete.

"'*Ma, l'amore?* But what about love?" I wanted to know, my voice cracking as though I'd just awakened from a long sleep. As though I'd been weeping in my dreams.

'Drying my face with the back of his hand, the stem of his pipe still between his teeth, he'd whispered, "*Povera cocca,* poor little one, it's duty that counts in life. *Amore. Amore.* Love. Love. Bread lasts longer than love. I want to offer you something better."

'The meekness in me thawed and boiled up like rage. Ripping his hands from my face, sending the documents and the onions flying from the table with a single sweep of my arm, I beat him about the chest that had been my refuge, clawed his cheeks, wrenched the grizzled black and brown pomp of his hair, tore the Brebbia from his mouth and smote it on the tiles. I bent to retrieve one of the bank books and, heaving it into the ashes of the hearth, I stood straight, laid a back-handed slap across his face and ran for the door. Flinging it wide and letting it bang against the wall, I remembered my coat, which he'd already gone to fetch. As he held it out for me, I snatched it from him, thinking of how many times I'd longed for that, for Niccolò to hold out my coat as he did for her. I walked away, shutting the door hard on his last words: "Lunch will be ready in an hour."

'My pace fast as my heartbeat, I traversed the few metres to the piazza. I turned back to see if he'd followed me, but there was only a small band of children from the kindergarten approaching in the bleak March light, harassing the pigeons while their teachers walked behind them, smoking hungrily. I sat down on the iron bench by the fountain, my grand revolt already on the wane, having exhausted itself on the truth that I had been Niccolò's seductress. If ever a woman offered herself to a man, I'd offered myself to him. A revelation. A plain truth. I wrapped my arms about my chest as if trying to find the repentance in me but there was none. I let one hand drop to lie on my stomach. On my womb. Big as a bean and not yet meat, a creature was ripening inside me and, while I'd been pining over a wedding dress, it had already shaken the kaleidoscope, rethrown the stones and the pattern they made was my future.

'Would I go back to the house now and take up my submissiveness? Invite Niccolò to the role of loving tyrant only just vacated by my parents? Would I surrender my child, too, to Niccolò's dominion? *I will hold financial responsibility, be a figure in the child's life, sustain both of you in every way save that of living together as a family.* No. Thank you, but, no. No, to every part of your offer, Niccolò. No.

'His back to me, he was slicing bread when I walked into the kitchen. Before he turned, I knew what I would see in those eyes and I longed to comfort him. I'd become someone more, someone less than who I'd been a scant hour before. Leaps of comprehension and self-trust, a capacity for empathy, if these deem to come in life, they come like lightning, *in un colpo*, in a flash. Unlike the sort of change that happens over time. Unlike change that is won by faithful pummelling – of one's self or of another. Nothing *fresh* about that kind of change. While I'd been sitting there by the fountain in the piazza in that bleak March light I'd vaulted the wall of the sanctuary. On my own, I was.

'"Also I, *Nicò*. I will never marry. I will be a bride a hundred times over but I will never be a wife." I'd meant him to laugh but as he turned, the bread knife poised, there was only desolation in his eyes. He looked at me. *Studied* me.

'"*Hai fame?* Are you hungry?"

'"*Sì.*"

'"*Brava.*"

'We sat and he poured wine. Not waiting for him to serve me as he always did, I took up the white fluted bowl of tiny purple artichokes and pushed some onto his plate. I took a few for myself.

'"*Ma, domani, cucinerò io*," I told him. "But tomorrow, I will cook."

'He stayed quiet. After a long time, he began a mild sort of protest but let it fall away.

'"*Va bene.*" His voice was a whisper. He raised his glass to me. "Your eyes are black in this light. They're purple in the sun. Your eyes make a man think, Paolina. Only poetic men will love you. The others will try to change you. The others won't be able to look in your eyes. I wish I were a poet, Paolina."

•

'It was a Monday morning, a fews day after our joint "proclamations": Niccolò's to me, mine to him. And my own to myself. I was sitting, dreaming, by the *salone* window when I saw them walking across the piazza on their way to me: the parish priest, his mother and his aunt. Don Umberto, Carolina and Luigia. Though the trio had been visiting me every Monday morning since my parents' death, I'd somehow not remembered on that particular Monday that it was their day. But there they were, the women in sedate frocks and elastic hose almost pink against their black lace-up shoes. Shawls, hats with veils and white cotton gloves, cloth-covered baskets hung from their wrists. As she was wont to do, Carolina minced ahead of the others, her head pitched slightly forward of her body, insistent as a lead goose. Apart from my parents and Niccolò, these three were as close to kin as I'd ever had. I went to put the kettle on, take off my apron.

'"*Buongiorno, bella*," they said in unison, commencing with the ritual unpacking of their gifts: *torte,* biscotti, *pane.* Jars of jam and little pots of savoury things to spread on bread. As though there'd been a flood or a war or some devastation that had emptied the shops which sat all along the piazza outside my door, they would replenish my supplies. The one constant provision was a thick green litre bottle of Marsala beaten with eggs and sugar. *Simpatia*, Carolina called it. Sympathy.

'Having been assigned to the parish just after his ordination when he was something less than twenty-five, Umberto celebrated the high mass when my parents were married, cleansed me from original sin in a bath of holy water, put the body of Jesus on my devoutly extended tongue when I was seven, inflamed my quest to be confirmed a soldier of Christ when I was twelve. Umberto said the euology for both my parents. He never left my side when they were being lowered into the ground.

'And Carolina. Unflinching, bold and yet refined, the kind of woman who would dress for dinner in the jungle, she'd fasten the fifty hooks on a boned corset before setting off on the twenty-metre trek from the parish house to the butcher. That was Carolina. When she was widowed at fifty, she departed Rome for San Severino to keep house for her son. Not to be abandoned in the family palazzo in the Parioli, Luigia – her elder and maiden sister – arrived days later at the station in Orvieto. "For a small month," she'd said back then – thirteen years ago.

'That morning, as she did always, Luigia made the tea while Carolina laid the table in the *salone* and Umberto and I, in a posture that had long become natural to us, sat leafing through one book or another. For the five years of my tenure in the *liceo classico*, Umberto had been my Latin tutor. But long before that he was drawn, I think, to the melancholy in me, mirroring his own as it did. Having himself been formed by the Jesuits, so would he form me, a bright, quiet lamb, black, among his flock. And so on that morning he commenced his usual imperatives: "It's time,

Paolina, that you should be choosing a *facoltà*, a major course of study." He spoke of enquiries he'd made to colleagues at the university in Perugia, said that he'd *alerted* one of them that I would need preparation for certain exams. "Were you to succeed in these, well, he would see to things. If you decide on Philosophy, I think we could manage to place you in that department."

"'I'm going to have a baby, Umberto."

'I said this without changing the tenor of my voice. I stood up from where I'd been sitting on the sofa next to him and said it again.

"'You see, I'm going to have a baby."

'Carolina and Luigia, both of whom had been still fussing with the table, heard the repetition of my announcement. Both sat heavily on the nearest chairs. Luigia began to laugh.

"'Of course you are. *Amore mio*, of course you'll have a baby someday and we'll all dance at your wedding and . . ."

"'In September. I'm going to have a baby in September."

"'This September?" Carolina had risen from her chair and come to stand in front of me. "This one," I told her.

'I turned back to Umberto and then looked at Luigia, both of whom were gazing downward.

"'My time will be up on the eighteenth. Dottoressa Ottaviano and I, we did the counting together. That is, I went to see her a few days ago and, well . . . I . . ."

'They were silent. I wept.

"'Niccolò?" Umberto looked at me, his eyes saying he hoped it *was* as much as he hoped it *wasn't*.

"'Niccolò," I said.

"'I'll speak to him . . . I'm certain his intentions are . . .'"

"'Niccolò and I have already spoken. We're . . . we've decided not to marry.'"

"'*Inconcepibile*, inconceivable . . .'"

'I fear the *conceiving* has already been done, Umberto," muttered Carolina.

"'Both of us have decided. I will raise my baby. Niccolò will be a part in some way but not as my husband. Not as the child's father. Neither of those. I can't begin to tell you how dearly I want this.'"

'Forever the lead goose, Carolina had left the *salone* to rummage in the kitchen. I began to follow her there but she was already returning, shaking the green glass Marsala bottle as she came. The bottle still in hand, she went to the credenza where the finer things of the house were kept. As though suspending the drama that had unfolded behind her, Carolina mused, humming, among the wineglasses. Rather than one of them, she opted for a cut-crystal compote dish from my mother's precious Bohemian collection. Setting it down on the table, she began to pour in the creamy sugared wine. So long did she pour, she had time to look up at me and smile and look down again before she'd poured enough.

"'Drink this," Carolina said. "I put more sugar than usual in it this week. And cinnamon, too. *Sapevo io*. I knew. *Siamo ancora in Italia, no?* We're still in Italy, no? If a man and a woman are alone together for more than twenty minutes, it has always been assumed that they have made love. *Sapevo*. I knew.'"

'Luigia hissed, "*Scema* . . . Fool . . .'"

'Eyes closed, I silently willed Carolina not to proceed with another indelicacy, not to be her haughty, disparaging self. *A half moment of truce, Carolina, I beg you.* Then I heard her words again. *If a man and a woman are alone together for more than twenty minutes, it has always been assumed that they have made love.* I couldn't tell if she repeated them or if I heard them from inside of me, from far away. Her words were a caption to images that began to slice fast as a guillotine across the back of my eyes. I saw my mother and Niccolò working in the kitchen when I'd return from school, their unpacking wine or oil or bushels of fruit from the boot of Niccolò's auto, my waking from a nightmare and, still half asleep, wandering downstairs to find Niccolò alone in the *salone.* "*Dove sono mamma e papà.* Where are my mother and my father?" I asked Niccolò.

'"Your father went to help cover the vines against the frost. The men telephoned . . . Your mother, I think, I think . . . she's, yes, she's bathing. Yes. Bathing. Twenty minutes. Of course."

'"*Amore mio, bevi.* Drink, my love," Carolina was saying to me. Already convulsed, the smell of raw egg and sweet wine brought shivers. I sipped daintily. Carolina goaded. I sipped again.

'Through all of this Umberto had kept his silence. He rose then, came to his place at table. Carolina sat next to me. All the cutting and pouring and passing made a reassuring noise.

'"There's so much to talk about, isn't there?" said Carolina.

'Adjusting her slipped shoulder pads back to their proper geometric formation, she asked, "Who would have thought we'd be having a baby in September?"

Over time I was able to calm, somewhat, Carolina's possessiveness of me and my "condition". I managed to convince her – and Luigia, too – that I could nicely manage my days, that I ate and slept properly, walked briskly for several kilometres twice a day, that I never raised my hands above my head (so as not to stretch the umbilical cord, which could then wrap about the baby's neck), that I kept nothing of the baby's layette in the house after sunset. This last meant that, as I'd finish knitting a cap or sewing tabs on some miniscule undershirt or cutting up sheets into diapers, I'd go dutifully to put the things in an old maroon leather trunk, which Carolina had especially provided and placed in the woodshed. Over it, she'd hung a print of a Botticelli Madonna in a wide gold frame. *Coincidenza,* coincidence, I thought . . . willing away images of my mother. Every time I went to open or close the trunk, I would carefully avert my gaze from her.

'I dined at the parish house once a week and our Mondays at my place were observed, sacred as mass. Though we spoke always about the baby, the subject of Niccolò we forsook, the moat too wide and deep around him. Umberto, however, I saw only by chance, he neither accompanying the women to me on Mondays nor being present when I dined at the parish house. "You know how it is, Paolina. He's always taking on more than . . ." When we did meet in the town, Umberto was remote but not uncharitable. My status with him had shifted from protégée to parishioner. I was reconciled to this.

'Niccolò continued to spend part of every day with me. And, as I'd earlier announced that I would, I began to cook for him, in my fashion. Boiling and roasting things to their wreckage. He was patient. I think his grand defence must have been to stop at one of his haunts before coming to me each day, to slurp down a plate of pasta or ravage the *bruschette* and *crostini* served in the bars with *aperitivi*. His single obstinacy about our cooking and dining arrangement was that he continue to gather up the provisions.

'Even before I was bathed and dressed in the morning, I would hear him trilling '*funiculi, funicula*' in the kitchen as he thumped down the morning's goods on the table. He'd fill the Bialetti, put it on a quiet flame, shout *buongiorno, tesoro,* and leave me, unencumbered, to my acts of destruction. Sometimes I'd find a scribbled suggestion, a few lines of method, a caveat. One day he wrote: "*Lascia il cibo essere se stesso. Non mascherare. Esalta.* Let the food be itself. Don't mask. Exult." I thought the words provocative. Almost like a dare. I remember tucking the scrap of paper in my pocket, pushing it deep into the bottom like a love letter. A charm. It was the only cooking lesson Niccolò ever gave to me. I'd recite the words over and over again every time I took up my knife or set a pot on the flame. It wanted time, though, before I began to act out the words. The first time I did, it was on a morning in July.

'In a large green basket with a broken handle, Niccolò left the first tomatoes he'd harvested from his own vines. Big and sun-split and smelling of heat and of the basil planted between the rows, these tomatoes. I fondled the warm satin skin of the misshapen things, turned them over and over, marvelling at them as though I'd never before seen a tomato. Carrying the basket on my upturned arms over to the sink, I began to rinse them, laying them on a nice white towel to dry and, as I washed the last one, I put it to my nose, and then to my mouth. Ravenous for that tomato, I bit deep into its pulp, gasping on its flesh as though I'd been starved and it was the last food in the world. Standing there over the sink, devouring the thing, careless of the juices running down my neck and into the bosom of my dress, all I could think was: *This is how I want our lunch to taste.*

'At first I meant to simply break open the fruits and serve them as they were – with knife and fork and a dish of salt. But then I took up a small, sharp knife and set to roughly chopping the tomatoes into the wide shallow bowl we used for pasta. I rubbed sea salt over and, holding my thumb over the olive oil flask, poured on thin threads of oil. Stirring it all together I was tempted to tear in leaves of basil and marjoram then, to cover the bowl and place it over a pot of simmering water as I'd seen my mother and Niccolò do when fixing *sugo crudo*, raw sauce. No. I would chase, further yet, this idea of revealing a food's own goodness. Better that these beauties be warmed under the sun that birthed them than over a gas flame. With the white towel I'd used to dry the tomatoes, I covered the bowl, carried it out to the garden and left it on a table where no shade would reach it. *Let the food be itself. Don't mask. Exult.*

'Moving in an epiphanous daze, wiping my hands down the length of my apron, stopping them to caress the place where my child was growing, I walked back to the kitchen. I was a mother. I was a cook. I was *becoming* a cook.

164

'I surveyed the other good things Niccolò had left for me and began tasting them, this way and that, in my mind. Out in the rustico – the summer kitchen – I built an olivewood fire in the hearth, the first one I'd ever made without my mother or Niccolò helping to tease the flames to their dance. The tomatoes out there in the garden and the good fire I'd set raised up in me a strange blend of conceit and awe so that, once back in the house, I set to my own sort of makeshift dance. Slicing finger-sized zucchini whisper-thin on the *mandolino*, I dressed them with oil warmed with a branch of *mentuccia* – wild mint – and left the bowl handy so I could give them a stir every time I passed by. As the fire began to smoulder, I laid tiny, fat, whole fennel bulbs on the grate and, when the stringy, sweet-licorice flesh of them had gone soft, I slipped the bulbs into a pan and set it down in the ash. As I'd seen my father do, I threaded the sausages that Niccolò had brought that morning from Mocetti onto vine twigs soaked in water. The sausages cooked and dripped juices onto the fennel resting below. I opened the wine.

'Niccolò arrived. Seeing that I'd left nothing much for him to do, he washed his hands, sat at his place. An elbow resting on the table, his hand supporting his chin, he watched me. Another Paolina, freshly pirouetted from her cocoon.

'A morning's sojourn in the sun had caused the tomatoes to give up their juices and, like soup, I ladled them into bowls. Beside each bowl I set down a long flat, crusty *ciabatta*, split and barely toasted over the embers. Dipping a branch of rosemary into a saucer of oil, I rubbed the charred crevices of the bread, dipping the branch again and again into the oil and painting the bread with it, pushing hard on the rosemary, bruising its leaves against the hot bread until the rosemary gave up its scent. Half a *ciabatta* for Niccolò and half for me. I brought in the sausages then, laid them over the fennel, wetting both with the pan drippings. More bread. The little salad of raw zucchini refreshed us and, as an end to the meal, we finished the wine and sat there plucking leaves from the bouquet of *mentuccia*, wild mint, that I'd set in a pewter jug on the table, chewing them like candy.

'Though I don't recall what I cooked or ate for lunch four days ago, I remember every morsel of that one in a July of more than forty years ago. I will always. It would have been enough, that lunch. Had the Fates never allowed me the peace and plenty in which to cook and eat that way again, I could have lived off that one. I was safe.

'Niccolò never said much about the food I set before him that day nor about the food I set before him on the days that followed. He knew and I knew that, by saying little, he was saying everything.

•

'Soon after the tomato lunch Niccolò began stopping by to fetch me at seven in the morning. "*Faremo le spese insieme.* We'll shop together," he'd said.

'Primped, lustrous, scented in neroli, Niccolò – already feverish over the glories that might be waiting in the markets – would appear while I'd still be pinning up my hair, looking for a sweater or my boots, the sleep just rinsed from my eyes.

'"Tonino should have figs today. Taste the borlotti before you buy them. Crisp and juicy they should be but not bitter. Take two kilos. And we'll need to put *baccalà* to soak today if you want to cook it on Friday. Walnuts from the Lazio truck, don't forget those."

'On Saturdays we'd go to both our own market and then to Orvieto, where we'd mostly just meander in the way one does when what's desired has already been found. We'd go to the wagon that dispensed *porchetta*, thick slices of wood-roasted suckling pig, boned and stuffed with a mash of its innards and wild herbs and I'd ask for one with crackling skin for Nicò, one without for me. Sitting on the steps of the Palazzo del Capitano, we'd eat and talk about food.

'"Before you cook a dish, you must be able to taste it. Go through the process first in your mind. Imagine yourself choosing the ingredients. Be sure of how you want them to look and smell and feel. Think about your pan or pot, your knife, get to work. Pour in the oil and begin warming it over a gentle flame; throw in a fine mince of pancetta or lard, wild thyme or rosemary or, better, both. Turn up the flame just a little; now the garlic, then the onions. When the pancetta is crisp, the onions and garlic are golden and transparent and the herbs are fragrant, spoon it all out into a large deep dish. Dry the pieces of meat and lay them in the pan, leaving them to crust in the perfumed fat over a modest flame. Leave them longer than you think you should. *Tanta patienza ci vuole.* You'll want great patience. When all the flesh is crusted, add it to the dish with the aromatics. Turn up the flame and pour the wine into the hot, very hot pan, stirring and scraping until the bottom of the pan is clean. Now tip the dish of aromatics and crusted flesh back into the pan. The wine in the pan should be enough to wet the flesh but not to drown it. When the wine begins to shimmer, lower the heat, cover the pot almost all the way. Leave the flesh to braise in the barely shuddering wine. Never should there be a more violent movement than that shudder. Every hour, add a few tablespoons more wine. After a time, that tiny aperture between the pot and its lid will have sent up sufficient winey vapours to scent the house. Your hair will smell of wine and rosemary. Go out for a short walk so that you can come back inside to take in the full effect of that winey steam. Now. Go through this exercise a few times and then you'll be ready to cook."

'I listened to Nicò's recipes as I would a fable, the words transporting me to a mythical kitchen where I could see the wine shuddering in that pan and smell the thyme and the onions. I went to bed that night and cooked myself to sleep, starving for that butter-soft flesh crusted in the fat and the wine and the herbs in which it had lolled for days and nights over a barely lit flame. I dragged a crust of imaginary bread into the imaginary sauce and then slept the angels' sleep.

'"Where did you learn those recipes?" I asked him one day.

'"In my grandmother's *salottino*." Niccolò told me that during the war he and his cousins lived with her, their parents having been otherwise occupied with the Resistance. He was the eldest of the grandchildren, a kind of surrogate uncle to seven younger children. From time to time he would defy his father's orders to stay and manage things for them and instead set off to join one *branco* or another up in the hills, mostly in Toscana. "But I never stayed away for more than a few days, time enough to enact some lesser violence against the *Krauti* before getting back to safeguarding my own," Nicò told me.

"'Better off than many, a little worse off than others, there was always some sort of supper for us. Mostly it was polenta, sometimes with a sauce. When it was cooked, my grandmother would pour it into a bowl, let it cool and then turn the great yellow dome of it out onto a pewter tray lined with a cloth. With all the pomp of a chef carrying a flaming pudding into a grand hall, she'd bring it to the fire, cut it into thick slices with a length of cotton string and set them to sizzle on the grate. Meanwhile, she'd tell us the story of one dish or another, of some luscious cake made with roasted walnuts and prunes soaked in Marsala or bread made with red wine and cinnamon, which her own grandmother would make at harvest time and bring out to the vineyards, still warm, with a pot of chestnut honey. The recipe she told most often, though, was the one I told to you. Only she told it better. Soft, breathless, her voice was the kind you had to listen hard to hear, and we sat there on the stone floor she'd laid with straw, looking up at her, rapt as a nest of starving birds. *Tristezza* – sadness – and joy watered her eyes and quivered about her lips and, young as we were, we knew. Young as we were, we knew her story was about more than food and so it became about more than food to us."

"'Listen with your soul's ear,' she'd tell us. 'It can hear the things that those foolish ones sticking out of your head can't hear at all.'"

'"When the polenta was crisp and gold and beginning to burn at its edges, she'd offer each one of us a slice from the tip of her toasting fork, so hot we'd burn our hands and then our lips and our tongues and she'd keep talking while spearing the next slices. We gorged on them. On the story. As much on the story, I think. She made cooks of all of us you know. Every one."

'"She died soon after the war ended. I remember helping my mother to wrap my grandmother's kitchen things in newspaper. Almost everything fitted into two small boxes; a meagre store of pots, the mortars in which she pounded her herbs, two etched blue goblets from her wedding feast, the shallow white bowls in which she served almost everything, mismatched table silver, all of it dainty and fine and gifted to her – a spoon and fork at a time – from the legacies of aunts and cousins. By comparison, my father left a noble's ransom to me, an estate which I've since managed to enrich. And yet I will never have as much to leave as she."'

•

'When Niccolò was with me it was good, and when he wasn't it was another kind of good: a wider good, better lit. I began to feel a quiet relief that he and I would not be repeating the *ménage à trois* I'd lived with my parents: mother, father and child, smooth as three paving stones carved and keyed to lock together. No. Not that for us. Having swerved easily enough away from thinking to be in love with him, my passions seemed inclined toward liberty. How I waited for the evenings when Niccolò would be off to the other side of his life, to his friends. To his mystery. Possessive of my solitude, nothing and no one would distract me from the wonder I was feeling about the child inside me. I would read or knit, take some small supper of broth and bread but mostly I would just sit and caress the place where the baby was. Niccolò's affection for me was a comfort that I brushed against but never leant upon. Even then, though, I'd understood that this liberty – this solitude – I was chasing would sometimes feel like *aloneness* and that the abyss between solitude and aloneness would be deep and dark. And so I wondered about love. About that absorbing kind of love. *You and me against the world.* Did I fear that? Did I believe in it? And if one risked such a thing, could even love save one from aloneness? I thought not. I think not.

'As I was then made of that fragile sort of thinness, more bone than flesh, and still wore mourning, the child growing in me had become quickly evident. Black dresses with padded shoulders and belted waists, the skirts falling to the calf, tea-length we called them. Oxfords with high thick heels, black cotton stockings. Even in summer. No more than I sought to display my baby did I try to hide him.

'As respectful to me in public as he was in private, Niccolò and I moved through some of each day as a couple might. We'd take breakfast standing at the bar in Ducchi, queue at the butcher's and at the post office, make the *struscio* – the evening stroll, up and down the corso, sit in the caffés for *aperitivi*, look in the shops. We were serene while the town clucked and wagered and watched, planting and harvesting rumours like so much wheat.

'Surely, the San Severese factored my tragic losses into the gauge of their censure. If some sewed me a scarlet letter, they pinned it to my turned shoulders and never to my breast. Carolina was my champion, after all. Her undisguised benediction of me – and Umberto's reserved acquiescence – suffocated the gossip, if not always to its death.

'Unmarried and with child in a small rural Umbrian town in the last years of the 1960s, I might well have scorched with shame at every social encounter and yet I never did. I suppose some of the locals thought Niccolò would eventually marry me or that I would surrender my child to the nuns or have the decency to remove myself to another town apart from their genteel sensibilities. Unreflected considerations, all of those. I shall never know how it was that, at the age of eighteen, I'd managed to grasp onto the truth that what others would say or think of me mattered less than what I thought of myself. I felt no mortification for my indiscretion with Niccolò, the shame in me being already engaged elsewhere.

•

'Stasia Lazzari. Even her name was lovely. Wherever she went, my mother brought all the light and took up all the air. Under the convincing pretence of devotion, my mother's every gesture was provoked by vanity, a superiority complex she wrapped in an often slavish humility. She accentuated her beauty by understatement. A natural actress, her long-standing and preferred role was Victim. The beleaguered mother. She'd buy her dresses from the used pile in the markets while mine were hand-smocked by a *sarta* in Florence. That escaped tendril, that fallen shoulder strap, were her at-home costume while my father's cast-off sweater and slippers with ankle socks, even in the rain, made up her public masquerade. *La Piccola Fiammiferaia*. The Little Match Girl. This one with green eyes iridescent as the neck of a pheasant. Stasia Lazzari was irresistible.

'Even those daily ten-metre trips to fetch my pastries were performances. She'd never simply stand in line to wait for them but groan and shake her head, reciting at studied intervals the same lament: "*Per la figlia, beata lei che è ancora a letto. Intanto la mamma fa tutto.* For my blessed daughter who is still in bed. Meanwhile her mother does everything."

'Her friends and my friends would tell me of this repeated scene, ask me how I could permit my poor mother to do my bidding. "I've asked, begged. A million times. *Ti prego, mamma.* I beg you. Don't bring me pastries. I prefer to have breakfast in the bar with my friends." How I hated those croissants. But should I leave them untouched, she would announce my ingratitude that afternoon in the shops, grist for the evening's supper table in who knows how many households. I took to leaving a few crumbs on the plate and hiding the rest in my knapsack to later tear up for the birds in the schoolyard. Unimportant in itself, this years-long pastry farce that Stasia and I practised was, though, a symbol of our *unrelatedness.* I was invisible to her save as an opportunity for the display of her virtue. The bleached-white, sugar-starched emblem of her excellence.

'As a small girl I'd been Stasia's devotee, shadowing her as she kneaded bread, ironed sheets. And when, before church or a supper out with my father, she'd perform a half-hearted toilette, I'd sit in the middle of her bed to watch: face powder from a gold tin she'd pat on with a pink puff and then, using a small brush which she'd wet on her tongue and rub across what looked like shoe polish in a tiny glass jar, she'd stroke her eyelashes – blonde and thick as a pony's – quickly, savagely, until they were black and curled against the green slant of her eyes. From the sack of her trinkets, I would choose her earrings. Sometimes a necklace. I remember only two dresses in her armoire, both of dark silk in more or less the same chaste form. Now that I think about it, there was another dress, black and made of some heavy fabric, perhaps faille. Straight and plain as a pencil from the front, she seemed so tall in that dress and when she turned there was a bustle, a small drape which fell from her waist to sit just above the curve of her derrierè. Not a proper Victim's dress. I think she must have worn it only on the occasions when she and my father would drive into Rome.

'I don't remember Stasia touching me, save when she dressed or washed me. Pulling, tugging, scrubbing, her affection utilitarian, purposeful. A good-night buss on the cheek, though not always. Nothing I could count on. When she sat to shell peas or tail beans or to talk on the telephone, I would sidle up next to her, rest my leg against hers, put my shoulder to her arm. I'd loop a finger possessively inside the hem of her skirt and just sit there, preening. Even then, when I was little, I'd always felt I was somehow older than Stasia, that I was the mother.

'Over time, my enchantment frayed, as it was bound to. She began to exhaust me and I consoled myself with finespun designs of wickedness against her. Among my most treacherous reveries, though, none were so extravagant as those that she and the Fates designed: the Match Girl flawlessness of her illness, her death. So you see, my shame back then, it was all used up on my mother.

'How did Stasia *become* herself? I still wonder about that. Do we become or are we begotten? What chance do we have? What was my mother's story? Did she mother me as she, herself, had been mothered? Is that what we do? Please God, no daughter for me. I fear that one evening my little girl would be sitting on my bed, humming over my jewels, and the next she'd be plotting revenge. I'd be doomed to make a daughter suffer. Who am I to think I wouldn't? Please God, no daughter.

•

'*Allora*. I spent that summer knitting and sewing, roaming the markets and cooking for Niccolò, talking and singing to my baby. But it was also during those weeks that, guided by a coverless and tattered illustrated volume Niccolò found in a vintage bookstall in Florence, I discovered the alchemy of cooking sweets. *The Traditional Convent Pastries of Sicily*. Transforming the kitchen into a laboratory, for the beating of creams and icings and the tempering of chocolate, I pummelled kilos of almonds with sugar into marzipan and crystallised gorgeous summer fruits and flowers in almond-perfumed sugar syrup. I tinted biscuit dough in the palest pink and pushed balls of it around in bowls of pine nuts or sesame seeds or roasted bitter almonds. Candied fruit and liqueurs I mixed with ewe's-milk ricotta and sugar and, after spreading the paste between rum-soaked layers of sponge cake, I covered the whole with a sheet of almond paste, glazed it with a thin pistachio-green icing and decorated the gorgeous mess with sugared violets. A fairly authentic reading of *la Cassata*. Loyal and willing beneficiaries, Carolina and Luigia would, at any given sitting, dispatch a dozen pastries, a tin of cookies, sugaring their heaving bosoms as they nibbled, crusting their lips with bits of pistachio.

'When I would go to supper at the parish house, I'd fill a kilo-weight tin with the day's lovely things and, resting it on the great mound of my stomach, make my way across the piazza. On one of those evenings, Luigia had gone with Umberto to an event in Perugia and Carolina and I were to dine alone.

'I remember how distracted she was, Carolina. We sat so long in the front garden with a glass of wine that I'd thought there'd be no supper at all until she finally hurried me inside and into the dining room, set down plates of soup. I remember it was a puree of green beans and basil and it tasted so good to me. Then there were thin slices of a veal galantine with a wine jelly that sparkled. *Rifreddo*, she called it. "One of Beppa's masterpieces made with bits picked from a Sunday roast," she'd said somewhat distractedly. Beppa was the parish-house cook. I was starving and so kept slipping another piece and another onto my plate, tipping a silver pitcher of sharp, vinegary sauce and skating crusts of bread through it. There was a blue-and-white-footed bowl heaped with tiny pickles. Carolina didn't touch the food. She would begin to say something, interrupt herself, look at me as though for help, as though I should know what she wanted to say. After a while I left her sitting there. I cleared the table, brought plates into the kitchen. I brewed espresso, carried in the tray and set it down before her. Still as stone, she sat.

"'Carolina? What is it, Carolina? Can you tell me?"

'Fluttering back from where she'd been, she laughed. Her skin rosy in the candle gleams, she seemed a Carolina more mysterious. I sat, poured out the espresso. Rising from her place across from me, she picked up her cup and came to sit next to me. With the artless sort of candour one might use to reveal one's self to a lone seatmate on a night train – unheated, unlit and speeding through a tundra – Carolina began to talk.

"'I don't want to be or become one who paints the past, rubs it to a glimmer so it bears no resemblance to the half-ruin every one of us makes of life. I want to do a good job with what's left of my time so that I won't have to do some kind of fancy mental restoration later on."

'She drained her tiny cup in a single sip, held it a moment longer in front of her mouth, looked at me over the rim, recognising that she'd already lost me.

"'I . . . can you tell me what it is that you . . . ?" I asked her.

"'Let me begin again. You, knowing me as you do – or as you think you do – how would you describe me to someone? What would you say?"

"'That you're maddening, that you're sweet . . . I don't know, I guess I'd say that you're audacious. Vivid. I'd say you were *vivid*."

"'Would you say that I was a hopeful person?"

"'Of course. Hopeful, yes . . .'"

"'I've always thought so. But what I'm discovering is that most people who think they live in hope are really desperate while those who admit to despair are quietly operating under hope. Case in point, I present myself an optimist, a sanguine, and yet what I truly am is a desperate person in convincing disguise. Most Pollyannas are, of course. Truth is skittish as quicksilver and I, for one, hardly know what was or is my own truth. Or if I have one and if I do, will it still be true in an hour? That was until this afternoon."

"'This afternoon?"

"'Umberto, he *proposed* something to me. An idea which, well . . . a *possibility* which . . . were it to become . . . well, it would change everything. I'm old, Paolina, and I trust there's time for me to grow yet older. Yet older or younger, I can't say which, though my sense, as of this afternoon, is the latter. In any case, there's something I'd like to do. And my *knowing* what it is I'd like to do makes me fortunate. Pollyanna is nowhere in sight, Paolina, it's only me sitting here saying all of this to you. And I'm telling the truth."

"'But *what is it* that you're sitting here telling me . . . I still don't . . .'"

'Carolina began laughing again and I – still not understanding and nearly past caring about her night-train confessions – laughed with her, bending forward in my chair, my arms twined about my stomach. I stayed like that, rocking my baby, and a moment passed before I realised it was only my own laugh that I heard. Carolina was suddenly grave.

"'Paolina, from the deepest part of my heart I would like to invite you and your baby to come and live here with Umberto and Luigia and me. You know, to be a family with us. For always, Paolina. For always until, well, until you decide you'd like to live somewhere else . . .'"

'I didn't say a word. I only looked at her. Searching now for clues from what she'd just been saying and not saying. What was it that Carolina "knew" she wanted? Was it to give me charity? To provide herself with diversion? Were my child and I to be some sort of mission to soothe her uneventful dotage? I felt suddenly disconnected from her and when she reached for me, I pulled away too brusquely.

'"Umberto said you might respond this way."

'"Umberto? Do you mean to say that he knows about this . . ."

'"I've already told you, Paolina. It was his idea. I'm sorry to admit it wasn't mine."

'"Have you left off telling the truth already? Umberto, he hardly looks at me, he . . ."

'"Paolina, Umberto is a Jesuit. Jesuits interpret, elucidate. Manipulate. A Jesuit believes in nothing so he is free to believe in everything and what you're perceiving as his . . . his diffidence, well, it's not that at all. What's at work is his *Jesuitness*."

'"Does he think I won't take proper care of my child, that I need . . ."

'"No. No, Paolina. *It's we who need you*. You're Umberto's *canto libero*. His *magnum opus*. He's been your teacher since you were learning to read. He adores you as he would a little sister. It's *magis*. More. You know Latin better than I. It's his Jesuit's *need* – no, his Jesuit's obsession – *to be* more, *to do* more. He paces the four-hundred square metres of this old palazzo in agony for its emptiness. He's begun scheming his remedies, though; among them is a program for seminarians in their final phase of study who, one or two at a time, would live and work here. All the better to understand the life of a parish priest in a small isolated town. He's in Perugia this evening to beg funds from the Curia to transform two of the *saloni* downstairs into a *nido* for infants now that mothers are beginning to work outside the home. He has already found licensed teachers and nurses to oversee it and . . ."

"'And so am I to be one of Umberto's *remedies* for the squandered space? Is that . . ."

"'How much reassurance do you need, Paolina? When he speaks of you, he speaks of *grace* . . . He says that you will grace our lives. *And that we must strive to grace yours.* An honourable intent, Paolina."

"'Yes, honourable, but . . ."

"'Is it that you don't wish to live here with us? Is it that? If so, I'll simply tell Umberto and . . ."

"'It's not that. I don't think it's that. But it's all so, so *fraught*. I guess that's a good-enough word. I'd be expecting Vatican guards to storm the palazzo in the night . . . The idea is preposterous. My coming to live here with my fatherless child . . . it would be flying in the face of Mother Church, of Rome. Of the Curia. *Of the San Severese.*"

"'Umberto is neither taking a wife nor entering, flagrantly, into sin. His behaviour is, well, I suppose I would call it *Jesus-like*. He's opening the parish-house doors to what he considers to be his extended family. Every family has some *eccentricity*. Some *anomaly* . . ."

"'Anomaly. A Jesuit's word if ever I've heard one."

'We look at one another, taking turns shaking our heads, speaking only with our eyes until I say, "Carolina, I can't think beyond the bishop and all those monsigneurs and . . ."

'"Whatever else they may or may not be, they're a troupe of gluttons at the Curia. You'll win them over with your pastries, especially those little round pink-iced things with the marzipan cherries on top . . . what do you call them?"

'"*Cassetine.*"

'"When I was a girl in Rome, I went every afternoon with my friends to eat gelato at Muzzi. I remember the boys would forsake gelato for pastries, for one sort in particular which looked very much like your *cassetine*. In dialect, the boys called them 'nuns' breasts'. Pile a plate with those and, next to it, prop a little card identifying them. Written in dialect, of course. That should strike a note familiar enough to distract the old piggish knaves from fretting over who's who in Umberto's family."

•

'Earnest as an estate agent, Carolina led me through the farthest corners of the palazzo. Originally the sixteenth-century country residence of a minor branch of the noble Monaldeschi, it was a descendent of that clan who left the property – handsomely and honourably restored – to the Church during the years between the great wars. Though I'd been so often in one or another of the *saloni* and the library and, of late, in the cavern of a kitchen, I knew nothing of the true immensity of the place until that afternoon of wandering through it with Carolina. She'd begun by saying that I should choose whichever rooms pleased me most, but when we'd climbed to the third floor where she and Luigia were situated, she lingered longest, thrusting wide the windows in each room, opening her arms to the rooftops of San Severino and to the wheat and the olives trembling in the wind beyond.

"'*Ecco*. Behold. Here you'll have morning sun and . . ."

"'What about the attic? Will you show me the attic?"

'Leading the way up the shallow stone steps of a narrow corridor lit by small, high windows, she said she'd been up there only once, maybe twice, in all the years she'd lived in the house, that it would be hellish in summer under the beams, that surely all the rats in San Severino assembled there, that I was too damn tall to even stand up anywhere but right in the middle.

'Nearly at the top of the stairs there was a door. "What's in there?" I asked.

'She told me it was for "storage". An oddly small room considering the dimensions of the others, it might well have been where the women of the house were isolated during their confinements. "At least that's what Umberto thinks," she said. "A rather morbid idea . . ."

'I opened the door to what would become my home for the next thirty-four years. The ceiling was high and vaulted, it's one window was a door opening to a small balcony. The floor was made of marble laid down in a design like a carpet. Here I could be as together with them as I could be alone with my baby. I would paint it red, a clear pure red with a trace of blue to keep it soft: carmine.

•

'On the agreed-upon moving day, Carolina and Luigia and I gathered together the things to be carried to the parish house: the baby's trunk, my books and clothes, a gilt wooden lamp with a grey-and-white-striped *abat-jour* from my parents' bedroom. Photos in silver frames and linens from my mother's chest. The Bohemian crystal. I don't remember that I took much else. At Carolina's insistence, we set about covering the furniture with sheets, turning off the water, the gas, unplugging the appliances. "You're moving house, Paolina, not just coming to us for a visit." Having arranged transport with two of the men who sometimes worked at the parish house, she was impatient when they didn't arrive on time and so we three began to walk the few cartons and sacks across the piazza and up the hill.

'On one of the trips up to the parish house, Ferrucci the baker – just returning from delivering the second bake and seeing us with our arms full – stopped his white van and loaded us and our baggage into the floured, yeast-smelling space. Leaving Carolina and Luigia at the parish house, Ferrucci and I went back to my house to fetch the baby's trunk, the books and then, rather than taking me directly back to the parish house, he asked if I'd like to ride along with him to Orvieto where he was to make the day's last deliveries. A kind of sentimental journey it would be since, when I was in elementary school and friends with his son, Ferrucci would often take us with him on his afternoon delivery. So I'd known Ferrucci forever, the small, sturdy white-clad figure of him racing on his wooden clogs into the shops and the *trattorie*, a brown paper sack of new bread in his embrace, shouting his arrival: *pane caldo, pane caldo.*

'As though years had not passed since the last time we rode together, we drove up into Orvieto and, when he'd delivered his goods, he parked the truck in Piazza Duomo. Reaching under the seat, pulling out the half-kilo *pagnotta* he'd tucked away there, he slapped a clasp knife in my hand.

'"Break it open, Paolina. I'll be right back."

'I sawed the bread in two and, with the halves resting on my lap, I sat there high up in the truck, pinching off pieces of crust, thinking how, from time to time, life makes such small circles. Wielding a paper packet like a trophy, Ferrucci soon came racing back and, opening the door on my side, he stood there laying slices of wild fennel *salame* in perfectly overlapping circles over the bread. Pressing the *pagnotta* back together with the heel of his hand, he tore the giant sandwich in two.

'"*Andiamo.*"

'He led the way to the steps of the Duomo and we sat with our merindina, eating and smiling and feeling no need for words until, as we stood to leave, he said, "I can't wait until your baby is old enough to ride in the truck with me. I can't wait for that, Paolina."

'I looked at little Ferrucci in his white paper hat, eyes solemn behind glasses dusted in flour, more of it caked in the furrows of his cheeks.

'"*Anch'io, Ferruccino.* I also can't wait."

'I didn't know back then nor do I now if Ferrucci, with his warm bread and his few words, meant to gift me my past and promise me a future. I think he did.

•

'It was the last Saturday of that September. Having pilfered Umberto's cherished Zenith radio from his study and set it on the bedside table in the little red room, Carolina sat feverishly twisting its dials. She'd been out in the shops that morning and had returned to find me installed up there in an early stage of labour.

'"You must have distraction," she kept repeating, though it was she who gasped and trembled while I sat folding and refolding baby clothes. She came upon some music and raised the volume. "*Quando, quando, quando* . . . When, when, when . . ." Uncorseted in her black woollen robe, still wearing her elastic stockings and town shoes, Carolina began to dance around the bed, making delicate samba-like moves, the pearl drops of her earrings jiggling in time with her bosoms.

'"*Amore mio*, dance with me. *Vieni, vieni*, come, come."

'She took my hands, strove again and again to wrench the great white bulk of me from among the pillows and each time she failed. I fell to laughing and begged her to leave me be.

'"Carolina, I hurt quite enough already without your . . ."

'"But it's this that will lessen the pain, you must move, move, move. When the contractions begin again, then you can be still. Come, try it."

'Carolina raised the volume just as Umberto entered the room.

'"I heard the music . . . Paolina, is there something I can . . . ?"

'"Ah, Umberto. Maybe she'll listen to you. Tell her that she must move, she must dance. Did I ever tell you that Anna-Rosa danced me through seventeen hours of *travaglio* before you were born? Yes, *la pizzica, la tarantella, la monferrina*. I don't remember a polka but . . ."

'Umberto and I laughed at Carolina and the more we laughed the better she danced and, when she pulled at me another time, I got to my feet and tried to do as she was doing. I'd never tried to dance before that afternoon. Never once. A contraction interrupted my debut and I fell back onto the bed. Intense as it was, Carolina had been right: the pain seemed less. After a few moments, *Quando, Quando* having given way to *Guantanamera,* I was on my feet again while Umberto, shaken by his first gaze upon a woman in her labours, was in retreat.

'"Umberto, don't you dare to leave me alone with her; you take a turn now while I rest. Keep her moving. She'll follow you. *Forza, forza.* Go, go."

"Neither had Umberto danced in his life yet there he was, facing me, his feet apart as though to steady himself. Tall as a cypress and pitifully thin, lank blond hair falling in his eyes – blue and wide with terror behind his wire-rimmed spectacles – Umberto took me in his arms.

'Heedless of the rhythm of *Guantanamera*, holding me in the formal stiff position of a waltz, his lower torso arched slightly backward to accommodate my belly, I danced barefoot with Umberto the Jesuit in the small red room under the black-beamed vault, the breeze from the open balcony door ruffling his Nordic hair, shivering the hem of my nightdress. No genius with a chisel and a stone could have carved such a moment.

'*Carmine*. Khar'-meen-eh. A beautiful word, don't you think? My son was born on Sunday morning. *Carmine Domenica*.

Carmine Sunday. All my sons were born in that red room and I named all of them Carmine. *Carmine Mezzanotte*, Carmine Midnight. *Carmine Pioviggine*, Carmine Rain. And my last, my baby, he's *Carmine Rovescio*. Born feet first, he's Carmine Backwards.

'But I've gone too far ahead, haven't I? Back to that Saturday, that Sunday morning.

'The midwife and Carolina having seen to my delivery, Doctor Ottaviano arrived in time to inspect my son and to congratulate me. I recall nothing save the dancing and the moment when Carolina laid my baby across my chest.

'Later that morning it was Umberto who came softly into the red room, asked me if I might sit up a moment. There was something I should see out the long window he said. I did better than that. With Carmine asleep in my arms, I walked to the balcony door to see that twenty San Severese, perhaps more than that, were walking in a free-form procession from the piazza up the hill toward the parish house. Every one carried flowers or some sort of parcel. Ferrucci had his arms around a great paper sack of bread.

'"Carmine's first visitors," Umberto said quietly.

'Through the gates they came and gathered in the front garden under my balcony, waving, shouting, "*Evviva Carmine Domenica. Long live Carmine Domenica.*"

'In both my hands I raised the baby above my head, held him there for all to see and the shouting mounted. Carmine slept. Carolina came huffing into the room and escorted us back to bed, saying that weeping and laughing as I was would sour my milk and leave my son to wail in agony. Umberto went to meet the delegation and returned with his arms full of flowers. Luigia brought in the bread and what looked like a small sack of sea salt.

'"There's a note," Umberto said. "Shall I read it to you?"

Life is a search for beauty and so we bring flowers.

And what would a life be without tears? And so we bring salt.

And so he will never be hungry, we bring bread to your son, great loaves for him to share.

•

'No one acknowledged Niccolò as Carmine's father and neither did any one deny that he was. Discreetly and with grace, Niccolò came and went as a visitor to the parish house. Claiming no special rights and no one offering him such, his was a mostly behind-the-scenes presence. Still, Niccolò's attendance rankled Umberto. Though not once – not then, not ever – did either of them openly indict the other, Niccolò and Umberto clenched jaws and crossed swords back then. And for the next thirty years – until Umberto died – they sustained those postures. I know, I'm going too fast again.

'Carolina, Luigia, Umberto, Carmine and I lived well together, as though we had lived well together always. There was screaming and shouting and laughing and tenderness in what felt like just doses. Emotions expressed, offences pardoned, kindnesses repaid in spades, all of it a revelation to me who, to avoid Stasia's dismay, had grown up so nimble a ghost.

'An eternal tragicomic opera, the household never numbered fewer than ten at table, what with the comings and goings of

Umberto's colleagues from Rome and the outlying parishes and the two or three live-in seminarians whose tenures rotated once a year. Catechism classes, pre-nuptial courses, child-care programs and thrice-weekly medical clinics provided the house chorus. The darling protagonist was Carmine Domenica, and Carolina, Luigia and I were his devout concubines. Though he reserved his fondest attentions for me, he did not withold affection from the others. As soon as he could tumble himself from his crib in the night or the early morning, he would go to one or another of us in our beds, tuck himself into our arms. At breakfast time, the victor in whose bed he had slept would carry the sleepy-eyed Carmine triumphantly into the kitchen. Of course, Carmine was only the first of my sons.

'There was a certain symmetry over the next nine years between the various residencies of the seminarians and my birthing three more babies. Coincidence. Chance. Providence. People still speculate and I am still Delphic. Opaque. Save to Carolina, I've never felt the need to speak of who fathered my sons any more than I felt the need to marry him. Them. Anyone. Whenever I faltered, Carolina could tell. She would say, "It won't matter in the end. What will matter is that you've wanted these babies with your whole soul."

'Yes. My whole soul. But would that suffice? Would that compensate for the affliction I am imposing on my children? And even if my love – the love of all of us – is enough for them, how would they manage outside that door? The candied faces of the adults, the open torment of their mates . . .

"'Remember what Umberto said at the beginning . . . always some anomaly . . . always a secret. A rune too old to read. We all get a cross, Paolina. Your children will have this one.'

"'A mother who is known as *la virginetta di San Severino*.'

"'They say it endearingly. You must know that.'

"'I do. I do but . . .'

"'What you're really worried about is whether they will love you? Whether they will forgive you? Whether your sons will forgive you. It's that, isn't it?'

'I couldn't answer her for the tightness in my chest. I nodded, yes.

"'They may neither love nor forgive you. Be clear about that risk. Of course, they may neither love nor forgive you no matter what you do or don't do. Be clear about that risk as well. Love them, Paolina. And not for the sake of the love they might return. Parental love, by its nature, is one-sided. Unusual as you are and as are your choices, your risk of love not returned may be greater. But as I think about it, because you and your choices are unusual, you may very well be easier to love, easier to forgive. Who knows? In any case, it has a nice ring, don't you think? *La virginetta di San Severino*.'

•

'All through the years that followed, the story of *la virginetta* remained the pungent stuff of local folklore. Even so, the prattle it caused was mostly confined to a small, tireless cabal whose disdain seemed made more of envy than of righteousness. I think it was sexual titillation that must have fed the men who gossiped. I'd never been a beauty. There was no prettiness about me to fade. And yet my femininity, my *femaleness*, grew more potent over time, that particular manner of moving and speaking and gesturing, of thinking and operating which is hardly generic among women and has not a thing to do with mincing or sashaying or the batting of eyelashes. I was strong and whole and peaceful and without any need of them and thus I was seductive. I bewitched them with indifference. Politely spurning their overtures – both subtle and not – I caused their hostility, their umbrage.

'The women's malice was made of another kind of envy. Unlike many of theirs, my life was never cluttered with angst over marital fidelity. I was never beaten or threatened or – most beautiful of all to contemplate – I was never lied to. There was, unfailingly, the little leather purse, fat with lire for the week's expenses, waiting on the kitchen table on Friday morning. A white envelope, often with a flower or a branch of herbs tucked inside it along with a generous sum of *argent de poche*, was slipped under the door of the little red room on the twenty-seventh of each month. Who knows how such a personal event could have made it to the *piazza*? And who knows how many other personal events, less real than that, also made it to the *piazza*?

'In winter I went to mass in a brown felt cloche with black velvet roses sewn along one side of it and wore a brown serge dress and matching coat. If it was cold, I wore a short silver fox cape. In summer my dress was of navy silk, a wisp of a thing no heavier than a handkerchief. My cloche was straw. When Umberto had business in Orvieto or Terni or Rome, my sons and I would ride along in his black Giulietta; I in front next to Umberto, the boys in back. As I've said, we all lived well together. More like a family or less like one, I can hardly tell you which it was.

'With the shelter – and, I suppose, the prestige – of life in the parish house, my sons managed their crosses and my mystery. Not always but often enough, they managed. There were even times when I believed they thrived on the unconventional circumstances of their childhood. In a way, they set a new standard by their living with the local priest, the priest's mother, the priest's aunt. And by their sitting at lunch and supper every day with seminarians who taught them Greek and Latin from the time they could speak and coached them in soccer and sang the Georgics to them before they slept and accompanied them across the piazza to and from school, their long black soutanes a uniform more majestic than a father's brown corduroy suit, my sons were elevated from their mates, their pain and embarrassment camouflaged so that their lives looked and, I think, *felt* ordinary. Ordinariness being the state for which children long more than all others.

'They look like me, my sons do. Tawny skin and hair black as a raven's, snub noses and good teeth. But their eyes are my mother's: slanted, green, iridescent as the neck of a pheasant. Never a day goes by without my thinking of her, she being there in my sons' eyes. Have I told you? Three are farmers who work the same land my father did. Niccolò's farms. Carmine Domenica is a paediatrician. They are all married and they are all fathers. They are the loves of my life. And who am I to them?'

Paolina is quiet now, sits up, pulls her shawl tighter, knots it, takes the cigarette tin from her pocket but doesn't open it.

'I would like to eat something. To drink some wine. Let's go back. Always something to rummage in the rustico.'

'The chocolate in my auto, it will stave off . . . I mean, until *aperitivi*. It must be . . .'

'The light's still greenish, not yet four, I'd say.'

Lithe as a geisha, Paolina shifts her weight to one knee then rises, *grows up,* tall and straight, from the weeds. She pulls me to my feet.

'I want more than chocolate.'

'I know. Bread and wine and oil.'

She lights the fire while I put back in place the things she'd moved before scrubbing the floor. Washing our hands at the kitchen sink with a slice of Miranda's private stash of clove-scented soap, which Gilda makes, Paolina says, 'How could I know, my sons, what they really think and feel? Do they talk to one another about . . . about the *uniqueness* of our lives? About me? Niccolò and Umberto were the men, constant, in their lives. As less than fathers, more than fathers, each one gave the boys what the other one couldn't. Umberto – bashful, studious, tender, wise, teaching, talking, endlessly talking to them, trusting them, even as tiny boys, with pieces of his own conundrums about right and wrong, good and evil. Niccolò was, remains their *vigor,* their laughter. As Miranda says of him, Nicò is an old oak. Tenacious, immutable. How strange, though, that the four are mine, resemble me, one another, Stasia. As though the others didn't.'

'Be careful or Miranda will accuse you of being prone to visions, *la virginetta di San Severino.*'

With a jar of Miranda's preserved pears on the floor between us, we sit by the fire, pull the fruit from its syrup, each with her knife, slice the fruit, wet the slices in tumblers of red.

'Great, deep lacunae you've left, Paolina. Did you mean to do that?'

'Have I? I suppose. I ... I went to the end, or almost to the end, as though you should know or remember what happened in between. As though surely I must have already told you. I think I have if only in my thoughts. Come to think of it, I've never even told myself the all of it. I don't know if I could.'

She looks away, then down, making a long, awkward show of slicing another pear. 'Is it about the men I've known? Are those the empty spaces you're wondering about?'

'Some of them.'

'Some of which? The men or the spaces?'

Questions that want no answer, I drink my wine. Screw the lid back onto the jar of pears. 'Shall I get us a candle?'

As though she hasn't heard me, Paolina says, 'Save his seed, I never needed anything a man might give to me. Or it might have been that I never needed anything more than what had already been mine with a man. With men. You see, I dreaded love more than I coveted it. It seemed enough to me to know that love existed. I lived my loves in scenes brief, perfect, unstained. With Niccolò. With others. Like when I danced with Umberto. Those were enough. I don't think I could have managed a cup any fuller. No, I don't think I ever wanted more than what was in mine.'

'You sound like a Franciscan.'

'The Franciscan impulse is purity. Mine was foreboding. I feared ruining a love by wanting it to be more than it was, more than it *could* be. Love seemed a devouring thing that must, perforce, grope its way always deeper into the beloved, finally throttling him, her. Niccolò believed that and, hence, all those years ago he refused the risk of *exclusivity*. And so avoided the death of love.

'And then there was my fear about wanting a man more than he would want me. We do seem to want them more than they want us, don't you think? Over the years one can't help but witness, here and there, how women are wont to chase after love, to beg for it, to try and *earn* it. I preferred to stay aloof. To keep love a stranger. But what I feared even more than begging a man to love me was that *I might hurt a man I loved*. Causing the beloved pain is the precursor to hating him, hate being easier to bear than guilt. That's what happened between my mother and father. I'm sure of it. Then the process of discarding the beloved begins. The casting aside.'

Paolina says this last phrase in English. *The casting aside.* She repeats it in a faraway voice.

'I love that English verb – to cast. I learned it a long time ago when . . . when a friend, a friend of Umberto's . . . when he was teaching Domenica to fish for mullet in the lake of Bolsena. He – this friend – had learned English in Boston. Boston College, I think that was where he studied.'

'A fine Jesuit school,' I say, implying a connection to Umberto's seminarists. She concedes the innuendo but only halfway. I get up to fetch a candle, light it from a hearth flame.

'Yes, this friend was, indeed, a Jesuit. In any case, he decided that Domenica should learn to speak English while he was learning to fish. "And now, Domenica, watch the movement of my arm as I cast my line." To cast. To cast aside. To cast away. I remember sitting there a bit behind where the two of them were standing. I would repeat the English words so that I could help Domenica to remember them later. From "to cast", it was an easy jump back to Italian – *castigo*. Punishment. Yes, one punishes the beloved – casts him aside – because one has wronged him. And when one is free of him, one strives to begin the process again with the next "beloved". Love, pain, hate, the casting aside. No, I would stay *aloof*.'

'I take it back. You're not a Fransiscan. Pure Jesuit you are, Paolina. Rationale, suspicion, theory, not even a Jesuit can apply logic to love, though. I don't believe it's you who's kept love a stranger. Love goes where it will. It may yet come to call on you.'

Paolina laughs, if without mirth, and I look at her, begin speaking in a sing-song parody of her voice: *No, I would stay aloof. I preferred to keep love a stranger* . . . She begins to really laugh then and I continue, mercilessly, to mimic her until we're both supine and breathless.

'Haughty Jesuit,' I say, sitting up to stir the fire.

'Haughty Jesuit,' she repeats as though the allegation intrigues her. As though she's never considered herself a 'pure' Jesuit, complete with rationale and suspicion and theory.

'So it's not too late, then. I mean, for me to . . .'

'Who knows, Paolina?'

Her laugh is dreamy. Pulling the elastic from her hair, she rebinds it, repeats the two steps.

'It's been half a lifetime since I've even tried to imagine what it would be like not to be alone . . .'

'Who ever said that love staves off aloneless? You might very well be in love and be still alone. Many of us are. I don't necessarily disagree any more than I agree with all your *Jesuitness* regarding love. I am only suggesting it's moot until love decides to have its way with you. *Basta*. Now what I want to know is, how did you come to be Umberto's cook?'

'That's easy. My little Beppa.'

'Beppa?'

•

'From the first day when I settled into the small red room, I dearly wished to earn my keep in the parish house. I wanted to work in the kitchen,' Paolina says. 'I opened the subject with Carolina. Before I'd even finished presenting my case, she was already bent on distracting me.'

'"*Ma tesoro*, wouldn't it be lovelier to work in the gardens?" she said. "Once the baby is born we could set its cradle under the olives or in the saddle of one of the oaks."

'I said I would prefer to set his cradle on the work table where we could see one another while I mixed the bread or . . .

Cringing, she said, "I'll speak to Beppa."

'"Maria-Giuseppa, 'Beppa', a widow past seventy, her old weeds faded from black to bronze, her hair so red it showed purple in the sunlight, Beppa walked into town from a neighbouring commune every morning to cook for Umberto and had done so since he'd come to live there. Her devotion to Umberto's supper was the fundamental substance of Beppa's life. And when Carolina arrived and then Luigia, Beppa dug her stick deeper into the lines around her dominion. The parish house kitchen was hers.

'Her body frail, her grit titanic, Beppa was famous for ravaging the shops, steering her wheeled plastic cart, string bags flapping on her wrists, negotiating with the merchants for every banana and stalk of parsley. Fierce as a scavenging bird, she would swoop upon the wilted, the withered, the perishing, demanding them for a pittance. Only meat and fish must be of exquisite quality and worthy of Umberto's lire. Trusting to no one for eggs, she brought them each morning, warm from her own hens, wrapped in newspaper. She baked bread every other day. These elements gave Beppa a certain culinary independence so that, with a few wild herbs from the imperishable stash in her pockets, the barrel of good oil in the pantry, the little jars and bottles of things she'd conserved in the summer, Beppa could perform a daily rendering of Loaves and Fishes. Thus, in the shops she could be ruthless, repeating ad infinitum to the merchants that the food she was gathering was to nourish God's own disciple and weren't they ashamed to take profit from the pocket of God himself. With equal repetition the merchants would roll their eyes, saying if only they could eat and drink with the abandon of the clergy: "*Magari, fosse vero,* if only it were true."

'Beppa's loyalty to her cause was unshakeable. Even before she would unpack her cart, she would march – her pigeon-toed step bouncing in jubilation – into Umberto's study. Under his desk lamp, she would tuck the morning's receipts wrapped around his change, patting flat the edges of the paper, smoothing the doily over it, her gestures as tender as Umberto's when he anointed a baby with chrism. Only then would she set to work.

'First Beppa would take stock of what she called her *caveau*. Her safe. A shelf in the refrigerator, forbidden to the householders, it was where she stashed her treasures: a precious half a litre of reduced broth; a cup or two of cooked white beans; pasta, cooked and undressed; dripping caught from roasting meat; a few spoonsful of one sauce or another; a heel of bread; the crusts from an aged cheese. In part, Beppa's menu was always based on the menu from the day before. An expression of frugality, her ritual saving was a kind of insurance stringing the house meals together, each supper promising there would be another one tomorrow.

'Not unlike a French cook who dips daily into a cassoulet that has sat on the back burner for twenty years or more, replenishing her withdrawals with fresh elements and mixing them together with the old so that her pot never empties,' I say. So did Beppa operate her kitchen.

'Whether cooking for two or fifty, Beppa's culinary battery was as scarce as it was sacrosanct: one knife, a great heavy pot, a sauté pan, a medium saucepan, three or four terracotta dishes for the oven, a slab of polished olivewood for a cutting board, one of marble for rolling pasta with a litre-size wine bottle, two ladles and a stoneware pitcher full of wooden spoons, all her exclusive property. And she liked to be alone in her kitchen, Beppa did. When Carolina told her of my desired "apprenticeship", suggested that, henceforth, I would be there to *help* her for a part of each morning, Beppa had turned from the pot she'd been stirring, ripped off her pinafore, started in weeping and howling. "*Ringraziamento,* gratitude," she'd sobbed over and over until Umberto came running in to quiet her.

'"*Beppina, amore mio, you are not being disenthroned but honoured. Don't you see that? Paolina wants to learn from you.*"

'Neither Carolina nor Umberto would prevail. Beppa dug her stick deeper yet into the dirt. I decided to try devices of my own.

'Next morning when she arrived, she found me in front of the burners frying sweet rice fritters.

'"*Sorpresa.* Surprise," I said and pulled out a chair for her at the kitchen table. "*Facciamo colazione insieme,* let's have breakfast together," I chirped as though the fritters and I would be welcome gifts.

'Saying not a word, Beppa allowed me to ease her into a chair, to pour her caffé. Sliding the sugar bowl to her, I said, "There was some cooked rice in the fridge and an egg and . . . well, I thought I'd just mix up a dose of batter and . . ."

'"One doesn't make sweet fritters with rice cooked in water. It must be cooked in milk."

'"Of course, well, I . . . I guess I didn't know that but, well . . ."

'I pulled a tiny pyramid of fritters from the oven where I'd been keeping them warm, set the plate before her and went back to the business of frying the rest. I kept my back to her. When finally I turned around, she was daintily snaffling the second from the last one.

'"Sono buone. They're good. A suspicion of cinnamon would have helped. If you'd thinned the batter with half a glass of white wine they might have almost been right. If there's milk, I'll cook some rice before I leave. We'll make fritelle together tomorrow. And never use that saucepan for frying. *Mai più*. Never again."

'"Never. Never, Beppa."

'I ran out into the garden and, prancing in raptures among the flowers, my arms tight around my belly, I kept thinking back to that day with Niccolò's tomatoes. And now, with *Beppina* . . . how much more I would learn.

'A brooder who rarely spoke save to mock and torment the merchants, Beppa was. But almost from the beginning of my tenure in her kitchen, she barely took a breath from her stories: memories, affirmations, revelations, mostly culinary.

'I think my favourite was the one about her birth. Beppa said she was born lucky. A sixteen-year-old sharecropper, her mother had been digging potatoes when a colossal pain rent her back, kidney to kidney. But, digging potatoes, one always had pain, her mother thought. And, anyway, the baby wasn't due for a month or more. And so Beppa was birthed in a potato field directly onto the rich black soil of Umbria. She and her mother were carried then to lie in the shade of an umbrella pine while the other women wet aprons and kerchiefs in the cool white wine from their lunch baskets and washed mother and child. They set Beppa to suck. The women fed her mother a pap of bread and wine and wild sage and sat with she and Beppa in a circle under the tree. Beppa's mother said the women sang and passed bread and onions and cheese to one another and drank their wine and told their own stories about birthing. They said the potatoes could wait until sunset, until Beppa and her mother had rested and the men came in from the farther fields with a wagon to take them home.

'Beppa would go quiet then, allowing herself to see the scene as her mother had described it. And then she'd get around to talking about the soup, the potion, the countrywomen fed to her mother: "Millennial elixir of the country people, as good for dying as it is for birthing, for healing heartache, nourishing joy, for calming pain. I'm happy when I'm bending in the meadows to gather herbs, to carry the fine-smelling things home in my pockets, to tear them then into a pot of good fresh water and let them heat and steep before I crumble in a heft of yesterday's bread. It's another kind of mass, the ceremony of ladling the broth into a bowl over a new-laid egg. The broth warms the egg, poaches it to a soft tremor and then, with a big spoon, one breaks the yolk, stirs it once or twice. Consoling. Yes, the little soup tastes of consolation. Don't you think mine was the most beautiful way for a baby to come into the world?"

'Each time Beppa told the story, she would end it with the same question: "Could anything be better, Paolina? Don't you think mine was the most beautiful way for a baby to come into the world?" And then, answering it herself, she would say: "Oh, it was, Paolina. That it was."

'I'm certain that the story of her birth shaped Beppa, that it formed her security, her self-worth, that it shaped everything about her, from how she cooked to how she made love to how she raised her children. Life to Beppa was the opportunity to take her turn in the ancient pageant of Umbrian tradition, abiding the spoken and silent ways and means her forebears had abided. Never wanting more than her portion nor would Beppa have accepted less than it. Beppa was born *Umbrian*.

'Also you were born, Umbrian,' I say to Paolina.

'I was. But my family – mostly my mother, I think – had been robbed of Beppa's sense of primal contentment with life. Like others of their generation, my parents were driven by other notions. The epic rural family with its miseries and its comforts perished with the end of the Second World War. Most of the sharecroppers escaped from the countryside to the fresh torments of urban factories. Happiness is, very often, a new set of problems. But even for those who stayed to work the land in the fifties and sixties, rural life was never quite the same. The greater world had chinked away at, and corrupted, the farmers' devotion to heritage and ritual. Beppina was one of the last of the tribe of genuine traditionalists. Miranda is another one. Gilda and Ninuccia, too, if in other expressions than Miranda's and Beppa's. I'm not of their ilk, though I wish I were and try to be. I think of Beppa's stories so often it's almost as though they're my own. She would like that. I know she would. As long as I knew Beppina – and that was for nineteen years, until the day she died – her fortune never ceased to astonish her. I have always sought to be astonished by my own.'

I rise to tidy up what few things we've used. Now that we've broken its seal, I bring what's left in the jar of pears out to the cheese hut where its cooler. When I come back inside, Paolina is on her way out the door.

'Where are you off . . . ?'

'Going up to Bazzica to use the phone. Niccolò will be home by now. Fernando, too, I would think. I'll call Ninuccia and she'll do the rest.'

'What *rest*?'

'Tell everyone to come here. Miranda and Filiberto and Gilda and Iacovo . . . I'd much rather have some little supper here than go out this evening. Wouldn't you?'

'Beppa's soup?'

'I think that was it. I'll be right back. Maybe Signora Bazzica has some eggs.'

I throw a lit match onto the wood and coal and crumpled newsprint that Miranda has layered into her old iron stove. Fanning the fire into life, I move the heavy iron plate halfway over the pot hole. I laugh to myself, thinking of the era when I moved on the line in front of all those eight- and ten-burner Wolfs and Vikings, shaking sauté pans, distilling broths, splashing in some wine, a little butter for gloss. Swirl and pour. Two donalds under the lights – two orders of duck, waiting to be served. Now, all those lifetimes later, I am here in a strange little dwelling a few kilometres beyond nowhere in a kitchen with a bedsheet curtain, coaxing the flames in a hundred-year-old stove over which I'll boil water and herbs into a soup on a Saturday night in Umbria.

It will want most of an hour before the stove is hot enough and so I look about for something to do meanwhile. Even though there's a great sheaf of sage hanging, half dried, by the kitchen door, I stick a candle in a lantern, and wander back out into the meadow to look for a few fresh leaves. I think of the soup

Niccolò fed to Paolina when she was grieving and of the soup Ninuccia's mother-in-law made with stones in the desolation of the Aspromonte. Of the pap Beppa's mother was fed under the umbrella pine. *Acquacotta.* Cooked water. Tonight I will ladle it out for an assortment of old-guard Umbrian countrywomen and some of their men, none of whom wear Alaïa extra-small or Gucci loafers with no socks. I, too, am astonished by my fortune.

When I return to the rustico with a pocketful of herbs, Paolina is there. I see that she has been crying.

'What is it? What . . . ?'

'Everything's fine. I stayed with Signora Bazzica until Ninuccia telephoned me back. You know, after she'd called the others. Signora Bazzica had seven eggs from this morning. Eight left from yesterday. She put them all in the same sack so we won't know who will get the day-old ones. Everyone's coming. Everyone's bringing something. Ninuccia was happy. Niccolò and Fernando have already gone to fetch Miranda and will stop by for Gilda. They'll all be here within the hour. I'll make a *dolce.* You make the soup.'

Who knows why but her tears bring on mine and we stand there weeping and smiling, taking turns starting and stopping to speak until Paolina says,

'So it's the ending you don't yet know. Only that. The various endings.'

'Paolina . . .'

'I want to hear the ending myself. I want to hear it, yet I don't know my way in the place beyond words. For myself more than for you, I will go there. I'll try.'

Paolina walks about the kitchen, pulling out the elements she'll need for the *dolce*. She scrubs the wooden table, dries it vigorously, dries it again, measures flour directly onto it, forms a well in the flour. With the tips of her fingers she begins mixing in butter, sugar, egg yolk, milk. She salts the mass with a marble-shooter's flick and mixes again. Her hands fly over the mass, touching it but almost not touching it and, in less than a minute, she forms a satiny paste, slaps it into a flat, perfect oval and covers it gently with a fresh white cloth. She pats the cloth. She looks up at me.

'It's as though I'd spent my whole life with Umberto and Carolina. Thirty-four years if we speak in linear time. But in a real way I live with them still. Nothing maudlin, nothing macabre, what I mean is that I think many of us tend to live always in whatever was the best period of our lives. We set up the next epoch, wittingly or not, by re-creating the earlier one, the golden one. And my sons have done the same; their households reflect how we lived together in the parish house: open doors, long tables, endless suppers, fiery discussions with not a whiff of taboo, a peculiar alchemy of rules and liberty, communal esteem. Trials made us stronger. A true test of family.'

A bowl of old bruised figs is in the armoire. Shooing away the fruit flies, I dump them out on a space near where Paolina has just worked, scoop out their flesh, add black sugar and vin santo. I have no idea what we'll do with it but I need to keep working through what must be three or four minutes of Paolina's silence. She washes her hands, makes room for me at the sink, hands me a towel.

'Luigia went back to live in Rome. I think it was just after Pioggia was born. She was failing and she chose to do so privately, making a grand appearance on the first Sunday of each month when Umberto's driver would go to fetch her. We'd run to the front garden to meet the old black Chrysler. We'd pull her gently from her prop of yellow cushions, taking care not to crush the two green- and silver-wrapped packages that the pastrybaker at Muzzi would loop over each of her wrists. He told us once how she would walk away after he performed this service, stiff as a soldier, arms held out like wings so as not to disturb her sugary loot and go then to stand in front of the shop to wait for Umberto's driver. She wasn't there on the sidewalk at Muzzi one Sunday. Luigia died in her sleep, just as she'd always said she would.

'The boys were fifteen, thirteen, ten and six when Carolina died. The love between their *nonna* and my sons was an epic love, a reciprocal adoration. Retrieving a ritual that had fallen out of vogue for generations, the San Severese – en masse and to the haunting drone of a lone Abruzzese piper – walked behind Carolina's hearse from the parish house through the narrow streets of the village, across the piazza and to the church. After mass we carried her casket together, Domenica, Mezzanotte, Pioggia, Umberto and I. Roverscio rode, sobbing, atop Domenica's shoulders.

'I will try to tell you of Umberto's passing. It was nearly six years ago, nearly six. He was at home and I was with him. The forewarnings of his leaving were not long. Not unlike my mother – though surely not in her manner – he dispensed with all notions of clinging to life. He'd stopped coming down to meals not more than a week before the evening when he asked me to sit with him until he slept. I did that. I closed his eyes, lit candles near his head and his feet, opened the windows and stayed with him until dawn. He'd left a box of letters for me, forty to be exact, written over the years, the last declaring – no commanding – his desire for a family celebration with nothing to mark his position in the Church. As I informed his colleagues of Umberto's death, so did I inform them of his wishes. Neverminding the wishes and my plea to honour them, the Curia set about staging the pageant it deemed appropriate. I was of little strength to fight the Church and I admit to wavering, myself, about the wisdom of sending Umberto off with a country funeral. But Niccolò would not permit Umberto to be betrayed. Niccolò was Umberto's cavalier. No fear of the Curia, Niccolò dictated and no one defied.

'At the funeral mass, the bishop – dressed in a simple black soutane – sat in a remote corner of the church with a contingent of priests from Rome. He and they, not unnoticed. At the sound of the sanctus they walked in single file to the altar, waited their turn to receive the holy eucharist and then, forming a tight knot, they stayed together in the front of the church. When the mass was finished, the group moved swiftly to surround the bier, Niccolò and the boys, joining them with a precision that could only have been conspired. Over their bowed heads, the priest who'd said the mass, a newly ordained Fransiscan, waved the censer, raising it higher and higher, swinging it as if it were the bell to heaven and he would announce the arrival of his old mentor. Midst plumes of frankincense, the bishop and the priests, his life's rival and his beloved 'sons', all together, they lifted Umberto the Jesuit to their shoulders. I did not bear Umberto's coffin on my own shoulder as I had Carolina's. I walked behind it. Like a daughter. Like a wife. The congregation were on their feet then and, in a rare, pure syntony, they began, slowly, powerfully, to applaud. During that long march down the aisle of the church, the scraps of odium that may have endured toward Umberto, toward me or any of his *own*, were washed away in the tears of the San Severese, obliterated in the unwavering beat of their hands. A family is made of love. Only sometimes is it also made of blood.'

Something she never does indoors, Paolina rolls two cigarettes, lights them, hands one to me, sits cross-legged by the hearth to wait the rising of her dough for the *dolce*. I sit beside her. We smoke in silence and without looking at one another. She rises then and I stay still. She walks toward the bedsheet curtain, pulls it aside and is about to pass behind it when I ask, 'Will you?'

'Accept him? I have always remembered, word for word, what he said to me on that long-ago day ... He'd been right then. He's right still. With nothing of spite or spleen, nothing of gall, this morning I told him, "*Tesoro mio, ti voglio tanto bene ma io non mi sposerò mai. Mai.* My darling, I love you but I will never marry. Never."

PART IV

GILDA

'GILDA AIDA MIMI-VIOLETTA ONOFRIO.' GILDA SAYS THE name slowly, lingering on each vowel, rolling the r's theatrically. She laughs, looks at me, repeats it. 'I was fortunate that my mother didn't deem to put *ciocio-san* in there somewhere.'

'Madame Butterfly?'

'The same. Mamma was a soprano. Promising, from what I understand. Understood.'

Gilda Aida Mimi-Violetta Onofrio. I try out the sound in my mind. For years she's been simply Gilda. Not even a last name. I look at her now as she sits at the rustico work table in front of a four-kilo hill of fresh borlotti beans, her tiny white fingers flying over the pods, slitting them open with a thumbnail, turning out the red marbled beans into a large pot. Two of the dishes for tonight's supper are being prepared by others, leaving little but the antipasto to Gilda and I. We'll stew the beans with a faggot of rosemary and sage and a whole *guanciale* – dried pig cheek – cut into the finest dice and then smeared against the wooden table so it forms a rough paste. Once the beans are cooked we'll pound the mass in a mortar with a pestle, adding drops of olive oil as we go. There are so many beans that we'll each work on half the amount: Gilda with a wooden mortar and a marble pestle, I with a marble mortar and a wooden pestle. It's the contrast between wood and stone that works best to smooth and crush. Some sea salt, a little more oil. The lush stuff is to be spread on potato focaccia, the dough for which I'll mix now while Gilda finishes podding the beans. Cornmeal, rye and unbleached flours, mashed potato, white wine, a natural yeast made from grape and potato skins, which I'd left to ferment for a week or so. Sea salt and white wine. No water. My hands deep in the glutinous mass, I say Gilda's name out loud now, repeat it in several tones and American accents. She likes it best when I say it with a Georgia twang. She tries saying it that way, too, but the sound she makes is more Smolensk than Atlanta.

'Tell me about your mother,' I say, without having decided I would.

Immediately I regret my request, innocent as it was and inspired by her own reference to her mother. By blood and temperament, Umbrians are often reticent. Umbrage, shade, shadow, darkness, ghost. An uninvited guest. A man – *hombre*. All these words and images are derived from the Latin, *umbraticum*. A half-nod, a quiet *buongiorno, buona sera*, the occasional, *come va?* It's these that suffice as social repertoire. In Umbria, it's hard to find a rhapsodist whereas, for instance, in Naples, it's hard to fine one who is not. As I've learned, the Thursday women can be exceptions; garrulous, rambling if it suits them, each one deciding for herself what she'll declare, what she'll withhold, to whom, when and if. Perhaps I'd risked invasion because, since the evening of the faulty gasoline gauge and the black velvet hat a year ago, Gilda and I have spent time together other than on Thursdays. We've taken to meeting at the markets, gone afterward to drink *aperitivi* and often she's come to supper at our apartment with Miranda. I express my regret by recasting the question.

'I mean, if it would please you . . . to tell me about her.'

Gilda looks up from the beans, her lips arranged in a smile, her eyes far away. She shakes her shoulders. Feigns nonchalance. After a while, she says, 'I think it would please me. To tell you about Magdalena.'

'Magdalena?'

'That's her name. Was. Still is, I guess. My mother is Magdalena.'

'Okay. Good, I mean, *good* as long as the telling is what you want to do.'

'It is.'

We both stay quiet then, each at our work and I think she might have meant that she'd like to tell me about her mother but not necessarily now. The only sounds in the old rustico are Gilda's stripped beans hitting the cooking pot and my one-handed slapping of the dough against the bowl. I look at her looking down. A narrow, well-made, pale-skinned woman, the bones of her face strangely strong among all that delicateness.

'As far as I know, that is. I can tell you only as far as that . . .' she says by way of preamble, of apology I think. As though she might fear what she knows is not enough. 'My mother was born in Orvieto, late in the life of her parents, adoring parents. Their own sun and moon, Magdalena was the darling of the Via del Duomo. Yes, in the street where you live, my mother was born.'

Gilda smiles, a borlotto pod still in her hand, she flicks her hair away from the whisky eyes.

'Not in your palazzo, though, but further up near the piazza.'

'Still . . .' I say, shaking my head, about to say something banal about how tiny is the world but stay quiet instead.

'Yes, *still*,' she agrees. 'So, Magdalena. Even at seven and eight, her voice was eerily potent. Sometimes people still talk about my mother's voice. About her. The neighbours would wait for her to sing, plan their tasks and outings around her practice times and, when she was, I think, eleven, some of them took turns walking her to Petrangeli palazzo in Via Malabranca. Up the eighty-six marble steps to the studio of a local maestro who wore a beret and smoked gold-papered cigarettes. Whenever she or my grandmother would tell the story they would always say *that* part – about the gold-papered cigarettes – in a whisper.

'Camili was his name. And when Magdalena was fourteen – precisely fourteen – this Camili paid a call to my grandparents' apartment, a beaver coat over his shoulders. He'd come to announce that he could do no more for their child. It was at Santa Cecilia in Rome where Magdalena must be trained. He'd already spoken with the director, already 'arranged' for her tuition to study at the famous academy. Only Neapolitans are better at 'arranging' things than Umbrians, but I suspect you've learned that by now. Who knows with whose soul Camili bartered for Magdalena's scholarship, surely not his own. And so, at fourteen, Magdalena was packed off to live with her mother's sister, also a woman of age, long a widow, childless. I, too, would one day live with that aunt, by then a perilously doddering old thing but . . . I'm not there yet, am I?

'I know little of Magdalena's story from that point. Safe to say, I think, her shift from cosseted princess of the Via del Duomo to struggling artist must have been violent, suddenly plunged as she was into a sea of talents formidable as her own. As the story went, Magdalena turned petulant. I suppose any princess would. And knowing the old *zia* as I eventually did, I can say that she would have been an unlikely pacifier, benumbed by life as she must have already been even then. She was of that ilk of Italian woman who abhorred the palest form of resistance to her will. Meeting it, she preferred to light another cigarette, unwrap another chocolate, say, to no one in particular, "*Che cosa devo fa? What can I do?*" Thus my mother kept her own counsel.

'Proof – at seventeen Magdalena quit Santa Cecilia and announced her betrothal to a barista in Sant Eustachio. Gastone Pepucci he was called. When I was . . . after my mother passed away . . . after she was gone, I mean, you know, when I was old enough to understand, the aunt told me that there'd never been a wedding but I didn't believe her. I still don't. I found a dress in Magdalena's trunk, it could only have been a wedding dress. There was nothing of photos but to what does that testify? Oversight, I'd say. In any case, I was born soon after . . . after the wedding or the elopement or . . . I was born soon after. And soon after *that* it was when Gastone Pepucci left Magdalena to seek better work in Milano or Switzerland. I've heard both versions. "Ostensibly to seek work" was a phrase still being bandied about by the aunt when I was old enough to wonder what it meant. I remember asking my mother, "Is Ostensibly a city in Switzerland?" She told me it was. I'm getting ahead again, I'm sorry.

'I must have been only a few months old when Magdalena left the apartment she'd shared with Gastone Pepucci to return to the old aunt, baby and baggage in hand. I think Magdalena withheld both my presence and the absence of Gastone Pepucci from my grandparents in Orvieto, the old aunt having convinced my mother that would be best. Consequently, I never knew my grandparents. All the while that Magdalena and I lived together with the aunt, grandparents were never mentioned. Only years afterward did I even begin to wonder about them. Who were they, where were they, why weren't we part of their lives, when did they die, what were their names? How can such estrangement happen in a family?

'What with the princess subdued in the still-adolescent Magdalena, the aunt, I can imagine the aunt, aloof, bovine, handing down embargoes and decrees upon my bewildered mother. That must have been the time when Magdalena began to sing almost incessantly, her voice haunting the small, fusty rooms of the aunt's apartment. Puccini being the perfect accompaniment to despair, Magdalena sang him. I remember trying to echo her, forming my mouth the way she did hers, hunching my shoulders, closing my eyes. Magdalena would laugh, place a finger over my lips. "Your little pipes make the sound of a piccolo played in a tempest," she would say.

'Years passed with no word from Gastone Pepucci and, slowly, Magdalena withered, dying of some ethereal complaint, which might have been suicide. I was eight.

'I remember her. Of course I do, if more as a drawing or a painting than flesh and bones. She was always there, but never there. Not all of her. Try as I would to make a conquest of her, to distract her from whatever or whomever it was that kept her away from me, to make her *see* me, to let me *be enough*, I never could. I can hear her singing, though. She left me that. That was real. My mother's voice was real.'

•

Though Gilda and I never break stride in task after task while she speaks and I listen, the pace of her story is reluctant, dreamy. She grows silent now and then, taking time to search her thoughts, to weed, I think, until she's ready to resume it, sustaining it with a kind of nimbleness if only for a while before she goes quiet again.

When all our work is finished, the fire laid, bread set to rising in the cheese hut, the stove lit, table set, we go to walk in the meadow, smoke the short, thin, clove-perfumed cigars I've taken to of late. We speak of who knows how many things, always high-stepping the edges of her story, both of us regretting her candour, Gilda for her revelation, I for its weight. We light two more cigars and I am about to launch yet one more inane attempt at distraction when she says, 'So, I was eight when Magdalena died. Or ran away. And to the old aunt's wintering life, I was a burden. She had no taste for the vigil it would want to keep me from echoing the disgraces of my mother. The disgraces of Magdalena. It was to the orphanage of Sant' Eufemia where I would go, the aunt decided. The nuns would shape me. They would protect me.'

Gilda giggles then, a girlish laugh rare to her and an overture, I think, to a pleasant turn in the story. We wander back toward the rustico, stop to sit on the stones of the sheepfold wall and Gilda takes my hand, turns it palm up as though to read its lines but rather she presses her own against it. To the millimetre, our hands are the same size. 'You're the first full-grown woman I've known with hands small as mine.' From Miranda, I think Gilda already knows something of my own shaping by the nuns.

'I would learn much later that half the aunt's pension opened the doors if not the hearts of the Sisters of Mercy to me. And – not to be outdone – the priests who came to say mass each morning in the convent opened the black bone buttons of their serge trousers to me as well. *Le punizioni.* Punishments. As standard on the curriculum as vespers, the punishments were the inviolate and holy fathers' historical if not just desserts, sacred spoils of their office. Though the ordeals were meted out upon only the youngest and prettiest of the little girls, all of the boys of Sant' Eufemia were subject to the holy fathers' summons. The boys were fewer in number and so were punished with a gruesome constancy. But there were so many of us girls under ten – ten seeming to be the maximum age of the girls who piqued the priests' lust – that our turns in the sacristy before or after mass came about rarely enough.

'But the punishments were only one of the ways to suffer at Sant' Eufemia: the everyday hunger and weariness, being cold, being hot, being alone . . . There were worse torments than being made to stand and watch while one priest or another set about his feats by himself or with the aid of one of the boys. They rarely touched us, we girls. I would look where I was commanded to look but I developed a sort of open-eyed blindness. I could look without seeing. I still do that.'

'You do. You still do that. It's true.'

Gilda laughs. 'You've noticed . . . I don't mean to, you know. It's only . . .'

'I understand. Now I understand.'

She smiles, shakes her head, shrugs a shoulder. 'A small relic of the punishments, I suppose . . . the faraway gaze,' she says, looking straight into my eyes. She proceeds: 'Abuse comes in many colours. Certain of its tints are all the rage now, aren't they? Popular polemics. A week in the hot light of the press and then the tortured are left to the business of their broken lives and the torturers are enfolded into some far-off flock, sent away if not to the stake or the gallows or down to the river with stones sewn to the hems of their trousers as they sometimes were in earlier epochs. Yes, now they are simply hidden. And wherever they are hidden, a fresh batch of babies is likely nearby. Civilisation. Ours. I've often wondered what the old aunt would have thought about the nuns' *protection* of me had she known of the punishments.'

'Did you ever try to tell her?'

'Of course. Not in distinct words. Eight-year-olds don't normally have the *distinct words*. I might have had them but even if I did, there was, even then, the suffocating sense that I wouldn't be believed. That my aunt wouldn't believe me. And not being believed was more frightening to me than were the punishments themselves. Telling and not being championed, not being rescued, that's what terrified me. Not being believed was akin to not being loved. They were the same thing to me: being believed and being loved. I think they still are. Anyway, back then I thought: *Better not to test it.*'

Gilda looks at me then, her gaze enraged. 'But I did try to tell the old aunt. Every time I saw her. But not in *distinct words*. Miranda was the first person I told. And not so long ago. It's easier to tell you now that she knows. That someone else knows. But I think the nuns knew. I'm certain they did. Perhaps they, too, were punished. More likely they were too deep in their own salaciousness to care. They did their duty, kept us from being not too filthy and not too hungry. They taught us our lessons, some of our lessons. The rest we learned by ourselves.'

•

We sit a while longer on the stones in the twilight, basking in a kind of complicity, shared if mostly unspoken. Her auto lights spent, it's Ninuccia who swerves onto the gravel.

'Why isn't the fire lit?' This her only greeting.

Gilda begins to assure her but I walk over to the auto, say, 'Ciao, Ninuccia.' I try to hug her but she is already bending into the back seat to fetch pots and sacks, some of which she hands to me before she leans in to offer her cheek to kiss.

Within the hour, the rustico is full to its sagging rafters on this November evening in 2007. Miranda, Ninuccia, Paolina, Gilda, Iacovo, Fernando, Filiberto, Pierangelo, Niccolò and I had just sat down at table when Miranda's most beloved trucker knocked at the door, told her he was *just passing by* to say hello. '*Non voglio disturbarvi, scusatemi.* I didn't want to disturb you, pardon me,' he says, eyeing the room and the table and us. Miranda sends him to the kitchen to wash while Niccolò finds him a bench and the evening begins with the passing of and the tearing at the potato flatbreads, the slathering of the pieces with the borlotti, which Gilda and I had pounded down to silk. It's potential richness having been the object of a somewhat harsh discussion between Ninuccia and I when we all planned tonight's menu, it's she who is first to finish her piece of focaccia, reach to tear off another and spoon more of the mousse onto her plate. Signifying 'delicious', she swivels her index finger into her cheek, nods her compliments to me and I wonder, *How long it will want before she begins to trust me?*

Tonight the tribe is deep in the annual strife over olives. Did the rain come too late, was the summer hot enough, the hail that fell three days ago, how cruel was its damage? Niccolò's groves are ancient, terraced on hillsides, and so receive sun and water obliquely, with more mercy than Pierangelo's and Iacovo's groves, which sit on flat land and so are more ruthlessly prey to the caprice of water and sun. It was Filiberto who planted Miranda's hundred-tree *oliveto* near the rustico eight or nine years ago and its most bountiful yield barely suffices for her sister's extended family and Thursday Nights. It is now less than a week before the November full moon and the beginning of this year's harvest and I, typically entranced by the subject, hear only a word now and then of their talk of quantity, quality, acid per cent, intensity of flavour and colour, the most current of the scandals over farmers who blend inferior Pugliese oil with the local and pass it off to exporters as pure Umbrian. It's Ninuccia who distracts me: *How long will it want before she begins to trust me?*

Four years have passed since that evening when Miranda announced her sham retirement and the tribe went to grief, the dialogue contemptuous about *La Festa di Babette* and murdered turtles and quail lying in state in pastry coffins, the air chastening around my two meekly spoken words: *I'll cook.* Surely that early chafe is gone but still Ninuccia drags a toe across the dirt. My side, their side. Maybe it's not Ninuccia who plagues me this evening. More, it is Barlozzo, who said: 'For you, my darling girl, being separate is being safe. You can hardly lament the status you've bestowed upon yourself. Separate you will always be. You're like Sicily. An island. Only you're an island born not of nature but of your own craving to be one.'

Miranda's gaze brings me back and, noticing that the bowl of mousse is nearly empty, I rise to take it to the kitchen, thinking to refill it but Miranda says, 'Leave the rest, thin it with a little broth and wine. Our soup for next week.' Waving her hands, palms inward, she says, 'Niccolò, you're on.'

A rare, maybe unique, departure from Thursday rules, a *man* has been sanctioned in the kitchen.

When we'd all sat at Bar Duomo after last Saturday's market to talk of this week's menu, Niccolò was there. Sitting at another table plying three farmers with grappa and old stories, when he heard me say that I would make *umbrichelli con le briciole*, he declared, loudly enough for the entire bar to hear, *'Devi fare quelli in modo mio.* You must make them my way.'

Alone now in a rampage behind the bedsheet curtain, we hear Niccolò slapping the flat of a knife on the work table, stirring, cussing – '*Questa maladetta cucina*, this damned kitchen' – the splash of pasta hitting the colander, then the soft plop of it into the wide shallow serving bowl, two metal spoons hitting one another as he tosses and tosses and then Niccolò begins to sing. '*Funiculi, funicula*,' and we all sing with him as Miranda herself holds aside the bedsheet curtain for his entrance.

This is a dish that causes Ninuccia's happiness. First of all, *umbrichelli* are the quintessential pasta of Umbria. Thick, imperfect, hand-rolled ropes of flour and water dough, these reflect the Umbrian character: rough, austere, wonderful. In the region of Tuscany, the very same pasta is called *pici,* these, too, reflecting the Tuscan character: rough, austere, wonderful. Yet should one be fool enough to suggest the similarity of their pasta, less the Umbrian and Tuscan characters, one could well incite hours of fist-pounding, shrieked threats, the biting of forefingers, endless and impatiently delivered litanies about how the water is different, the earth in which the wheat has grown up is of a another colour and texture and composition, the very manner in which the *trebbiatura*, the threshing, is conducted is not the same. And let's not even speak of the different 'hand' in mixing and rolling. Far more than a geographical border separates Tuscany and Umbria. Italy is not a united country but a group of individual 'city states', much as it was in the medieval.

Having chosen to soften what I knew would be her displeasure at the suavity of the borlotti mousse, it's the sauce for the *umbrichelli* that pleases Ninuccia: stale bread – roasted and pounded to rough crumbs – the best oil, half a large head of perfectly crisp, perfectly creamy white garlic smashed to a paste, a pair of well-rinsed anchovies preserved under sea salt, also pitilessly smashed, a little of the pasta-cooking water. Mixed together with the hot, hot pasta, the result is sumptuous and yet it's *a supper made of sticks*. Certainly this way of dressing pasta is a take on *aglio, olio, peperoncino,* a sauce so simple that, when concocted out of it's territory, it's likely to be desolated by flawed elements used in erring proportions: acrid, green-hearted garlic, chillies older than most marriages, who knows what oil. *Only a masterful hand can make supper out of sticks. Anybody can make good food from extravagant elements:* Ninuccia's mantra.

Of Niccolò's pasta, the tribe eats as one, smelling, absorbing, tasting, chewing, their eyes gone glassy with the very comfort of it. I think to a long-ago night, a Venetian night when, as Fernando slept, I cooked pasta for myself, lit a candle, opened the window to moonlight, sat and slurped, inhaled, twisted the strings about my fork – just as he'd instructed me never to do. That was the last time that pasta tasted this good to me.

'And now for the *secondo*, the main plate,' Niccolò says, with a whiff of challenge in his voice.

'Contrast,' I'd pleaded as we sat last week over the menu for tonight. 'After the simplicity of the pasta, let's make a . . . more complex dish.'

It was Ninuccia herself who said, *fagiano in salmi*. She went on to say that Pierangelo had four fat pheasants hanging in the cantina, nearly 'ripe' enough to be cooked. 'And *salmi* is a family recipe invented by my father's sister. Or his aunt, I can't remember. If someone could barter a black Norcia truffle, we'd be set.'

Though words collided in my throat, shackling the breath in my chest, I knew better than to free them. I would not tell Ninuccia Santacaterina née Marchesini that her family's *fagiano in salmi* is an adaptation of the Franco-Piemontese repertoire of the early 1900s, that it came to fame when French gastronomy held sway over the *borghese* – the upper class – in northern Italy. I won't say that *salmi* is a reworked French 'civet' – a ragout of game cooked in butter and wine. Even the word *salmi* is derived from the French *salmigondis*, which signifies melange, amalgam, concoction. I will not say that, over the years, the dish was claimed and rusticised by the Tuscans and the Umbrians – among others – so that now it lies among the celebration dishes in the most modest kitchens. I will not say that salamagundi is an Anglicised word for hodgepodge, muddle. I allow myself to say, 'Wonderful. I'll find the truffle.'

This evening Ninuccia brought a potful of dismembered pheasants, which she'd earlier wrapped – while still whole – in pancetta and roasted at a high temperature only ontil the flesh was rosily undercooked. Cutting them into pieces then, she'd set them to cool in a bath of red wine. In the rustico kitchen, she put together the sauce. With not the smallest justification for the impiety of it, she melted what looked like half a kilo of butter in Miranda's braising pot, scraped in a fine mince of the pancetta in which the birds had been wrapped, carrot, celery, porcini, rosemary and sage, and began the slow dosing of the fats and aromatics with red wine. Each time the wine reduced, she added more. After two litres of wine and nearly an hour's worth of distillation, she spent the flame, stirred in three or four anchovies, rinsed and mashed, covered the sauce. '*Ecco, fatto.* There, it's done,' she'd said, not even asking me about the truffle which, though I'd tried every reputable supplier in town, I had not been able to find. 'Too early, only *scorzone* now,' they'd said.

Ninuccia thickly sliced the great round loaf she'd bought in Ciconia, readied the trenchers for the grate and, while the rest of us were at the business of Niccolò's *umbrichelli*, she'd added the pheasant to the sauce, slowly reheated the mass and set about roasting the bread. I'd gone into the kitchen to help her plate the *salmi* but she smiled, told me to stand by should she need me. Ninuccia Santacaterina née Marchesini was in her glory, laying quarters of the birds on the hot bread, ladling the sauce, which, after its rest, had gone so deep a red as to seem black. Glossy. Redolent of the wine but as much of the woods, of pine needles and oak leaves crunched underfoot, and maybe some whiff of the apples on which the birds had fed in the orchards bordering Pierangelo's hunting fields. How I wanted to stick my finger in the sauce, pull a sliver of flesh from one of the breasts. With the tail of an eye, she kept vigil over me. As she finished plating the first two portions, I began to pick them up, to take them to the table but she slapped my arm. 'They must always be brought out together on a tray. You'll take one side of the tray. *Un onore.* An honour,' she told me.

Maybe she has smudged the line between us, at least for tonight. Or have I?

•

'I've never known anyone to hunt porcini at dusk,' I tell Gilda.

'Which is why I always do. Nothing worse than some old *fungarolo* brandishing a pointed stick at you as though every oak in the copse was his own,' Gilda tells me as she hikes herself up next to me onto the sheepfold wall.

It is the Thursday after the grand Niccolò–Ninuccia supper and we are just returned from a tramp in the woods. Between us on the broken stones where we sit, there is a large lidded basket filled with loam-smelling wild mushrooms. Gilda shakes one of the fat creamy-coloured things against a stone, loosening clods of wet black earth and, with the metal bristles of a small brush, she cleans it, being careful not to touch the tender underside of the cap. As she finishes with one, she hands it to me to wipe with a strip of old linen she keeps in the basket for that purpose. With a single sharp twist of my wrist, I separate the caps from the stems. Leaving the caps whole, I lay them in Miranda's old, well-seasoned tin. The porcini 'legs' – as the stems are called – I stow in a cloth sack. Once we're in the kitchen, I'll mince the legs almost to a paste with some rosemary and garlic and a rasher of *lardo di Colonnata*, fresh pig fat perfumed with wild herbs and flowers and aged in marble vases in a village that sits at the feet of Michelangelo's mines in western Tuscany. I'll scrape the paste into the caps, and set the tin in the embers until the porcini give up their juices. My thumb over the bottle, I'll splash on some white wine then, urging the mushrooms to drink and plump a while before I spoon them and their thickened sauces onto roasted bread. We'll begin supper with these tonight.

Straight up from the cluster of rosebushes rambling along the wall, small birds swarm and rustle, fly into the west. A breeze shivers the rosehips, carnal red on the naked brown arms of the bushes, and I feel the end of autumn. Long after we've finished with the mushrooms, Gilda and I stay there looking at the light. The trees across the road are thin black sticks against a reddening sky and the light seems like old light, light from the past. I feel as though I can see into the past. As though Gilda and I are there.

When the bells of San Bernardino in Canonica ring five and the sky has gone nearer to dark, we head back to the rustico. Filiberto's dogs bark, chase some fool creature across the meadow and its final hellborn shriek precedes a sudden silence. Gilda whispers '*Poveretta,* poor thing', and makes the sign of the cross on her breast. Through the kitchen window we see Miranda already working on the fire, once again breaking her own rules about Thursday suppers. We wave but she is oblivious. We enter the kitchen just as the hot crescendo of *Bamboleo* wails up from Miranda's disc player. Tonight's supper we have mostly prepared over the past few days, leaving little to do now but light the stove, the hearth fire. Still we putter about, Miranda, Gilda and I.

There's a fine old grey stone crock I've filled with a mousse of goat cheese, butter, Cognac and unshy turns of the pepper mill, and which I'd set to ripen in the back of my armoire at home several days ago. We'll roast walnuts at the last moment and warm the walnut-cornmeal *focacce* I baked this morning. I've cooked the duck at home. Slow-braised duck. Very slowly braised duck. This we will rewarm over the fire along with a pan of potatoes roasted with butter and thyme. There's another bread for that dish, one enriched with a few spoonsful of the duck pan juices, which render the crumb tender and moist, as though it's already been smeared with fine savoury fat. Even tonight's *dolce* will have benefited from its day or so of rest: a cornmeal cake made with white wine and olive oil. And just before we serve the duck, we'll set to warm by the hearth a bowl of blood oranges sautéed in salted caramel dark as molasses, the red flesh of the oranges and their juices, the nearly burnt-sugar intensity of the caramel saved from cloy by the tenuous crunch of salt. '*Una cena ricca*,' Miranda says; a rich supper. Nearly every dish made with butter. There is amnesty from the tribe's butter rancour since once a year, maybe twice and only when the weather is turning cold, one of the farm wives brings butter to the Saturday market, kilo loaves of it tied in kitchen towels and piled in a bushel basket lined with asphodel leaves.

We take stock of what's done, what is still to be done. We set the table. Gilda says she'll go home to bathe and change and be back at half-past six. I want to do the same but I can tell that Miranda would like company and so I content myself with a quick hands-and-face wash in the kitchen sink. A swipe of Russian Red across my lips, I brush bitter chocolate on my eyelids and draw a thin black Cleopatra line close to my lashes and out toward my temples. I unbraid my hair, gather all the tight waves the plaits have made into a chignon. I go to sit by the fire where Miranda waits.

•

'You two are so much alike. Deadpan as *la Gioconda*, both of you. Skin white as the dying Camille's, your faces with those jutting bones, chins square as a warrior queen's, I wouldn't do battle with either one of you despite those voices all whispery. Your mouths are different though, yours a full-blown peony, hers a rose, just come into bud.' It's clear that Miranda much prefers the rose just come into bud to the peony. 'Ninuccia wears the guise of harpy but she's all butter inside. Paolina is pure butter. You and Gilda could be sisters.' Miranda nods to the glass of wine she's poured for me and left on the hearth stone.

'I suppose. Sometimes even we notice what's alike about us, tell one another so. Still, our lives, some things in common but . . . more contrast than sameness, Gilda and I.'

'I think it's only the trappings that are contrasted. Time and place. A few circumstances, maybe. No matter, though, the two of you are built of the same stuff. Even the way you dress. Your long skirts and your old-lady shoes, boots made more for combat than for walking the meads. Gilda mostly does her own sewing, though. One dress or one skirt for each season; I've never known her to have more. She even sews her underthings, freshwater pearls smaller than grains of *carnaroli* edging her nightdresses. She makes one for me on my birthday every year. Wide as a tent but still feminine. 'How long have you known her?'

'She was fifteen when she came to live in Orvieto. She was born in 1953, so forty-one years have passed since the day she appeared at the back door of my sister's *forno*. Giorgia and Flavio used to bake for a living, did you know that?'

'I did.'

'It's one thing for a fifteen-year-old to set off alone, to escape from dire straits, real or perceived. Real, in Gilda's case. It's quite another to bolt with three children in tow, essentially abducted ones. There she was, toting one baby on her chest, the others secured by their wrists to ropes she'd looped onto her belt, a cardboard suitcase in either hand. I repeat, she was fifteen, Gilda was.

'It's a hundred times I've heard my sister tell the story of Gilda's unexpected arrival: "Signora Giorgia? I'm, I'm . . . It's me. I'm Gilda." Giorgia telephoned to tell me that I'd best come to town, she said there was a surprise, four surprises. I wept that day for all the times I'd kept myself from weeping. I wept for those babies, for Gilda, how beautiful was Gilda that day. I wept for Nilo. I wept for his son, I wept for *l'altra*, the other one. I wanted to scoop up all the babies in the world that day. I wanted to rock them and feed them. *Jesumaria, era un pianto atavico.* A barbaric weeping. Ancestral, primal.'

I place my hand on Miranda's wet face, one cheek, then the other. I pat her tears onto my face.

'An Etruscan rite. They having believed tears to be the blood of the soul. Never to be wasted.'

'The Etruscans used to wear tiny bottles around their necks, catch the tears in them.'

'Yes, well, since I didn't happen to have a tear bottle . . . Gilda has told me the story. Pieces of it. I would never ask about the parts I don't understand, the ones she passes over.'

'That's what I mean when I say the two of you are alike. At ease with shadows. Me, I want to know everything. Or tell me nothing at all.'

'What about . . . Well, you don't know so much about me.'

'You being *foreign*, well, you must, perforce, remain in the realm of the exotic and I'm content for you to stay there. Besides, I may not know so much *about* you, yet I know you – yourself – very well.'

I think she does but I don't say so.

Miranda continues, 'But Gilda, she's tight as a morning glory at twilight.'

'It's because even she doesn't know. About herself, I mean. Her mother was called Magdalena. Did you know her?'

'I did. She and Giorgia and I were together from the *scuola materna* straight through until Magdalena went to live with her aunt in Rome. She was, maybe, fourteen. Lovely. Tall, smooth dark hair like an Indian, prettier than us and timid as a lamb until she began to sing. Lord, what a voice.'

'Puccini. *Ciocio-san*. Gilda says when her mother wasn't singing from Madam Butterfly, Callas was. Either the mother or the phonograph.'

'From what I understand, more did Gilda grow up hearing her mother's weeping. Gilda still suffers from her mother having loved a man more than she loved her.'

'You mean, Gastone. Her father.'

'Maybe he was. It's just as likely he wasn't.'

'Is that a conjecture Gilda shares with you?'

'As you said, Gilda knows less of the story of her parents than most of us do. Or think we do. All she's had to go on is a gathering of trifles.'

I sip my wine, stand up to poke at the fire. I won't let Miranda see my eyes. She doesn't need to, though. Very softly she says,

'Now I've gone and struck that tender chord of yours again, haven't I? I'm a clumsy old thing, Chou . . . I wasn't thinking about . . .'

I turn to her then, bend to put my arms about her. My gesture is awkward, embarrassing both of us. I go again to stand by the fire.

After a while she says, "Leering like a chorus of shades", we all have *questions*. Save small hard evidences, all any of us know is what others *let* us know. And so we're wont to shape our stories to suit ourselves, pass them down as history. Over time, inventions become memories. And we tack our own onto the invented memories of those who came before us.'

Comforted by her use of the collective, I say, 'I sometimes feel a kind of *nostalgia* for the little scenes I've invented over the years, little fablesque vignettes to play in the dark. Short delicious scenes in which I'm the heroine or . . .'

'We all do that. But Gilda . . . her apocrypha she keeps stashed in a biscuit tin. The heirlooms that furnish that rattrap of a house of hers she's bought or bartered in the markets or the *antichità*. The portrait of Gastone that hangs in her *saloncino*, for instance.'

'And those books with the green leather covers that were her mother's?'

'Maybe so. And her Christmas dress. That blue velvet thing. That was supposed to have been Magdalena's wedding dress, though I know better who's dress it once was. And there's the gold pocket watch that she bought in a shop in Sorano because it's engraved with her own initials, which she says were also the initials of her maternal grandfather. A sepia portrait of him in a gold frame, wholly dissonant with her otherwise frugal decor, hangs over her hearth. She got herself a father, a grandfather, gave herself a past. The chasm that separates lies from invention is vast. Gilda escapes, fantasises; she does not lie.'

Shifting her gaze from the fire to me, she says, 'What does it matter? The portraits, the books, the dress, the biscuit tin full of husks. They may be as much Gilda's history as someone else's. Who can say? As one wanders toward the end, time dwindling always faster, I can tell you that not much of what was or wasn't, who was there or who fled or . . . *Jesumaria*, it all becomes a smudge. Only children never forget. I am loath to see Gilda using up her days in grieving for *interludes* she can't fill up with gospel.'

'I've never thought her dreaminess to be a kind of grieving,' I say. 'I don't think it is. Romantic. Gilda is a romantic. Byronic. She trusts pain more than joy. Doesn't she say that all the time? *Pain is more loyal than joy. It lasts longer, stays close forever.*'

'Yes, always close, pain is, but no less close than *delight*, both always nuzzling nearby. But we're apt to give more attention to pain, as though we were partial to it. Like being partial to a wayward child, never minding the one who's good as bread and whom you haven't given a thought to since the day before yesterday.' Miranda closes her eyes, shakes her head, pinches her upper lip, her preferred gesture of dismay. Her eyes still closed, she says, 'Girded, expectant, I suppose we tend to steel ourselves for tragedy. I worry that Gilda . . .'

'I have never known a person less *girded* for tragedy than Gilda. She wears pain like skin and yet all she *sees* is beauty. All she lets in under that skin of pain is beauty. And, like a child, she's roused by whim . . .'

Miranda opens her eyes, laughs softly, repeating: *whim, whim*. She looks at me, says, 'I'll tell you about one of Gilda's whims. It happened about a year ago by now. She gave a five-hundred-euro note to a violinist who'd set up on the corso in the rain. The whole of her earnings for a month, that five hundred euros. He played Paganini.'

'Well, yes, there's proof that she . . . How do you know? About the violinist and the . . .'

'He was a student at Santa Cecilia. I forget his name now, his first name, but he's a Baraldo, kin to Giacinta Baraldo . . .'

'The egg lady in the market?'

'The very one. This young man had come to Orvieto for a cousin's funeral. He busks all the time in Rome; most of the students do. Not so many of them are their daddy's spoiled little boys. That day he ran straight to Giacinta, showed her the note, said it was a woman, blonde, wearing a fedora. Giacinta understood which blonde, which fedora. The boy tried to give the note to Giacinta but she, knowing Gilda as she does, assured him that the note was *meant* to be his, told him that he'd given the lady in the fedora the greater gift. Of course Giacinta was right.'

'Only beauty matters to Gilda. She chases it, she . . .'

'Yes, that's what Gilda does.'

'What does Gilda do?'

'*Ah, sei qui?* You're here?' Miranda rises to take a bottle Gilda proffers as she steps from behind the bedsheet curtain of the kitchen.

'A private *aperitivo* for the cooks to while away the time before supper,' Gilda tells her merrily. 'I stopped by to see Ninuccia and found Paolina there, the two of them working on persimmon jam. I caught a lovely whiff of quince from the cantina kitchen.'

'*Cotognata*. Quince paste. Our *dolce* for next Thursday, no doubt,' Miranda says, fetching a corkscrew from a pocket in her apron, another treasure living there with The Gypsy Kings among the herbs and weeds.

'They'll wait until eight-thirty for Pierangelo to return from wherever he went. Rome, I think. If he's later than that, they'll come along without him. The evening being wonderful, I decided to leave my car at Ninuccia's and walk up the creek road. That's why I came in through the back doorway . . . I apologise if I seemed stealthy . . .'

This evening Gilda's costume is a black wool, ankle-length dress, the lace-up, thick, high-heeled shoes we call *le Francesine*, a long silk scarf, which she also uses as a shawl. She's pulled the battered grey fedora so low on her brow it flaunts the whisky eyes, and her hair, still damp from its washing and, as much, from her hike along the creek road, curls against the high flush of her cheeks. Sometimes she wears a choker of baroque pearls but tonight her neck is bare. When she wears the necklace, she touches it, adjusts it, pats it, calls attention to it, always finding a moment to slip in a word about her mother. Magdalena's pearls. Gilda doesn't need jewels. 'I didn't mean to . . .' Gilda's voice trails off as I shake my head, smiling at her, pulling a chair from the table near to the fire for her. Gilda sits, tucks one foot under her, letting the other dangle, holds out both her hands to the *calice* of red, which Miranda brings to her. There is a single thin crystal wineglass in Miranda's armoire, remnant from some other era. It's only Gilda who drinks from it. *Beauty matters to Gilda.*

Gilda takes a long quaff of the wine, asks, 'And so what is it *that Gilda does?*'

'I was telling Chou what I've already told you . . .'

'That I'm *closed tight as a morning glory at twilight?*'

'That and . . .'

'I've always loved that image. It pleases me as much as it suits me. It's rather pretty, don't you agree?' Gilda looks at me. Willing me, I think, to join her in deflecting Miranda from a harangue.

'It's lovely. And maybe apt once in a while but . . .'

Gilda cuts me off, says, 'Yes, once in a while or often or even always . . . It's who I am.'

Now she looks at Miranda who says, 'I'm taking a mother's liberties, aren't I, Gilda? Fretting over you. An ineffable habit by now since, for a grand part of my life, I've loved you as my own. As has Giorgia. We still quarrel over you, over who is closest to you, who has more *rights* to you. Over which one of us you love best.'

'I know.'

'You do?'

'Not so difficult to glean. When I was young I would profit from your rivalry, nimbly provoke it, but, by now . . . *Jesumaria,* Miranda, it's as though we've all arrived at more or less the same age and . . . well, I just wish that you . . . that you would *fret* less. *Un'anima solitaria,* a lone soul, a rogue woman. More than I'm some furled flower, maybe that's who I am.'

'Could be that. More, I think, that you've worked hard and long at contriving solitariness. How perfectly splendid a job you've done, Gilda. Your raw materials were formidable, I admit. Let's see . . . You must not have been a loveable child or else your mother and father would not have *abandoned* you. Horrid word, *abandon*. Even the sound it makes is hollow. Surely it was your fault that they went away. And if a child is not loveable to her own, how can she be loveable to anyone else? A pariah. A scrawny little creature not even the nuns wanted. Time passes, pages flutter and our Gilda is always more persuaded to this *reality*. It hurts so deeply, this *reality* does, that Gilda invents others. Though these invented realities comfort her, that other one – that *truth* which she's buried under the inventions – is the one that haunts her, scrapes its claws across her heart at three in the morning. And so our Gilda stays mostly separate from the world, wandering forth only guardedly. Suspiciously. Running back to sit by her fire, riffling through a tin box of memories.'

Gilda rises, takes up the bottle of wine and refills her glass, a metal glitter in her eyes, now more gold than whisky. She turns to Miranda.

'And you would have me do otherwise? Miranda, do you understand that I hardly know who I am? Who was this Pepucci, this father of mine? *Was he my father?* If so, did he wonder about me? Does he? As I do about him. And she, Magdalena, I never knelt beside her, never said goodbye. What I mean is that *I never saw her dead.* I'm certain of that. No funeral, no people who came to mourn or to comfort. No grave to visit. Why did the aunt tell me this story about my mother having gone to live with the angels? Why did she lie to me or *did* she lie to me? Was it that Magdalena was no longer able to tolerate life without Pepucci and so she ran away to find him? But why didn't she take me with her? And did she find him? If she did, why didn't they send for me? If she didn't find him, why didn't she come back? Because I wasn't his? Sometimes I think I may not even have been *hers*. The truth, what is it?'

'A shifting thing. A liar. Even truth lies,' Miranda says, her voice hushed.

'Yes, yes, of course, there is no whole truth and if there was, one would never tell it. Not the all of it. Still . . .'

Now, close to shouting, Miranda says, 'You want – no, you demand – precisely what you can never have: a flower-strewn, starlit road to your past. Here's a truth for you, Gilda: your case is hardly a particular one yet the whole of your sympathy you keep for yourself, checking your wounds, poking at them like stigmata, just to be certain they're still there. What do you know about Magdalena's past? Maybe she couldn't leave a path flowered and lit for you because she, herself, never had one. So many of us never have.'

Miranda becomes quiet then, pats her upper lip with the ends of her apron, closes her eyes, presses the apron on her tears. The apron still in her hands, her face contorted, she says, 'Have you ever thought how you would fare as a mother?'

'No. Why would I?'

'Empathy. I suppose that would be a reason . . .'

'So I could shift my pity to Magdalena, away from myself?'

'Something like that.'

'I'm not so generous.'

'Not a question of generosity but of fear. You fear you'd fare no less well than any other mother. Mothers do wrong. They must, perforce.'

Gilda rises, goes to Miranda, crouches before her, rests her head sideways on Miranda's knees, still wearing her fedora. Miranda pulls off the hat, covers Gilda's face with it. A stick in the wheels of the discourse. Gilda sits up then, smashes the fedora down low on her brow.

'And so *what is it that Gilda does*? That's where I came in and you've still to tell me.' She looks to me, then back to Miranda, stands, hands on hips. Softly she says, 'It's Iacovo. All this is about Iacovo, isn't it? I didn't understand until . . .'

'Which Iacovo? *Our Iacovo*?

As though I am sitting in the upper tiers behind Goliath in a top hat trying to follow a Chekov play recited in Portuguese, I'm lost. Neither notice me or the question.

Miranda is saying, 'He'll be here again this evening, I don't know whether you knew that or not. I mean . . . Gilda, he's . . .'

'Why should it matter if I knew or didn't know that Iacovo would be here . . . We're a group and all are welcome without official announcements or warnings.'

'Perhaps he misinterpreted your expressions of affection.'

'And which misinterpreted expressions were those?'

'When he brought the wood. The invitation to . . .'

'It was raining and cold last Saturday and nearly one when he finished unloading and stacking and so I did the normal thing, inviting him to lunch.

'You will remember Gilda that he's been grieving for half a decade. Iacovo's social machinery has always been somewhat antiquated, but since Fabiana's death it's been shut down. You're the first person – no, the first woman – who seems to . . . to *interest* him. You're both still young and . . .'

'I see. We're both still young, both without partners and so what else is there to do but to take up with one another? That's the thinking, is it?'

'You're afraid.'

'Of?'

'Being abandoned. Again. You won't risk it.'

'You insist on that word, Miranda. You insist so fiercely that one might begin to think it's you who aches with it.'

'Aches with what?'

'Abandonment.' Gilda's voice is soft, her thrust delicate. Deliberate.

'Of course, it's my ache, too. *Pacifico*. Fundamental. The undisputed and grand commonality of which I was trying to convince you a few moments ago. Otherwise known as broken trust. You know my story well enough . . . Better, I think sometimes, than I know yours.'

Gilda rises, busies herself with the table settings, moving things this way and that a centimetre or two and then back to where they were. She begins to say something but Miranda speaks over her.

'I am loathe to think of you alone in that burrow you call a house . . .'

The two are back on safe ground, the parrying strong and equal again.

'And would you name this place a palazzo?'

'This is my play house.'

'You're making me out to be pitiful and . . .'

'Not pitiful. Not that. Niggardly, I'd call it. Concocting supper from roots and berries and wandering among the oaks like some druid. When was the last time you dined in a restaurant, bought a new hat, went to the cinema? Put gasoline in your car? I know why you left your quaking old thing at Ninuccia's this evening. Empty, its tank dry. Your *gauge* acting up again. And while I've got your attention, what's happened to your will to work?'

'I've worked all my life.'

'You worked until you were fifty, which is not *all your life.*'

'And what do you call those four or five hours a day I spend at Bernandino's?'

'You should be doing other than scrubbing that gargoyle's noble bathrooms.'

'Miranda, that's unfair. You know very well that I work in the gardens and sometimes help with the housekeeping. I bake for them. I do what there is to be done, it's . . .'

'I can't abide the sight of him roaming the markets in his red velvet slippers and that tweed coat draped about his shoulders, deigning to sniff at a farmer's tomatoes but not to wish him good day. I know he canes his dog and most likely that addled wife of his. How can you, Gilda, when . . .'

Miranda stops herself, looks at me, says, 'Gilda cooked in the *scuola materna* in Orvieto for years, one of her many incarnations.'

'Eighteen years. It was the incarnation I loved best.'

'Gilda and . . . How many others?'

'Three.'

'She and three other women, they cooked divinely for those children. A hundred or so of them . . .'

'Eighty, sometimes a few less. Never more than eighty.'

'Giorgia and I would go to help once or twice a week . . .'

'Not in the kitchen. They would help serve and wash up.'

'No, we were never *permitted* in the kitchen but we sat with the children, ate with them. Some of the best meals of my life were in that cold, awful basement room of the elementary school. Like no other school lunch I'd ever known, they served handmade pasta and cakes and pastries. *Lumachelle* with pecorino and prosciutto, tiny ones to fit in their little hands; how they loved those.'

'The soft anise cookies were their favourites. I'd go from table to table, helping the children cut their food, spooning it up to the few reluctant ones, cajoling, applauding clean plates, measuring muscles. I sang Puccini to them,' Gilda says. 'When State funds were diminished and we could no longer shop locally for the kitchen, we were sent boxes of frozen chicken and fish, already fried, powdered eggs and milk, even our bread was frozen, baked who knows when in some commissary kitchen and trucked down the peninsula. Animal feed. I left, took to the woods.'

'Which brings us back to the present, to . . .' Miranda says, but Gilda is heading backwards.

'Do you really think that my life is, what did you call it, *niggardly*? No, don't answer that. Try this: do you really think that the *consequence* of a life – it's significance – can be measured by what I wear or how I eat? If I had a new hat and went to dinner, would my life take on more greatness? Would I need a vintage

Bentley? Would that do it for you? Or a man? Ah, have I got to the crux, have I . . .'

Miranda steps in. 'Iacovo is bright and kind and when he swings his axe to the wood, he could be Ares himself. Wraparound eyes, long as a Greek's. A man less likely to break a trust I've yet to meet. And if he did betray you, well . . . there'd be another layer of memories to fill up your tin.'

'Ares, himself.' Clucking her tongue at Miranda as though to shame her, Gilda aims her gaze at the window pane again, this time prowling after some canker on the scrupulous man with the wraparound eyes. Her fingers tremble as she picks at the knots on the laces of her shoes. She unties the laces, re-ties them with a vengeance. She presses a middle finger to the bridge of her nose. Then, her voice feeble with defeat, she ventures, 'Iacovo doesn't even bathe.'

'Would you truly set up honest sweat as an impediment to getting to know a good man? Draw him a bath some evening, Gilda. Pour him a glass of wine and leave it on the rim of the tub with a slice of soap and one of your clove-smelling candles, why don't you?'

Miranda's mordant solution to Iacovo's presumed antipathy to soap and water causes Gilda to flush from her décolleté to her downcast eyes. To hide the now greater trembling of her fingers she reaches up to push a strand of hair behind her ear. Her hand lights on the old fedora she is still wearing and she removes it, hangs it on the back of her chair, makes an elaborate business of smoothing her hair, a device that enrages her already hot red cheeks. Still not looking at Miranda, Gilda says, 'He's younger than I am.'

Miranda throws up her arms, rises clumsily from her chair, adjusts her balance and heads toward the kitchen. She turns back, says, 'You're hopeless, Gilda, perverse as a cow who will kick over a full pail of her milk because the milker is wearing mismatched socks. You're, you're . . .'

'Miranda, wait. What you refuse to understand is that, for me, there's a . . . I don't really know how to explain it . . . For me there's a kind of *thrill* in being alone. In loneliness. Why would you have me risk that? For what, for whom?'

'I would have you risk it for your own sake, Gilda. I would have you interrupt the daily ravaging of your wounds. But if you truly find loneliness thrilling, then slam shut the door and draw that tawdry old hank of stuff you call a curtain and take to your bed. I'll be long gone when you're finally moved to answer an urgent banging on that door to see that Accident, Destiny and Chance have come to set up in your garden, that they've come to taunt and whisper, *You're almost out of time, Gilda* . . . What will you do then?'

'*Sei cattiva,*' she says. 'You're evil, Miranda. Why can't you just let me be?'

Miranda moves to stand very close to where Gilda sits, bends to run her hands down the length of the heavy lanks of her hair, pulls at it and smiles. She bends to kiss a lank of Gilda's hair. She tells her, 'It's that ineffable habit I spoke of a while ago. That I have long loved you as my own.'

Wandering into the kitchen, Miranda pulls the bedsheet curtain across the rod, a sign that she will stay apart for a while. Neither speaking nor looking at one another, Gilda and I stay where we sit. We hear Miranda setting about her evening's ablutions out in the garden behind the kitchen door where Filiberto has constructed a primitive shower of bits and pieces, loot from his habitual moonlit pillages of reconstruction sites along the deserted private roads. Thick oak planks form its walls, these faced on the inside with marble – black, white and grey. A square of prestigious Verona green marble is the base and a plate-sized showerhead, attached to a rather grand gold-coloured hose, sends down a drenching and never more than lukewarm rain upon the lavish form of the goddess of Buonrespiro. Filiberto has planted blue hollyhocks around the bathing place and painted the same on the outside walls. A brass Moor's-head knocker, meant for the door of some Englishman's villa, he's driven into the stone wall of the rustico to hold her towel. We hear Miranda priming the pump, muttering just loud enough so that her oaths against the lunacy of 'youth' reach us. When the water stops, Gilda shouts to Miranda, 'What did he say that causes you to think he has *interest*?'

'What did who say?' Miranda asks in sing-song.

'Tell me.'

'No, I won't.'

'Tell me, Miranda. Please. What did he say?'

Out of the shower now we hear her moving about in the kitchen.

'Please, Miranda, I . . .'

Flinging back the bedsheet curtain in a move so brusque it falls half off its hooks, an impudent Victory wrapped in the curtain's companion sheet stands before us, dripping lavender water onto the stones of the kitchen floor. Plaits loosed, the white skin of her shoulders gleaming from olive oil soap, the blue-black eyes gloating, Miranda says, '*I want her to have the most beautiful peaches.* If you must know, that's what Iacovo said.'

'What? *Peaches?* And for that you think he is . . .'

'Think about it, Gilda,' Miranda says, heaving the wounded curtain back across its rod.

Gilda laughs, calls Miranda daft. She stands up, scrunches the brim of the fedora with both hands, pulls a face. She goes silent then, rips off the hat, letting it fall where it may. She's flushed again, this time a deeper shade of red.

'*Jesumaria.* He was twelve. I was fifteen.

•

As the others begin to arrive, it is a Gilda less demure than usual who steps forward to fuss over them, relieving them of coats and offerings, pouring wine, lighting candles. The colour stays high in her cheeks; the memory of a peach? Her beauty is heightened.

Ninuccia notices. 'Gilda, you're lustrous. If I didn't know better I'd say you were post-coital. Who did you meet on the creek road?'

Wearing jeans and a crisp white shirt, it's full pleated sleeves and narrow waist trademarks of Crivelli-the-shirtmaker in Viterbo, Iacovo looks up from stacking wood near the hearth. Fastening a fresh blue pinafore over her flowery market dress, tucking her rewoven plaits under a kitchen towel, Miranda goes to sit by the fire where Iacovo is still at work with the wood. Accepting a glass of wine from Gilda, Miranda's laugh – usually robust – is a thin jet of water splashing in a fountain below a half-opened window.

•

'I want to know how you cooked that duck. Every step. I even want you to shop with me and then to show me what to do.'

'Which duck?' My still-sleepy mind thinks Gilda refers to a specific bird rather than a recipe. It's very early the next morning and Gilda has telephoned me. Having always left our communications to chance or to Thursdays, it is the first time Gilda has resorted to this urgent form of intercourse.

'Last night's duck. I ate it with a spoon it was so tender and . . .'

'You don't need me, Gilda. Just remember how it tasted and then . . .'

'No, no, the flavours were too complicated, too . . .'

'Complex but not complicated. And the method is long, nothing we can start and finish in a day. It can't be rushed, that's the idea of the dish, that it wants nine days and that one's appetite for it grows and . . . I'll write it all out, I'll . . .'

'No. Come here and *tell* it to me. It will be better if you tell me . . .'

So unlike Gilda, first a telephone call, then this persistence about a duck. Iacovo. All this must have something to do with him. I begin to laugh.

'Can I ask *you to tell me* something in return?' I say.

She's laughing, too, knowing where I'm leading her.

'Not if the something is about Iacovo.'

'It's about peaches. And about Iacovo. I'm curious about the peaches. You're curious about the duck.'

'Don't bargain with me. We'll see. Just meet me at the market, high noon tomorrow, and plan on coming home with me.'

'Go to Cotigni for Moulard breasts and have some thyme ready. I'll meet you at your place after lunch.'

•

'From Cotigni?'

'Of course. Moulard breasts, just like you said.'

Gilda and I are standing in the single room where Gilda lives. Once a village wash house, it is long but narrow with soaring smoke-blackened beams and a slate floor cracked in places so that little weeds grow up between the stones. There are the remains of a sort of balcony where the clothes were once hung to dry in the winter but mostly the space is all open like a loft. The kitchen end of the room is crowded with an Aga, pre–Second World War, two deep stone sinks and a magnificent oak table recovered from a monastery chapel in Viterbo, a piece that Gilda insists was a mourning table, a bier on which the dead were displayed to their brothers. Miranda says this is another of Gilda's fantasies, but I wonder. Twelve chairs are placed around the table even though, according to Miranda, Gilda has only three plates. I have never dined in Gilda's home.

'Rinsed and dried, the skins scored. *Brava.* I'll need a knife to trim this excess,' I tell her, tearing at the nuggets of yellow fat adhering to the inside of the duck breasts.

'It's in the drawer near the stove, right behind you,' she tells me. In the drawer I find a wooden spoon and a ten-inch Wusthof. 'Something smaller?'

'Only my clasp knife,' she says.

'This will do.'

I remove the fat, ask Gilda to save it carefully, tell her we'll need to render it later.

'Now, where's the thyme?'

'Take your choice,' she says, 'dried from the hillsides of Amiata, still on its branches, or the meadow kind, which is milder.' She holds out a basketful of the herb.

'A little of both.'

I slip the thyme leaves from their branches directly over the skin side of the duck breasts, rub coarse salt over the thyme, blending them together over and into the score marks. I turn the breasts flesh side up and do the same. I grind white peppercorns with whole allspice and repeat the double massage until not a millimetre of the skin and flesh escapes the cure. I place the breasts back in the white china bowl and look about for plastic wrap, which, of course, Gilda does not have. I find a plate of the right diameter to fit tightly inside the bowl and ask Gilda to set it out in the shed where three hens roost and her wood is stacked. When she returns I'm washing my hands.

'That's it for seven days,' I tell her.

'What?'

'I told you it wanted time rather than trouble. All you have to do now is, once a day for seven days, massage in a few more crumbles of thyme – very little – and another pinch of the white pepper–allspice mix. Once a day for seven days. I'll be back next Saturday and we'll do the next step. Meanwhile, now it's your turn. Tell me about the peaches.'

'Why didn't you just write that down and . . .'

'Because it was you who said, "No. Come here and tell it to me. It will be better if you tell me . . ."'

'I suppose I did.'

'Peaches, Gilda,' I say, going to fetch the bottle of Terra Vineate I'd earlier placed in her refrigerator, a machine half the size of a hotel bar refrigerator in which I've never seen anything but water. 'Peaches and Iacovo when he was twelve,' I tell her merrily, but when I turn to her, she flinches, looks at me almost solemnly. Her stare bruises the moment, maybe it humiliates me because all I can think is: *these damned Umbrians*. I'm forever stepping into their traps. Silent as stones they are until they want to talk. And when they say they want to talk, I settle in, believing they do while they've already begun pitching daggers at me for the sin of forced entry into their souls. I fire a solemn stare back at her.

'Gilda, let's just drink some wine and, well, it's hardly necessary that you . . .'

'No, no, it's not that I don't want to . . . it's not that.' From a wall shelf she takes a Camparisoda tumbler and a lovely cut-crystal goblet, her entire stock of glassware. She sets them on the table.

'But I can't tell you about the peaches until . . . until I tell you of other things. Until I tell you about the farm.'

'The farm?'

'If you're going to interrupt me, I won't be able to keep things straight. Just listen. Be patient. A story can't be rushed any more than a duck can. It may want nine days to tell you.'

'Touché.'

I open the wine and follow Gilda to the other end of the room. To her *salotto*. As opposed to the bare stone walls of the kitchen end, here she has papered over the stones, bouquets of blown yellow roses tied in red ribbons, the paper peeling, water-stained, smoke-blackened like the beams. A wrought-iron chandelier with three tiers of handmade brownish candles hangs over a single bed, its iron head and foot shaped like a sleigh. Two, maybe three paces from the bed there sits a clawfoot bathtub raised up half a metre on a kind of wooden platform from which extends a thick elbow pipe and a long, thin pipe that trails all the way to the kitchen end of the room, exiting somewhere under the sinks. A wonder of plumbing conceived and executed by Filiberto. There is a wing-backed chair and a hassock. On a square gilt baroque table there is a candlestick lamp with a red shade, a teapot and a cup, and an untidy stack of leather-bound books. Against the small hearth, its fire nearly spent, Gilda has leant a black marble mantle. Over the mantle, hung from a tasselled cord, is a Dutch-school portrait of a man in a red velvet Garibaldi cap. A length of unsewn yellow velvet she's flung over a butcher's hook to the side of a many-paned door; both the door and the marble mantle, Gilda once said, are spoils from Filiberto's Robin-Hood-ish expeditions. Filiberto, shepherd-craftsman-pirate. From a second butcher's hook near the open door, a haunch of prosciutto swings in the mild December breeze. Every time I have been here, there is always this unexpected ornament, sometimes carved to the bone, other times a fresh, fat one, yet to be cut.

In every corner of Gilda's house, there is the lush, titillating scent of cloves. Oranges stuck with cloves are piled in deep baskets here and there on the flags, more are lined up on the mantle shelf while a mortar full of bruised cloves she keeps by her bed. The candles and the long loaves of soap she makes are clove-scented. Essential oil of cloves is Gilda's only body perfume.

While Gilda pours the wine and stirs the fire, I look out from the door into the yard where the hens peck among the rows of a kitchen garden, harvested save a few pumpkins lurking under withered leaves. We touch glasses, sip the wine and Gilda beckons me into the chair while she settles herself against the head of her bed.

'I've never really known very many men. I don't mean in the *carnal* way, though I've never known one in that way, either. A fifty-three-year-old virgin, does that shock you? My tribe is small but not yet extinct.'

She pauses only to smile. *'Allora.* Men. Gastone Pepucci. My father. He was *absent.* The priests with their punishments, they were the only males I knew until the cousin came to take me from Sant' Eufemia.

'Cousin?'

'Chou, I don't have a text for my story. Nothing to read from, nothing in a straight line. Just give me a chance. I'll try to make sense.'

'Gilda, it was only the peaches I'd wondered about. Since Miranda had . . . But this, what shall I call it, this *excavation* of your past, it's not what I . . . that was not my aim, not what I meant to . . .

I stand up, look about for where I've left my jacket.

'Don't be put off. Please. Wait, I'll go with you. Let's walk. I'd had a mind to search for pine boughs today and to cut some *vischio*, mistletoe, from the oak by the creek. Will you walk with me?'

'I'd best be going. I'd only meant to stay a short while in any case. Fernando and I are taking the 17:10 into Rome, staying the night. We can catch up on Thursday. I'll be at the rustico by . . .'

'Who's cooking with you this week?'

'Actually, I never know. Mostly everyone shows up at some point or another during the morning. Miranda is always the first one there, up to her elbows in one dish or another. So much for her retirement from Thursdays.'

'I'll be there this week with the last of my pumpkins. What shall we do with them?'

'Maybe roast them, caramelise the flesh for tarts.'

Gilda walks me to the door, out to my auto, her Camparisoda glass still in hand.

As I drive away, she shouts, 'Don't forget our date . . . The next episode of the duck . . .'

•

It is the next Saturday. After their week-long thyme cure, Gilda had brought the duck breasts in from the shed to warm a bit while she and I gathered up what I'd need to proceed.

'Now, about the peaches,' she'd said, tilting her head to one side, presenting the unqualified spectacle of the whisky-coloured eyes. 'Okay, the famous peaches . . . but, meanwhile, we have these lovely breasts . . .'

Without reserve, Gilda began to talk. As I moved from one task to another, the tattoo of the knife on the board, the quiet sizzle of fat in a hot pan, the familiar backdrop seemed to comfort her. Pacing up and back upon the stones of her long, narrow house, she would break stride each time she arrived at the kitchen end, alighted long enough to smile, nod perfunctorily, perform the ritual Umbrian swivelling of her index finger into her cheek – the gesture signifying *deliziozo* - resume her pacing, her talking.

'This cousin, he just appeared one Sunday at the convent. He came with a letter from the old aunt who had only recently died. Smooth black hair caught in a strip of leather on the nape of his neck. Dark clothes. I remember that everything about him seemed dark. I remember thinking that his teeth were beautiful. He remained standing, silent while one of the nuns sat with me there in the reception room, quietly explaining that this man, this relative of mine, had come to take me to live with him and his family. A farm up in the Castelli, in the hills above Rome. Though she sat so close to me, the nun's voice seemed to come from far away. I remember looking at her as she spoke, trying to fathom her words. "How lovely it will be for you, Gilda, to live in the countryside." I tried to grasp that the old *zia* was truly gone, she, my one link to even the most tepid of familial affection. Dead. Standing over there, that man with smooth hair, the beautiful teeth, now he was my family. Questions about Magdalena, Pepucci, about life before the convent, who would answer them . . . ? Who knew the truth or even pieces of it? I stood, walked toward the cousin, stopped close to him, looked up at him as though he were inanimate. I gazed at the cousin until the nun, taking my arm, led me, still looking back at him, up the stairs to the dormitory. I watched as she packed my belongings in a cardboard valise, deep like a doctor's case. I still have it somewhere, that valise. I remember how warm it was that day.'

'The thing to do at this point, Gilda, is to render the duck fat you've saved. Would you fetch it for me, please.'

'Yes. Yes, of course. The fat. I'll go to . . . where is it?'

Clearly still back with the cousin, Gilda searches in the tiny fridge, opens the pantry door, stands in front of it for a long time, then turns to me, 'I know I still have that cardboard valise somewhere. I'd never have parted with it.'

'Are you saying that the duck fat may be inside the carboard valise?'

'It's in the shed. Must be there. Just be a moment.'

'The duck fat or the cardboard valise?'

'I wish you'd stop interrupting me.'

I place the fat in a small, heavy saucepan, add a spoonful of water and set the pan over a low flame on the gas ring that Gilda keeps on top of the Aga. Slowly and without stirring, the fat releases its oil until only crisp golden bits of it are left floating about in the rendered fat. I put the pan aside while I chop half a dozen peeled shallots with a few thick slices of lean pancetta to a coarse dice. I scrape the shallot/pancetta mixture into a large, heavy sauté pan – Gilda's one and only, in which she cooks everything she doesn't roast in the hearth. I add the rendered duck fat, the *ciccioli* – the crisp bits – and, still over a low flame, stir the mass about until the shallots go transparent and the pancetta is nicely coloured. I scrape the mass into a deep oval terracotta dish and set it aside while I get back to the sauté pan in which a bare film of fat remains. I heat the pan over a medium-low flame and slip in the dried, very well dried magret, skin side down. I turn up the flame to seal the skin, checking it after five minutes or so, waiting patiently for it to take on a deep mahogany colour. The wild thyme has perfumed the fat, the fat has perfumed the shallots and, already, they've raised up the heady, hot moist air of a good kitchen. I turn the magret, gild the flesh side to that same deep colour, then slip the breasts into the terracotta dish with the aromatics.

Gilda peers over my shoulder, resumes her pacing, her talking. 'The aunt willed her legacy to this man, a grandnephew, her sister's grandson, a third or fourth cousin to me, he and I being all that remained of her kin. A monthly trust and all her worldly goods she'd left to the nephew. And me she left to him as well. There was a great deal of money, a great deal it must have seemed to the nephew who was poor but, with hindsight, I suppose it was a pittance. In the notarised letter to him from the aunt's attorneys, there was a caveat: the trust and the goods would be released to him only after he'd taken me from Sant' Eufemia, brought me to live with him, his wife and his two children. There would be legal controls, State visits from time to time to ensure my proper integration into his family. I was his *quid pro quo*, measure for measure.

'Docile as a good convent girl must always be, I carried the valise, walked three paces behind the cousin through the streets of Rome to a waiting bus in the Largo Argentina. Watching our approach from the windows were grappa-soused farmers bound back to the hills after the morning market in Campo dei Fiori. I noticed the farmers watching. Me in my uniform, my perfect braids, my tiny gloves. I wore a straw hat. I was twelve, halfway to thirteen. The cousin was called Giulio. Giulio told me that he was twenty-five. He told me nothing more. During the hour it wanted for the bus to arrive at his village, he stayed silent. He looked at me, though, appraising my fancy convent clothes. I think my quietness he took to be *compiacenza*, complacency. As I'd learned to do during the priests' punishments, I shifted my gaze to the middle ground. And then to the far side of the window.

'A kilometre or so beyond the village, somewhere on a yellow-dust road slashed through a sprawl of wheat fields, the bus stopped. Giulio and I descended the bus across the road from a low stone building, oilcloth curtains flapping on glass-less windows. We waited for the bus to pass. How hot it was. How desolate. Where is his family? Who is here to welcome us?

'More a hut than a house, Giulio's home is a single room. Sitting upon shards of post-war linoleum laid over packed earth were various wooden chairs, a table, two beds, a stove. The hearth was large and deep. A *soppalco*, a raised platform, ran above half the room, a flight of stairs, steep as a ladder, leading to it.

'The cousin's wife was twenty-two and heavy with child. Isolda. His wife was called Isolda. They had two little daughters,

Livia and Dafne, aged four and two. As though I had just been dispatched from an agency – still in hat and gloves, my valise in hand – Isolda informed me of the ways and means of the household, outlined my tasks: to tend the children while she and Giulio worked sun-up to last light in the fields, to prepare their evening meal, see to the washing and the general order of things in the house. Isolda told me they were subsistence farmers, as were most of the families who lived in the area. They worked a small parcel of rented land and sold the yield to pay the monthly land and house tarrifs. What remained in either produce or funds fed them. Having gleaned some gist of the discourse about the transfer of funds and goods between the nun and my cousin, I – brightly, consolingly – told Isolda that surely the old aunt's legacy will make life easier for them now. Arms embracing the roundness of her belly, rocking to and fro as though in pain, a kind of disdain flashing in her eyes, Isolda conceded only to say: "There are two goats, chickens and, when we can afford to feed it, there might be a pig."

'The first thing I did was to take off my hat and place it on the older girl's head. Livia. I crouched then to the littler one, to Dafne, pulled off my gloves and urged her baby hands into them. Dafne's lower lip jutted, the tiny gloved fists kneaded her eyes. She wept and it wasn't until later that I understood she'd been weeping for joy. Having silently witnessed this little pageant, Isolda, with a tilt of her chin, sent me up the stairs to the space under the eaves. Once a dovecote, this is where she'd meant me to sleep. The pigeons long gone, only the silver-white sheen of two centuries of their shit remained, embellishing the parched beams. There was no bed.

'I remember very little about those first days except the silence. Giulio and Isolda barely spoke to one another, less to me and almost never to the little girls. I think it must have been the second night I was there that the children, dragging behind them the rags that served as their blankets, climbed the stairs to me. The next day, maybe it was even the same night, I folded the thin wool-stuffed pallet that was the little girls' mattress, pulled it up the stairs. We three never slept apart from that night.

Isolda and Giulio would bring home a portion of whatever they'd been harvesting on a given day and that would compose the family's supper. In summer we ate watermelon. Evening after evening, there was watermelon, bread and wine. When they harvested tomatoes or green beans or artichokes, these would be on the table. In late September Giulio began arriving with some great round tough-skinned squash in a sack, dumping it, wordlessly, onto the oilclothed table, and I would slice and roast it over the embers with a few drops of oil. Sea salt, big crystals of it. Always wine and bread. We managed.

'A few pieces at a time, the contents of the apartment in Rome, the old aunt's *alta borghese* furnishings, were transported to the farmhouse in the neighbours' trucks where earlier in the day had been piled sacks of potatoes, cabbages, wire cages of chickens, hutches of rabbits to sell in Campo dei Fiori, each load further transforming the stone hut on the yellow-dust road into a shambled revisiting of the aunt's *salone*. Turkey rugs were laid over the linoleum and the packed-earth floor, sofas and chairs – maroon and green – and a walnut Lombardy bedstead were stacked against the walls. Wooden fruit crates packed with china. Tipped against a painting from the Macchiaioli school in a forty-centimetre gilt frame was a chandelier, its crystals tinkling as Isolda swiped it with her skirt every time she walked past it. Nothing was arranged in a way that it could be sat or lain or even looked upon; nor, as far as I knew, did the cousins ever try to sell off any of the goods. Half treasure trove, half hovel, that old stone house.

'In the last of the truckloads from Rome sat the bed that was mine at the aunt's. Iron, painted white. I dismantled it, hauled the pieces up the stairs to the dovecote, used the head and foot as clothes' lines, the feather mattress to make a better bed for Livia, Dafne and me. It was months later when the old aunt's best gift to me was delivered to the farmhouse.

'According to the aunt's instructions, her attorneys arranged for a trunk to be sent from Rome by train to the village and then, by cart, to the farmhouse. A grand trunk it was or so it must have seemed to the farmers who watched its progress from the station through the village and along the yellow dust road. Red leather banded in brass, green silk tassles hanging from its handles, it could only be the convent girl's dowry, the farmers agreed. Faces scrubbed raw, Sunday shirts boiled white, widowers, boys who would be men, men too poor to afford a wife, they queued at the cousins' door to beg my twelve-year-old hand. Guilio drank wine with the men, sent them back from whence they'd come, over the old yellow road.

'As it turned out, inside the grand red trunk there *was* a kind of dowry, my convent girl's estate, my solace, all that remained of my heritage: an oval red and silver *amaretti* tin of grand dimensions, the sort that would be displayed in the window of a fancy caffé, its silk-lined depths crammed with *oubliettes*, symbols, letters, photos, music scores, libretti. Under the tin were two black dresses wrapped in tissue paper and one blue velvet one, Magdalena's wedding dress. Black satin shoes with velvet ribbons to tie about the ankle, various of Magdalena's nightdresses and frocks, a grey squirrel pelisse still scented in Cabochard, so familiar I'd thought it was the smell of my mother's skin. There were twelve leather-bound books: Manzoni, Verga, Calvino, Moravia ... It was Giulio who carried the red trunk up to the space under the eaves, brushed the brass bands with the sleeve of his shirt. He stood back from it, almost smiling.

It was under the eaves where I read more often than I slept, where I sat sifting through Magdalena's things, the Cabochard-scented trove from which I might compose a life. Slipping into her dresses, winding the ribbons of her shoes about my ankles, draping the squirrel pelisse over one shoulder, I'd mince up and down the room as though it were the via Veneto. As though I was Magdalena. I know it wasn't a real 'dowry' in the pretty red trunk but I don't know how I would have fared without it.

'I suppose many childhoods are made of mischance and, at some point, a measure of humiliation. As was mine. What I mean is that I was not unprepared to live the tempered form of slavery into which I was established in the cousins' household. Then it was an almost universal role for older children in poor families. The cousins' abuse of me was benign enough, akin to how they parented their own daughters. Less cruel than they were diffident, they lived in the centre of themselves, in a fog of fatigue and hunger and what seemed their own private lust. Perhaps this indolence was, itself, a kind of cruelty.'

As though she is considering the potential cruelty of indolence, Gilda stays quiet, directs her beyond-the-window-pane gaze at me. I see that she is tired. 'The Aga is taking a long time to heat, Gilda. We need it to reach one hundred and eighty,' I tell her.

I uncork a bottle of dubious white, unlabelled, its nose musty, its colour a turbulent yellow. I taste it, recork it, go to fetch the bottle I'd brought for us to drink later on. Trying to retrieve her from the indolence-cruelty question, I say, 'If you ever cook this again, best to use classic sauvignon blanc: chalk, stone, new grass, distinct cat pee aromas.'

She laughs but I tell her it's true. I add about a third of the bottle to the casserole, just enough to float the breasts without drowning them; I place a piece of oven parchment directly over them, cover with a tight-fitting lid and place the casserole over a medium flame only until the wine begins to shimmer. The Aga still twenty degrees too cool, short of 180C, I put the casserole in anyway, leave it to braise.

'At forty-minute intervals, dose the duck with additional wine, a quarter cup or less, each time turning the breasts to bathe them well in the wine and the rendered juices. Shall I write that down?'

'No. Forty-minute intervals, a little more cat pee. *Ho capito.* I've understood.'

Wanting the person and the dish to succeed, I cannot help but become mildly pedantic if I'm trying to talk someone through a recipe. Hands on hips and with a bit more volume, I proceed: 'Depending upon the age and quality of the duck, it will want three dosings and turnings until the flesh becomes velvety and falls to pieces with the slightest touch of a fork. Remove the casserole from the oven and allow the mass to thoroughly cool, uncovered. Then cover the casserole with plastic wrap and then with its lid. Transfer to the fridge for four to six hours or overnight. In your case, to the shed.'

Jesumaria, if I'd known how tortuous it would be just to cook a duck I would never . . .

'If you think about it, nothing tortuous at all. *Long*, as I told you in the beginning, but very little *active* time. Mostly the beast rests in the shed or in the oven.'

•

'Claudio was born in October, late in October. Having come back early from the fields, Isolda stayed prone on her bed all the afternoon, her silence interrupted every now and then by a brutal moan. The little girls hovered, fretted. The tea I set to her lips she waved away. "*Fuori da qui.* Get out of here." With the *levatrice*, the midwife, and another woman in tow, by the time Giulio arrived it was dark and Isolda's moans had become screeches from hell. Up under the eaves Livia trembled and keened and Dafne bent over the red trunk, searching for the little gloves, which had, by then, become the magic balm for her two-year-old's heartbreaks. I tried to help her but she pushed me aside, knowing already that she must manage the hardest things by herself. Finding the gloves, Dafne sat next to me on the feather bed, finally allowing herself to weep, gloved hands crossed in her lap.

'"Call the girl down here. Best she sees this." It was the midwife's voice. "Gilda! *Subito*. Quickly."

'The neighbour woman pushed me to stand next to the midwife, centimetres from Isolda, a woman like Isolda but this one made of wax, yellow, melting, eyes empty holes. The only light was a candle. "Bend down. When I tell you, hold out your hands. I'll help you, I'll help you."

'Claudio was born into my arms. I remember only that I held him tight against me, struggled to keep him there as the midwife, laughing, pried him away, tied the umbilicus in two places, swiped a pocket knife through the candle flame, handed it to me, held the cord taut. "Cut it. Go ahead, cut it between the knots. Now."

'Livia and Dafne, hearing the different sounds, came scrambling down the stairs, went to stand by the kitchen table where, having lain him there, the midwife was washing a wailing Claudio. Taking off her gloves, Dafne then set to the work of gently fitting them to her brother's hands. "Don't cry, baby. I'm here. Shhhh."

'More wet nurse than mother, Isolda fed her son, offering him one breast then the other, she smoking through the ordeal then handing him back to me. As were her daughters, her son was more mine than hers. When he cried in the night I would carry Claudio down to Isolda, lay him on her breast, take him away when he was sated. Never having fully awakened, Isolda would curl back into the embrace of her husband. Though I tried to hate her, all the sentiment I could muster for Isolda was pity. For her torpor, her always being *elsewhere*. As I cared for the baby, especially him, I would think almost constantly of Magdalena, imagine her with my newborn self with myself at Dafne's age, at Livia's. Magdalena, also, had been not so much present as she was *elsewhere*.'

•

With only brief respites back to the present, Gilda has been telling her story through the first and second forty-minute interval between wine dosings, during which time we've variously sat by the fire, stood in the kitchen, stepped outside to feed the chickens, brought in from the garden three pumpkins, which we've peeled and cut into chunks, set to boil on top of the Aga, she intending to caramelise them to fill cornmeal-crusted tarts for the next Thursday. Gilda performs the last dosing and turning of the breasts, heaves the casserole back into the oven, heading directly to the nest of pillows against the head of her bed. She's already back into her narration when I stop her, ask for a piece of paper, a pen.

'Business first. You're on your own from here so I'll write out what's next.'

'Next? Next I take the braised duck out of the oven, let it cool, cover it and let it rest for a day. Then I can finally eat the damned . . .'

'No, you can't. After a day's rest, take the casserole in from the shed and scrape away all the fine yellow fat that has risen to the top, reserve the fat, transfer the breasts to a bowl and set them aside while you finish the sauce.'

'But the sauce is already there, three doses of cat pee and all.'

'That's only the sauce base. A piece of paper, please a . . .'

'You say it, I'll write it.'

So I dictate: 'The better part of a bottle of good red wine, one and a half tablespoons of butter, two teaspoons all-purpose flour, a tablespoon dark brown sugar, a quarter cup red currant jelly (better, red currant preserves), four whole cloves crushed to a paste, two teaspoons genuine *aceto balsamico di Spilamberto*. Place the casserole over a low flame to warm the braising juices. With a slotted spoon, take out the bits of pancetta and shallot that have not already melted during the braise; *do not discard these bits.*'

'I discard nothing, least of all bits of pancetta and shallot.'

'If there is any remaining white wine used in the braising, add it to the casserole. Add two cups of red. Keep about a half cup for the final sauce refreshment just before the dish is served, and reduce the sauce by one-third. While the sauce is reducing, work the flour into the softened butter until the two are well amalgamated into a smooth paste. Set the *beurre manie* aside. Add another cup or so of the red and reduce again, this time by one-fourth. Add the dark brown sugar, the red currant jelly and the cloves, stirring well. Taste and correct for salt. With the sauce still at a simmer, begin adding bits of the butter-flour paste, stirring constantly until the paste melts; continue adding the paste, bit by bit, until you've used it all. You will find that the sauce is nicely reduced, slightly thickened and glossed. Off the flame, add the balsamico and stir. Reacquaint the magret with its sauce, then allow the mass to cool, and cover and refrigerate as usual. Have you got all that? Read it back to me.'

'Here's my synopsis: I take out the now properly rested duck, skim its fat, save it. To the casserole, I add red wine, a little black sugar, a few more cloves, boil it down, meanwhile manipulating some butter with some flour then adding that to the pot. When the sauce is thick and shiny, I turn off the heat, add some balsamic vinegar which I don't have and won't buy. Ditto for red currant jelly, whatever the hell that is. Reduce, amalgamate, manipulate, reacquaint, refresh, gloss, correct – I'm truly desperate to be finished with this wretched duck.'

•

'Through the winter Isolda and Giulio worked in the landowners' villas or in the barns repairing tools or shoring up the outbuildings and I would bring Claudio to wherever Isolda might be, sometimes kilometres distant from the farmhouse, the girls trailing along, chattering with the hope that their mother would be scrubbing in someone's kitchen that day where the cook would invite them to sit by the fire. "There you go. Such big girls you're getting to be. A bowl of broth? A slice of cake smeared with jam?" Into the pockets of my sweater and my skirt, a half kilo of polenta, a few potatoes, figs dried and threaded on a string. Back then people who cooked in other people's kitchens often did so because they were hungry. They knew what it felt like, that corroding grief, not of having nothing but of never having enough.

'I learned to wring the necks of Sunday chickens and to milk the goats, though it was Isolda who would go out to the shed twice a week or sometimes three, cook the goats' milk, pour it into small baskets woven from grapevine and lined with wild grasses, set the molds to drip in a chest with wire-mesh shelves and doors. Isolda never took her cheeses to market but brought them with her in the mornings, sold or traded them to the other workers, to the villa housekeepers. I don't know what she did with her earnings save that they never showed up on the table. By January Isolda was again with child. And by March, I'd secured myself a job.

'Mornings I'd tramp into the village with the children and, depending on what funds Giulio had left for me, I'd shop for the day, often having lira enough only for bread. Tullia was always at the head of the line at the *alimentari* even before the truck arrived from the *forno* in Genzano, the bread still warm. "Two *pagnotte di mezzo kilo*," she'd call out, her voice too loud for a noble though she looked like one. The daughter of sharecroppers, *una lavandaia ambulante,* a travelling washerwoman, Tullia was seventeen, long-limbed, pale, blonde.

'One morning, as she turned to leave with her bread, she stopped where I was waiting in line with the children. "Come to work with me, Gilda," was the gist of what she said.

'Having weaned Claudio from Isolda's to the goats' milk, I'd get us all packed up and ready by seven and we'd strike out to meet Tullia the washerwoman as though heading for a day at the fair.

'A copper tub set on an iron grid attached to a tricycle of sorts, Tullia rode the contraption along the yellow dust roads to the farmhouses where she'd been hired. Fetching water from a well or a pump, lighting a fire under the tub, heating the water, adding wood ash, we'd boil every shred of cloth the family owned, pull it through the wringers attached to the tub, spread it over rosemary bushes or festoon it on the lower branches of the olives. While we waited for the wash water to heat or the clothes to soak, I'd feed Claudio, set the girls to some task, bask in being away from the droning purgatory of the farmhouse.

'Sooner or later, Tullia would run off. "I'm going to forage," she'd say, though I knew it was on some barn or fallow field she was bent rather than the meadows. Boys, often a man, they were what Tullia was off to forage for. For the price of a pack of cigarettes, a man could have a few private moments with Tullia. Never gone long, she'd come running back, hair flying, fingers jingling the lire in her apron pocket. "Not a leaf of wild thyme. The *puntarelle* all pulled. *Chè miseria*," she'd say smoothing back her hair. "Is the water hot?"

'While the wash was cooking in the copper tub, I'd set to cooking whatever the woman of the house had put out for the evening meal, a chore not officially Tullia's and surely not mine but one that helped to pass the time and ensured I could feed the children. People who cook in other people's kitchens often do so in order to pinch bits to feed their own kin, themselves. Potatoes, rice, polenta, a heft of dried pig cheek if times were good. A basket of the morning's ricotta dripping in the stone sink. Hung from iron hooks over the stove were faggots of wild oregano, marjoram, little braids of garlic and onions. Sometimes there would be veal bones for soup. Almost always there were tomatoes, fresh and sun-split or a dense basil-scented paste of them. I'd sit the girls down in front of a good lunch and stand by the stove, eating a few spoonsful myself, Claudio on my shoulder. I loved those times watching the babies eat. I suppose it was stealing, my feeding us from other people's stores. I'd scrub the kitchen floor, set wildflowers in the window. I comforted myself saying I'd left more than I'd taken.

'Tullia would set off then on some other of her business while the clothes dried and, my part done for the day, the children and I would head back to the farmhouse. Tullia would return in time to heat the irons, smoothing and folding the sun-dried, leaf-embossed things, leaving them stacked all neatly on the kitchen table. Wait for her pay. Two hundred lire. Fifty cents. "Half for you, Gilda."

'All this glory happened 70 kilometres up the road from the centre of the world, the caffés in the via Veneto, the Pope and his league supping on songbirds, matrons in the Parioli stuffing Pucci into Gucci, a weekend in Taormina. Historically cheek by jowl in the southern regions of the Italy of the mid '60s, the haves and the have-nots existed in an especially contiguous formation. And always more contiguous the further south one went.

'In any case, Tullia was a fine instructress. Apart from foraging for men, she knew every wild grass and leaf and how to turn them into virtuous drenches or, when there was an egg, luscious little *frittate*. Bitter weeds she'd fry in oil with garlic buds and raisins soaked in wine. I learned about food from Tullia. I learned about thieving, too, and begging in the markets. Bending into a bushel of his onions, Tullia would beguile a farmer while I slid great, long-stemmed purple artichokes, one by one, from his table into my sack. Once or twice a week we'd loot the markets, stash our haul here and there under our skirts or leave our 'purchases' for half an hour with the few farmers whom we didn't pilfer while we went off to the *bancarelle* of used clothes. Pressing some unattainable treasure against one another, I remember laughing, the sound of it strange to my ear. *Is that me?* Not even so often with the children, it was only with Tullia that I laughed.

•

'"I know what you do when you go away. I know about it."

'"Do you?"

'"How can you? I mean, how can you let them?"

'"Let them? My father was first. I never let him. He would push me down wherever we were, whenever there was no one else ... whenever he could contrive to be alone with me, one great rough hand pushing himself into me, the other hand flat, crushing my face. I couldn't breathe, couldn't scream. He'd roll off me, call me *puttana*. The way he'd look at me when we were all at supper. My mother knew. Why didn't she stop him?"

'I'd thought, once I was free of priests, I'd be safe from the punishments. I began to think I might have been lucky that Pepucci went to Switzerland. Tullia said grandfathers, uncles, brothers often did the same but priests were second only to fathers in their lechery. Tullia said she'd yet to know a man who was not prone to punishments. Tullia's mother had often confirmed this. "So why not get paid?" Tullia had said. "My boys are more polite. Mostly, they are. Certainly more polite than my father."

•

'Each day when we returned from assisting Tullia, I'd begin all over again, seeing to our own washing, to the supper if there was anything to cook. The girls would help me to bathe Claudio and put him to rest so I could bathe them, if in some less than thorough fashion, fix their hair, tumble them into their nightclothes. Awaiting the entry of the wooden couple, I'd feed them a pap of bread and goats' milk with a little sugar. I'd sing Puccini.

'Isolda and Giulio would stop first in the shed to peel away their sweat-soaked clothes, decoration for the dirt floor until I'd gather them up the next day. They'd wash, dress, come into the house; she going first to fill a pitcher from the demijohn, he to place on the table whatever food he'd brought. Isolda was always centre stage, all of us watching her, waiting for her to set the tone of the next hour or so. Would she speak? Would she grant the half smile that had the power to pierce a breathing hole in the shroud her silence stuck to our faces? I would make some instinctive, protective gesture to the girls, a tug on their braids, a quick kiss between their shoulderblades – Dafne's more tensed than Livia's – all the while keeping my gaze on Isolda.

'Tall, taller than Giulio, she was thin like a dancer is thin. Unbound adolescent breasts, dark almonds for eyes, two beauty marks, one under her left eye, one just to the right of a corner of her mouth, I could never tell if the marks were painted on each morning or were moles, birthmarks. I was never close enough to her to see for sure save on the night she birthed Claudio and then I didn't notice. Flat, velvety beauty marks, perfectly placed, her makeup. Those and her disdain. No matter that she'd bathed, still she stank of old sweat and even that seemed only to add to her allure. I don't think Isolda did anything without first being certain of her audience. Whoever was near would have eyes only for her. Once, from the stairway to the dovecote, I'd watched her, unaware I'd thought, as she combed her hair. But she knew I was there and, as much to the air as to me, she said, 'My hair was cut on the day of my First Communion. I was eight. Never since.' She wore it in a single plait, thick as an oak branch, and it flicked like a reptile's tail across her derrière as she walked. I have always hated how I look because I don't look like Isolda.

'Some cursory touch Giulio would give to the girls. Never returning it, they continued to speak to me as though the others were not present, save when Dafne, in her best rendition of an adult voice, would say, "*Buonasera, Giulio.*" Despite himself, this never failed to turn the corners of his mouth into a stifled smile. She never missed a thing, which was, of course, why Dafne continued to say it; her clandestine greeting and her father's more clandestine response composing the whole of their relationship.

'Only much later would I understand it had been Isolda's own vividly absent sense of parenthood that had kept Giulio from his. His wife's price was dear. She would have all of him and he would pay it.

'Though he rarely spoke to me, Giulio would look at me, maybe say something with his eyes. I used to believe he tried to talk to me that way. It helped; it was enough. I'd get to work on the supper or, had I cooked earlier, I'd serve he and Isolda, the girls preferring more of the sugary pap to a bowl of green beans or cabbage. Never eating with them, I always stood, Claudio on my shoulder. No matter how much sugar I'd stir into that pap, though, the house was still purgatory.

'I would tell myself that I stayed on the farm because of the children. I loved them and they loved me. We were the family; Isolda and Giulio, the outsiders. Were it not for the children, I'd have found my way somewhere else, though I never did let myself think where that other place might be. Another of my voices would defy, entreat: *Just go; the children are not yours. Their parents managed to keep them alive before you came; they'll do it after you go. You're using the children as a shield for your fear. That's it, isn't it, Gilda? You're afraid to be alone.*

'The strand of truth in that voice was a bane, a rift in the purity of my motives. The other voice won, though: *The children will be better off with you than with Isolda and Giulio.* So into the amaretti tin I stowed my washerwoman's pay.

'My plans were humble, no dawn flight on a swift horse. I was too hungry, too tired. The first step to freedom would be prosciutto, a whole haunch of it swinging from the dove-shit-shined rafters over our shared bed. I dreamed of that haunch. In the dream I kept a long thin-bladed knife in the sleeve of my nightdress, pulling it out at will, reaching up to carve a slice of the rosy, salty flesh, or a slice from the cheek of a man bent on punishments.

The girls, each curved into one side of me, Claudio on my chest, they were the shape of my life. Still, Tullia's words chilled me: "Let them? My father was first. I never *let* him." As I said, an instructress, Tullia. Her words framed half an epiphany: *Stay far away from men.* The other half I'd already heard from inside me: *Feed hungry children.*

'I worked with Tullia through that spring and into the early summer, the lire growing in a thick pile at the bottom of the amaretti tin. We were happy enough, the children and I, our time with Tullia diminishing the nightly anguishes of purgatory. But as Isolda grew big with the next child, so did fresh agonies begin to ripen in me. I was fifteen, an ancient fifteen, and I knew that if I didn't escape the farm before that baby was born, I never would. Or worse, perhaps worse, when I did find a way to leave, I'd take this next one with me, too.

Tullia and I spoke endlessly of my flight, she always in a froth over a new plot: her kin in Puglia would take us in until I found work; I should go to the hostels in Rome for homeless mothers and their children; or to a refugee program established post-war and still in operation in the north where her mother's cousins had cousins. Dedicated as a *partigiana* aiding a refugee to the safety of the other side of a mountain, Tullia entangled others in her mission. She'd speak openly of it in the markets, in the village, in the public bathing house, which served as a kind of club for the farm women.

Even for those few who had their own in-house plumbing, Saturday night at the baths was ritual. Soaped and dripping upon the rotting boards of the bathhouse floor, fleshy matrons, nubile daughters, *le nonne, le zie,* all of them championed Gilda, shouting through the gushing water of their own dreams of somewhere else. Someone else.

To dine in a ristorante.

On a terrace overlooking the sea, to dance in a blue satin dress with a Corsican prince whose hair smells like oranges.

Yes, he must be a prince.

No, no. He need only be a man, not just male but a man, one of that rare species of human.

Yes, a man who wouldn't beat me.

A man who would make love to me rather than to take me in all the ways he pleased then leave me while he farts and burps and snores through the night.

A man who wouldn't endlessly keep me with child and then go off to the taberna on the nights when one of them died.

I could better tolerate the taberna than the brothel. Before Marcello's machinery broke down, the brothel was his sanctuary: Fortunate you were, knowing where he was. It was only after I'd planted Giangiacomo that I knew his whereabouts.

All men, their concentration is singular, constant. The next opportunity. Where and how and with whom The where and the how and the with whom being less urgent than the when. Of course, most men make do with fantasy and use the one handiest on which to play it out. I think I was Luca's fantasy for a night or two. Not much longer than that before I began to feel, you know, disembodied. A device. Useful only from the neck down.

I know that feeling. There was always something false about Marcuccio, false or indifferent. Maybe that was it . . . I used to feel as though all of him was never there . . . and, more, that it wasn't me he was with but it . . .

Fabio never kisses me. A graze in passing once in a while but . . .

A wrapped-in-his-arms-wanton-hungry kiss? Never. First I was the unassailable Madonna and soon after I became the shrew. A wife is relegated to these two states.

It's true but it hardly matters. We have so much more than they do: children, family, friendships, house, Church. If we work things right, a lover or two. Most of a man is his sex. Think how tragic then for a man when his chassis begins to break down. It's his tyranny, a man's sex.

So little awaits him beyond his lust. I used to feel so sad for Gianni when he first found himself on the wane. He was so like a boy who'd lost his mate, a child whose favourite toy was broken. And there was all that apologia, the self-acquittal. It was me, it was me who'd broken his toy for I was aggressive, I was passive, I was fat, I was cruel. When he tired of castigating me, he turned to the gods, to the fates who'd put the harvest at risk, soured the wine, let his beloved dog die. And my impulse to soothe him he spurned bitterly. I withdrew. I waited. He seemed to pass over the lurid phase common to aging men although pornography and an intensified kind of ogling took him over from time to time. I can say, though, that he never deteriorated into the pathetic, the whoring, the desperate lechery. However cunning he may be, a woman knows the signs that mark a man with these.

Amen.

It wanted two years, closer to three, until Gianni moved from the brutal phase back into a kind of humility, which, when he directed it at me, sometimes felt like tenderness. He found himself amazed when, if only now and then, his chassis would rally to a flickering renaissance. Otherwise I think he was mostly content having made a kind of peace with that wilful thing between his legs. An ancestral relic, nostalgic, outworn, precious. How fortunate

*we are that our sex doesn't age the way theirs do. When it feels
like an autumn leaf down there rather than a juicy fig, olive oil
is all it wants.* Ecco. Siamo a posto. *All is in order.*

Amen.

Verissimo. *There is no parallel for us, that disastrous diminishing for a man. When our own 'impotency' sets in, we are mostly
ready for it, for the ending of fertility and all that it signifies.* Anzi,
hallelujah. *How strange the difference between us: he remains
fertile but can't perform, we can't conceive but our desire and our
satisfaction are spurred with a caress. Our own or someone else's.
Wouldn't it be grand if a smear of fine oil could do that for a man?
For all the good it would do him down there, better he should use
his oil on his beans.*

*There's one thing more uniquely ours: mystery. That's not to
say men are not grand liars, skillful betrayers. But rarely are they
mysterious. Her mystery, it's really all a woman can keep safe from
time. Mystery and olive oil.*

*Yes, Gilda, go. For all of us, go and find yourself a young one,
a charmer, an . . .*

An enchanter.

'The women in the bathing house couldn't have known how
uninhabited by charmers and enchanters were my dreams, though
I suspect their own were as well, all that reproach made mostly of
bombast. What with hunger and dying babies and endless fields
to bend to, their countrywomen's notions kept them safe from
the peril of romanticising a man, less themselves.

'As the children slept and my eyes would no longer let me
read, I'd sit to rifle one more time through Magdalena's things.

I'd read all her letters a hundred times and then I'd read them again. There were many from a girl called Giorgia, my mother's classmate in Orvieto. Giorgia Filippeschi. Our own. Miranda's own. It seems that, after years of silence, my mother – during her epoch of desperation after I was born, after Pepucci had wandered off – had taken up correspondence with Giorgia. Tied with a length of string, there were twenty letters, at least twenty from Giorgia. Tucked in among the clothes, one letter was loose, dated after my mother *went to live with the angels.* In this one, Giorgia pleaded with Magdalena: *Come to Orvieto for a visit, Magda, you and your little girl. Stay with us for a while. Let me take care of you.* One night as I read that letter, the last two lines leapt from the page: *I'm here waiting for you. My arms are always around you.*

'I took up a pen and wrote a letter of my own:

Cara signora Giorgia,

Though we've never met, I feel that I know you and that you will be pleased to hear from me. I am Magdalena's daughter. I am Gilda. Among my mother's things I found your letters . . .

•

'Just before dawn, the August day already hot and dry, Isolda was preparing to leave for the fields when I hurried down the dovecote stairs, scrubbed and braided, my out-grown boots pinching, Tullia's brown poplin dress hanging from my thin white shoulders. Swaddled to my chest with a shawl, Claudio was sleeping. I moved, stood between Isolda and the door. A cheeky move, to confront the princess.

"'I will be leaving the farm today," I said, holding out my hand to her, offering a piece of paper on which I'd written Giorgia's address. Here's where we'll be living, for the time being. That is, if you should want to contact us."

"'Us?" Isolda looked at me then quickly shifted her eyes to some point beyond me. A crack in the wooden princess, a snag in her breath, aural. Still looking away from me, Isolda waved her hand toward the baby, toward my chest, which was already tight with pain.

"'I will be taking Claudio with me. The girls, too."

'Composure regained, Isolda had no questions. Not a single muffled regret. She took the piece of paper and, looking away still, let it flutter in the direction of the oilclothed table behind her. A nod, her farewell, Isolda stepped beyond me and her son. Out the door, her stride was long and sure.

'I would have stayed, you know, that's the strange part,' Gilda says to me, her tone pleading, trying to convince me of what I already knew.

'Until that last moment, part of me longed for Isolda's inter-cession. Two words of entreaty and I would have continued on as before. That's how dearly I wanted to belong somewhere, *anywhere*. A prisoner pardoned, lingering in his cell.'

'I know. We are wont to give prisons, almost any prison, the shape of refuge. The only way we can endure them.'

'I . . . yes, I suppose. Prison, refuge. A small twist of will or vision and one can become the other.'

'*Già*'.

'Chou, you should have seen Livia and Dafne on that morning. Six and four they were by then, resplendent in pinafores of white organdy, white stockings and shoes gifted by one of the bathhouse women from her now grown-up daughters' stores. Wide white ribbons I'd tied around their heads, bows flopping just above their eyebrows. Perhaps not understanding the import of their journey, perhaps having understood it indeed, both were nearly faint with giggling anticipation for it.

'Two lengths of rope I fastened to my belt, the other ends of the ropes I tied into loops to slip over each girl's wrist, thus leaving my own hands free to carry two cardboard valises packed with the children's clothes and my own wreckage. I unwrapped Claudio, slung a large cloth purse across my chest, retied the baby. I banked the fire, and closed the door.

'Small knots of bathhouse women waited along the edge of the yellow dust road and, as our little party reached them, they joined in, walking in a body to the village where the autobus would stop. The women sang, wept, stopped to press kisses upon the children, to stuff the girls' pockets with pistachios. In a woven basket that Tullia slipped over Livia's free arm, there were thick cuts of Genzano bread, a paper-wrapped package of mortadella, a heft of pecorino, biscotti filled with marzipan. The autobus would deliver us to Stazioni Termini in Rome from whence we would ride the train to Orvieto.

•

'I saw her on the platform, Giorgia. Her own two boys hanging on her skirt, the first thing she said to me was, "*Jesumaria*, you're so tiny, so blonde. I'd been expecting Magda. All this while I'd been imagining Magda. Welcome home, darling Gilda. And who would be these little beauties?"

'Slipping her wrist from the loop of rope tied about my waist and likewise freeing Dafne, Livia reached out for Giorgia's hand while, Dafne, leaving no doubt of her dominance, flicked her fingers, palms inward, at Giorgia's five-year-old twins. Taking the little boys' hands, Dafne settled herself between them, swung their arms high, pulled them along in a triumphant march. While holding tight to Livia, Giorgia nuzzled Claudio, took my arm and, in tight formation, we seven walked out of the station. Though none of us could know it then, save Giorgia, we were already a family.

'Not as forlorn creatures but as cherished kin, Giorgia embraced us. No less did her husband. You know Flavio. Had I written horrid things about the conditions of our life with Isolda and Giulio? No. What sentiments I'd let fall between the lines of my letter which Giorgia was able to interpret, I'm not certain. I'd asked if the children and I could stay with them until I could find us a place, until I could find work. I'd told her that I had funds, never mentioning a sum. What with my savings plus the envelope thick with lire that I'd found in the trunk, my name written on it in the old aunt's shaky hand, I'd thought I was flush. Significant enough back then, today all those beautiful lire notes the size of a dinner napkin would total thirty euros.

'Giorgia and Flavio baked bread for a living. Situated on the ground level of a narrow three-storey *palazzo* off Piazza della Repubblica, their *forno* perfumed the *vicolo*, the steamy frangrance of it reaching into the marketplace, and I wanted to sleep on its flour-dusted floor. I remember thinking that. They lived upstairs and, above, in the attic, a seamstress had her atelier. I don't think she ever paid rent but traded mending and sewing for Giorgia and her sons and then for us. They lived well, if hand to mouth.

"'Do you need help in the bakery? May I put up a sign offering myself as a washerwoman? There are so many shops that surely I can find . . .'"

"'It's the school you'll be off to find, *amore mio*," Giorgia said. "Two years you've been away from the nuns, time to catch up.'"

"'But the little ones . . .'"

"'Soon enough the twins and Livia will also go to school and then I'll have Dafne and Claudio all to myself; though I expect Dafne will soon enough be running the bakery if not the neighbourhood.'"

'Rules, chores, manners, expectations. New bread, a laden table, baths and fresh towels, embroidered linens and goose-down quilts, soap and toothbrushes and doctors' visits and never a word from Isolda, from Giulio. Livia asked me once if her parents were coming to live with Giorgia as well. Before I could respond, Dafne, her black eyes wide and round, "If they do, they'll have to sleep on the floor."

'Even amidst a paradise, old habits die hard. I suppose I found it difficult to trust that my fortune would last. Someone would come to take us back to the farm or me back to the convent, and the children, who knows where? I began to hoard bits and pieces from the table, mostly bread, cheese, sometimes a few potatoes from the sack in the pantry. I took candles, soap, bars of chocolate. Strolling the markets with Miranda and Giorgia, I would long for an hour's plundering with Tullia. Such richness there. Soon enough Giorgia sent me to shop on my own and it was then, that first Saturday in the markets by myself, when I stole the peaches.

'Theirs was the most beautiful table in the market, the one belonging to Iacovo's father and his uncles. Peaches piled in pyramids and rolling out of baskets and strewn across a length of red brocade, scenes awaiting an artist. I would approach the *banco*, step away, gaze at it from afar, put myself in the queue only to step away when my turn came. Giorgia's list did not include peaches. And then I saw my chance. The three men who'd been selling motioned to a young boy. The men went off toward the caffé, leaving the boy in charge. I waited for other shoppers and when the boy was serving them I struck: three peaches on a branch. Just as Tullia had taught me to do, I smiled, kept my eyes on the the people around me, even spoke a word or two to no one in particular, never looking down, letting my hands do their work. Into my sack. Three heavy peaches on a floppy, leafy branch. Wandering slowly away, looking this way and that, not a care in the world and then I heard someone calling, "*Signorina, signorina, aspettami, ti prego.* Wait for me, wait, please."

'I turned to see it was the young boy shouting, running toward me. Too mortified to notice the newspaper-wrapped parcel he carried, too mortified to notice that he was smiling, I stayed where I stood. "*Per voi, signorina.* Queste sono le più belle. For you, miss. These are the most beautiful. Posso? May I?" he asked, opening my sack, taking out the branch, placing the parcel inside, then replacing the branch on top. "There, now we're in good order. *Buongiorno, signorina. Buongiorno. A presto.*"

•

On the next Thursday Night, Gilda Aida Mimi-Violetta Onofrio wore Magdalena's necklace, a triple string of baroque pearls clasped in the hollow of her throat with an unpolished ruby. On the Thursday after that, she left the pearls behind but wore the blue velvet dress that she'd worn before only on a Christmas. On the last Thursday Night of that November, Gilda wore the pearls and the blue velvet dress. There was about Iacovo on that same Thursday Night the unmistakeable pungency of cloves.

•

Early in December Gilda, Ninuccia, Paolina, Miranda and I meet to plan the supper for the Thursday before Christmas. There would be no other Thursday Night Suppers in December before that one, honouring a traditional, seasonal hiatus. Rather than meeting at the rustico, Gilda – surprising us all – suggested that we gather at her place. Usually at these planning sessions one brings along some little morsel to share. Gilda said we shouldn't.

When we arrive at one o'clock she leads us to the kitchen end, the windowless part of the room where candles are lit, the table set with branches of mistletoe thick as a wrist, paper plates, cups, napkins, these last raising a snuffle from Ninuccia. We talk about the December supper, argue, compromise, drink the red wine, which Gilda tells us is Iacovo's own. There is no sign of food.

Still snuffling, Ninuccia asks if she might stir the white embers of the fire. 'At least we can be warm if not fed.'

'Not just yet. Not until the potatoes are cooked,' Gilda says. Ninuccia brightens. From the wall shelf Gilda retrieves a dish of grey sea salt and one of dried wild fennel flowers. Ninuccia pours more wine all around. 'I'll just be a moment,' Gilda says.

Bending into the hearth, Gilda digs in the embers to uncover a chestnut pan of potatoes the size of plump grapes, fifty or sixty of them, their skins bronze, oil-shined. Carrying the pan to the table, Gilda walks it around, helping to scoop ten or twelve of the little things onto each plate . . . We know what to do with the salt and the fennel. We eat the potatoes out of hand, popping them whole, scorching fingers and mouths. No further snuffling from Ninuccia.

'I'll just be a moment,' Gilda says again and we sit like children waiting for a birthday cake, watching her excavate deeper into the embers for the second pan. She repeats the ceremony of serving them.

Sated and a little 'in our cups', the others say *buona sera* and go off together in Ninuccia's truck. I laugh when I realise how foolish I sound as I ask Gilda if I can help her with the washing up. We throw the paper things into the hearth, sit in our usual positions for a moment before I, too, prepare to leave.

Save to say that we were drinking his wine, Gilda – to the dismay of the others who'd been hoping for a Christmas engagement, some sort of open recognition of a romance – never spoke of Iacovo. Tempted to ask her about him, I don't. I find my shawl. Then Gilda says, 'It's twilight out there, almost the shortest day of the year. Let's walk, just for a few minutes.'

We light one another's cigars, link arms, head a few metres down the creek road toward the pine woods. Withered leaves twisting in a low-slung breeze make a taffeta rustle under our boots. We fold down a patch of high grasses near the creek and sit. The mist rises pink and wet like smoke from just-crushed grapes seething in the tubs, silvering the weeds all around us and the pines and the ancient oak leaning across from the far side of the water. Nodding at the oak, Gilda says, 'In its hollow, that's where the mistletoe grows. Has for centuries. It's because of the oak and the mistletoe that Miranda calls me druid. Oak woods were their sanctuaries, mistletoe sacred, a curative. Magical.'

She turns to look at me, smiling, and I tell her, 'How love has changed you . . .'

'*Pian, piano,* Chou. Slowly. Whatever you're seeing or sensing in me, let's not give it up to something fickle as *love*. Iacovo the Brave has not awakened the aging druid to eternal bliss but to a lesser aloneness. More, he's chinked away at my arrogance.'

'You, arrogant?'

'My feeling wronged, as Miranda calls it, has bred a kind of arrogance in me, which I hide behind timidity. *Poor little Gilda.* An effective device, generally compelling though not upon Iacovo. Nor has it been upon you, I understand that now.'

'Now? Effective as it might often be, your masquerade has never convinced me. This feeling *wronged*, it's a bygone thing by now, long past due for repeal.'

'Time heals all wounds?'

'With our permission. Do you think about her?'

'Her?'

'Your mother.'

'Do I *think* about her? I'm obsessed by her.'

'No, not about your mother in relation to you or to what she did and didn't do for you. Just her. Magdalena the woman. Before you, after you. Do you think about *her*?'

'I hardly remember her.'

'Could you hazard empathy? Can you even begin to see her and the other absent culprits of your life with any sort of form other than the one you've already drawn of them? Having lived with Isolda and Giulio, having seen another kind of abandonment, one which must have been more hideous than the sort Magdalena visited upon you, can you not muster some generosity, some reprieve? I would have thought your own injury would have dissolved in your sympathy for Livia and Dafne, for Claudio.'

'It did. For years it distracted me. The rasp was always there but, like the bathhouse women, I had other things to occupy me. And now I have less.'

'More time for angst.'

'What do I do with my string of culprits? Magdalena, Pepucci, the aunt, the nuns, the priests, the cousins.'

'A *string of culprits* . . . I guess you could cut the string, let the culprits fall away. Beads of a broken necklace, bouncing, rolling, scattering. All of them lost.'

'Wouldst it could be so simple.'

'Not simple.'

'And then? What comes next? Some piercing grief for those I accused? Do I line them all up in my mind, brushed and combed, smelling of rosewater, my censure having taken on a tinge of affectionate grace?'

'Maybe for Magdalena.'

'Never for the priests, all of whom I hope have long ago suffocated themselves on their own lasciviousness.'

'Never for the priests.'

'Priests, culprits, beads, broken strings, I'm still lost, Chou. I live in a half-painted picture, always looking for myself but . . .'

'Paint *yourself* in it, Gilda. Mist the edges if you must. Draw and erase and redraw until your likeness suits you. You won't be any less real than the rest of us.'

'Is that what you did?'

'Do. Still drawing and erasing.'

'Do you remember when Miranda asked me: *Who would you be as a mother*? It haunted me, that question. I tried a thousand times to imagine myself a mother and, harder still, to imagine how my child would perceive me. I couldn't do it. Not honestly. Not wholly. I couldn't get a single thorn to stick to my self-portrait as a mother. I began painting myself a Madonna, frantically scrubbing out any notion of a flaw, just as another one would appear. The exercise was a firebolt: as sure as I would pass on my blood and bones would I pass on my weaknesses, adding mine to those I'd assigned to Magdalena. Families bequeath ancestral pain. I began to laugh, scrub all the harder. *Not me, never, not me. I would be different. I would be better.*'

'Mothers do wrong. They must, perforce.'

'Miranda always says that.'

'Miranda does.'

'The closest I've ever gotten to motherhood was to be a kind of passing saviour to Livia and Dafne. Claudio was too small to remember me as that. It was Giorgia who raised them, though. And Giorgia and Miranda raised me. I got to be the girls' heroine, their idol in a way, I could do no wrong. *Mothers do wrong, perforce.*'

'What happened to them, to the children?'

'Have you never met Claudio?'

'I guess I'm just this moment putting him together with *your* Claudio. I'd always known him as Miranda's nephew, Giorgia's son.'

'Isolda and Giulio's son.'

'And the girls?'

'Have you ever seen me on a Sunday? You never will unless you come to Rome with me. I go to my little Dafne. She restores frescoes, removes crystalline accretions from water seepage, smoky deposits, repairs structural cracks. Sometimes she applies the paint, only red. Dafne works in red; other members of her team work in the other colours. She's forty-three. She's lived in the Monti with Jan for nearly eleven years by now. Jan Sobieski. A Pole with a king's name, he is nearing sixty. A sculptor, Jan Sobieski. They are always more in love.'

'Livia?'

'You must have met Livia a dozen times or more. *Olivia*, she calls herself, having added the "O" at some time during her adolescence.'

'Olivia, Giorgia's housekeeper?'

'Same.'

'Isolda. Did she . . . Did the children . . .'

'Not until Livia was sixteen. A decade passed from when we left the farm to when Livia decided to make contact with her parents. Giorgia and I helped her.' Giorgia went with her.

'And?'

'All Livia ever said about the visit was: "I have two brothers. They were in the fields with my father. Only she was there. She poured wine, sliced bread. Her hands were shaking." They live alone in Genzano now, Isolda and Giulio, both in their sixties,'

'Did you ever manage to hate her? Isolda?'

'I must have back then. I don't any longer. It was years after I'd left the farm when Tullia, making her yearly trek up here to visit, told me about Isolda, what she'd learned about her from those who knew her family, who knew about her childhood. Isolda was seven when she watched as her father beat to death her nine-year-old brother. Being hungry, her brother had stolen from the markets, brought bread home to share with his sister. Their mother watched, too. I think Isolda died that day and it was the ghost of her who remained, a ghost full of dread for her children. If provoked, what might she do to them? And so she chose the passive way to kill them. I think that's what happened to Isolda.'

Gilda has been looking out over the water and when she turns to me, she says, 'My stories have made you sad. I'm sorry. Then again you're always that way, just this side of wistful, especially when you're laughing, making us laugh. Miranda says you think in a minor key.' In a quieter voice, Gilda wants to know, 'Why do you never speak about yourself? To me, to Miranda. The others. Apart from your funny little stories about meeting Fernando, your early Venetian days at the Rialto tipping down *ombrette* with the fishmongers, the marketeers, it's as though you didn't have a life before Fernando.'

'Oh, but I did. A life lovely in its way. Always good work and mostly without my having to seek it, one thing steering me to the next. And good people, some of them superb, passionate, generous. More than my share, I would say, of good people. Less than my share of tormentors. And here I am, landed in the Umbrian wilderness, still not quite knowing how, but again surrounded by good people.'

'A watery distillation. *La nostra Gioconda*, Miranda has named you. Our own *Gioconda*.'

'You, as well. That makes you *la Gioconda, tight as morning glory at twilight*.'

'I think you hide inside your czarina clothes.'

'And you behind *Poor Little Gilda*. We all hide. Congenital self-preservation. My camouflage is more apparent.'

'I, we were all surprised, not particularly in a happy way, when Miranda invited you to join Thursdays. We wondered why we needed, you know, a *stranger* among us.'

'I knew that. I'd been, for a year or so, declining her invitation for that reason but she finally . . .'

'Miranda recognised you at first sight. Over and over again on Thursdays, she would tell us about that evening when she met you and Fernando at the *sagra*, your marching, uninvited, without introducing yourself, into the communal kitchen, *buona sera, buona sera*, and how you just began doing what needed to be done as though you *belonged*. She says you're Mother Russia, never carrying a purse, never having a euro to your name, always with a corkscrew in your pocket, rosemary in the other one, always out to feed someone.'

'Cardomom pods and anise seeds. In my pocket.'

'The funny thing is that we're all becoming little czarinas. Those two dresses you gave to Paolina, they're all she wears now. And she's taken on your walk, have you noticed that? And on that last Thursday when we were together in November, Miranda changed her eternal gold hoops for those amethysts and pearls that swing like little chandeliers. Where did those come from?'

'Giorgia. They belonged to their mother and their grandmother. She says they've passed them back and forth over the years.'

'Paolina wears mascara now, Ninuccia, too. And not only on Thursdays. Miranda wants mascara in her Christmas stocking.'

'As long as she hasn't asked for a tube of Russian Red.'

'No. Not that, not yet.'

'And you? Any czarina desires?'

'I've decided to look about for some plates, maybe a whole set. Rosalba has some in the window, flowers on the rims, probably English, blue, green, pink. There was another set for *dolce*. I'll need wineglasses. And I want to tell you something else, something wonderful . . .'

'So it's true then, what we've all been wondering about . . .'

'I'll be starting a new job, not a job, really. Soon after the New Year, I'll be riding the train into Rome three days a week to cook

and serve and wash up in a *mensa* in the Monti *rione*. A Caritas
project for pre-schoolers, Dafne and Jan put me on to it. I'll take
the 17:57 back to Orvieto, be home for supper. Iacovo says he'll
cook for me on those nights. I'll always be home on Thursdays.
There'll be three- and four-year-old Romanians, Moldovans,
Ukranians, Kazakhistani, North Africans, and I'll sing Puccini
to them. I'll sing Puccini to Magdalena.'

•

'Gilda, before I forget. About the duck.' It's late, very late on that
Saturday evening but, just the same, I telephone her.

'Not another word about the . . .'

'After all that business of reducing and glossing, you'll need
to let the whole thing rest again. Another day or so. Splash in a
half cup of dry Marsala secco, then. Never sweet. Give it a good
stir, cover it and heat it in a quiet oven. The Marsala exults the
richness of the sauce, connects the flavours. A smoky, musky
liaison. *L'ultimo trucco,* the last trick.'

'And then do I get to eat it?'

'Well, that's what I was just about to say. It'll taste all the better
if you let it rest one last time. Even half a day.'

'*Jesumaria*, will I never be rid of this narcoleptic beast?'

'Not beast. Bird. Parts of several birds. Not narcoleptic.
Delicate.'

'*Ciao*, Chou.'

'*Notte*, Gilda.'

EPILOGUE

FLAILING HER TOASTING FORK, SHE BOSSES US INTO OUR places at table, stoops down then to the small hearth on the wall behind it to turn the thick spluttering slabs of pancetta crisping on a grate over olivewood embers and branches of wild sage. As she moves about the ceremonial rites of a Thursday supper there is a lustre about Miranda-of-the-Bosoms on this evening in February 2008. The goddess of Buonrespiro in her prime, it is her birthday, her seventy-sixth. The eighth, perhaps the ninth or tenth, anniversary of her seventy-sixth. Her one wish? That only the women be present in the rustico on this Thursday.

Without having planned it so or told one another we would, we are dressed astonishingly alike, our sartorial kinship making us laugh, symbol of other less conspicuous affinities. Long skirts, boots, some form of a men's-wear jacket, our hair braided or caught in a chignon. Earrings, long, gaudy. As we set the table, Gilda whispers, '*Vedi*? See? Czarinas, all of us.'

My gift to Miranda is her own tube of Russian Red, fresh from it's little black MAC box. In the past, I'd given her tubes worn down, ones she'd seen me using and asked to try. There is no mirror in the rustico but she wants to wear the lipstick *now*.

'You do it for me, Chou.'

I take a tissue from my sack, blot her lips dry, draw the red along the edges of her mouth, fill in with more colour. Pushing the tissue against her mouth, I then rub a corner of it all over her lips, wiping away most of the colour I have just applied, leaving her mouth more stained than painted. As though she's just bitten into a cracked pomegranate. Ninuccia and Paolina, their lips already Russian Red, do the same with a tissue, wiping off most of the colour. They admire one another. Only Gilda refrains until Paolina pushes her down onto a chair, does the same business on her that I've just done on Miranda. Gilda touches her lips, smiles, says lipstick makes her feel taller. Czarinas, all of us.

We serve and pour for each other, dine slowly, luxuriously, on the simple things Miranda loves best: pancetta, sausages, potatoes roasted with rosemary, our own thick-crusted, wood-baked bread, our own oil, our own wine.

Tilting back on the hind legs of her chair, Miranda looks at us in turn as she is wont to do more often these days.

'I wish life could end all even, like a supper when there's that last little roasted potato with a single needle of rosemary clinging to its crust and the end of a sausage, charred to a crunch, a heel of bread, the last long pull of wine. Even. Everything in harmony.

I have always preferred the last bite of my supper to the first, the beginning being frought with hunger, the last with serenity. As life should be. Every supper can be a whole life.'

'Supper ending, life ending. Sated, quiet.' This is Ninuccia. 'I suppose it's the nearness of death that *graces* life. Endlessness would be a kind of horror.'

She waits, we all wait, and then she looks at Miranda, asks, 'Do you think dying is easier than being born?'

'I think it may be. The lonely journey down that narrow road from the womb into the light, I think being born is the hardest thing life asks of us. Which is why we're born old and, if we work things well enough, why we grow young.' Miranda looks somewhere beyond as she speaks.

'But what does that really mean? *If we work things well enough.* No one's born a white canvas awaiting a brush, the Fates having long before seen to a creature's portion.' This is Ninuccia again.

'Penchants, proclivities, capacities, birthday gifts from Destiny. From Clothos,' I say.

'True. We hit the light uniquely ourselves, as we'll be always, save the effects, mostly tame, of what we bring down upon ourselves. Wise or not, our choices are mostly powerless over the original design.' Miranda has taken up her goddess voice.

'Powerless. Mostly that.' Gilda seems unsure.

'I worry about my lasting as long as life does, what with all the walking dead, waiting-room lives. *Nec spe, nec metù.* No hope, no fear. No regrets. A coward's closing down. A passive suicide.' Paolina looks to Miranda for accord but it's Ninuccia who speaks.

'How smug a life would be without regrets. As though one proceeded sure-footed. A goat climbing a hill. As for fear, it's the sentiment we're best at hiding, avoiding.'

Still looking far away, Miranda smiles, tries for her goddess voice, which cracks into softness.

'Fear. Of being alone, of being together. Of love, of no love. We fear joy because we know it won't last, we fear abundance because emptiness always lurks. Certainly we fear life at least as violently as we do death.'

'So fear is good.' This is Gilda.

'I don't know about it being *good* but without it, without understanding that life is finite, we'd succumb to the torpors. So many do, as Paolina has just said.'

'So . . . regrets, fear, hope . . . all of them *good*.' Again, Gilda.

'Good. Yes, and right, somehow right. I do well understand I've not exactly been a woman of the world for these last seventy-six years, having been born and lived all that time within eight kilometres of where we sit right now. I don't know how much more I could have learned about the point of life had I wandered farther. I think that wherever I might have gone I would have found you. Souls like you. We are magnificently the same. Not only us, all of us. Without pain, without fear, who would any one of us have become, what would we have to show for having lived? Any five women, wherever, whomever, put them together at supper around a fire and, *ecco, ci saremo*, there we'll be. The point of life is to do what we're doing right now, what we did yesterday, what we'll do with what's left of our time. Surely we are not barren of fantasy or dreams and yet none of us seem to be swanking about, reaching for *great things* or, worse, perceiving ourselves to be doing *great things*. There are no great things. After the myth of security, the second greatest myth ever inflicted on humans is the myth that we were meant to triumph. How wonderful it is to be content with holding hands around this mangled old table, with some nice bread, some wine, a candle and a fire, a blessed sleep waiting.'

'A highly concentrated recipe. Within the holding-hands part and the blessed-sleep-waiting part there are other components. I mean, about the *point* of it all.' Ninuccia says this.

'Yes. But those other components are implicit, instinctive in the holding-hands part, the blessed-sleep part. We wouldn't be doing what we do if those other components were not in place. They hardly need naming, do they Ninuccia? Like saying, *taste for salt*. We already knew that.'

Già. Indeed.

Paolina says, 'I wonder if that woman of Lampedusa's, the one in the brown travelling suit, I wonder if she rides up there right behind the man on the black horse, keeping one another company on their endless route. If so, maybe that's why we're sometimes taken to the brink and then taken back, maybe they disagree. A man and a woman on the same horse, they're bound to disagree. Especially with old Atropos waving her scissors at them.'

'It won't matter. There'll only be that half moment of meeting, maybe less. They arrive as we leave. Atropos must have grown fast enough with her snipping by now. Ships in the night, isn't that how it is?' Gilda wants assurance.

'So they say. *When you are, they aren't. When they are, you're not,*' Ninuccia says.

'I forgot about Atropos.' I say this but it's not true.

'She is forgettable. Especially in springtime. I can tell you now I'd never go in springtime. Having once again snatched her baby girl back from Hades, Demeter in all her glory then raising up the grasses and weeds from their sleep in the dark, wild asparagus in the meadows, *puntarelle* on the hills. Never in springtime.' This is Paolina.

'Less would I go in autumn. New wine, new oil, all those chestnuts, fat porcini smelling of loam and the ages, figs dripping honey, the leaves on the vines gone yellow as saffron, rounds of *pane della vendemmia* cooling on the shutter over the windowsill, pheasants hung from a wire in the cheese hut. Never in autumn. It would have to be summer.' This is Ninuccia.

'Parched gold, the hills. Light limpid as apricot tea, the beauty of it stinging my eyes, bruising my soul, I could never go in summer. I shall outwit them all in summer,' Gilda says.

Blue-black eyes wet, fierce, Miranda says, 'I shan't even consider winter.'

'And you?' Gilda asks me but I don't answer.

Out of words, we listen to the candles beginning to splutter, to the plash of wood char upon the embers in the hearth.

'Open the window. Fill the pitcher,' Miranda resumes command.

Moonlight drinks in the darkness of the little room and the window panes shudder. The lantern swinging from the metal arm above the old green door strikes it in tempo. *Lento, lento.* Sea beating upon sand.

Miranda says, 'A strange sensation, just now. A memory, I think. Maybe not a memory. A little girl, not me, holding tight to a woman's skirt. Her mother's skirt. I could see and feel the stuff of it, black, soft, but it wasn't me touching it. I think it was my mother as a child. Yes, it was she, trotting along beside her mother, holding tight to her skirt. Now where did that come from? How strange to be old and to recall your mother as a child.' Miranda looks at Gilda who looks away.

Rising, taking off her apron, Miranda says, 'Let's go to walk now.'

'It's past . . .'

'Midnight. Past midnight in Umbria, get your things, go on.'

Ninuccia grumbling, we others happy for Miranda's impulse. A small tribe of aging czarinas, earrings swaying, lips still mostly red, we find our shawls, trade hats so no one wears her own, step out into the night. Into warm greenish air, gusty as before a storm, we start up the Montefiascone road under the umbrella pines. Miranda and Gilda lead, Ninuccia, Paolina and I are close behind. Miranda stops, turns to face us.

'I wonder if any one of you will remember that pinch of cloves in the ragù of goose for the *trebbiatura*. I doubt you will, if only for orneriness. I know you won't cook the old dishes as I do. The bread won't rise because you'll forget to close the back door and no one will remember to roll a demijohn into the kitchen on Wednesday so the wine won't be too cold for Thursday. *Pian, piano*, you'll slip away from how things are tonight. You'll begin meeting in restaurants on Thursdays. Not meeting on Thursdays at all. What was it she used to say, Chou, that little girl you wrote about . . .'

'I-love-you-don't-forget-me.'

'As though it was a single word. I-love-you-don't-forget-me,' Miranda says in English, her accent somehow Hungarian. 'Hold tight to one another, now, all in a single row. Good, that's it. Tighter.'

Miranda stops abruptly then, looks at Gilda and Paolina to her right, to Ninuccia and I on her left. She looks straight ahead.

'They'd never dare come for me on a Thursday.'

THE RECIPES

ABOUT THE RECIPES

WITHIN THE NARRATIVE MANY OF THE *SUPPER CLUB* DISHES are described in detail sufficient to guide a home cook to a fine result. Even so, I've chosen to further elaborate some of these, to put them down in more traditional recipe form. Also you'll find dishes not recounted in the narrative, dishes which, over these long years of my Umbrian life, have become well-loved emblems of our table, dishes guests expect to find there.

There are two caveats: first, I'm wordy but not complicated (as a cook, as a woman). In the pages that follow, I talk to the reader as though he or she were in the kitchen with me. I want you to know more than the means to the end and so I take liberties, assuming that you, too, want what I want for you: the stories and the chatter which can be passed on.

I've made no attempt to offer a balance of starters, main dishes, sweets. As I tell you in the narrative, we often ended Thursday

Suppers with an espresso cup of fresh ricotta drizzled with dark honey (or a piece of honeycomb) or mixed with a few crushed espresso beans and, perhaps, some dark sugar. Miranda almost always set out a tin of biscotti for dipping into the heel of our wine or into a tiny glass of ambered *vin santo*. That said, you won't find 'desserts' here but rather several *dolce salata* – sweet and salty – dishes which are more often served at the end of a supper than a traditional sweet.

And caveat number two. Over and over again, I will offer you dishes based on wine, extra-virgin olive oil, pecorino and bread, the elements which form – and have for centuries formed – the cuisine of Umbria. We have sheep and pigs, we have grapes, we have olives, we have wheat. And so this is what we cook, how we eat, what we drink. Though all the dishes, in the narrative and in this section, are inspired by the gastronomic patrimony of Umbria, they are almost never lifted from the canonical repertoire of the region. Rather I've interpreted recipes to suit the marketplaces, the sensibilities and lifestyles of readers who do not live and cook in rural Umbria or those who do not have the Umbrian hand – *la mano* – as it's said here.

After what I can now quite honestly term a lifetime's passion for food and cooking, I admit to practising a very personalised cuisine, an amalgam of tradition and instinct. Hence these recipes represent the slowly distilled juices of my cooking not only here in Umbria, but in all the places to which I've travelled on my stomach, where I've lived and worked and cooked and fed people.

Bruschette with Sun-struck Tomatoes

One of the finest dishes of my life (and one which I recreate as often as its components are to be found) is nothing more than bruschette served with little soup plates of tomatoes. Only tomatoes. Glorious tomatoes. Ripe, sun-struck, skin-split beauties – broken and crushed more than sliced – set to warm for a few hours under a hot sun. Spooned into the bowls, a dish of salt flakes or fine sea salt nearby, the bruschette almost too hot to handle, a dry, almost chalky white wine chilled down to a degree somewhat below that which the winemaker would advise. And there you have it. Don't be tempted to tear basil over these tomatoes. Save that luscious idea for another moment.

TO SERVE 6

INGREDIENTS

As authentic a crusty country loaf as you can buy or bake, sliced into 3cm thick trenchers and laid on a baking tray in a single layer or upon a grate if they are to be toasted over embers

Extra-virgin olive oil

Fine sea salt

One kilogram of very ripe, nearly over-ripe, garden tomatoes which have never been acquainted with a refrigerator and which you've either grown yourself, or selected from a farmers' market or a trustworthy fruit and vegetable seller.

THE METHOD

To begin, it seems fitting that one should learn to say *bruschetta*: bru-skett'-ah. A bruschetta is nothing more than freshly toasted, oiled bread spiked with sea salt. Hardly an Umbrian or Tuscan supper begins without one or two trenchers of honest country bread, lightly toasted on both sides under a grill or over the hearth embers then drizzled with fine oil. The goal of 'toasting' is not to harden the crumb or crust of the bread, but to enhance its good flavour and texture as only a gentle charring can do.

Once the bread is toasted – and without missing a beat – pour the best oil in thin threads (in a circular movement) over one side of the bread, take pinches of fine sea salt or salt flakes and rub them between your fingertips over the oiled bread. Again, with no delay, get the things to the table around which everyone is already seated, the wine poured.

These and only these, unornamented, are true bruschette (plural). All manner of vegetables – cooked or raw – cured meats, savoury pastes, and even sometimes the flesh of a fine juicy fig, can be laid upon the hot oiled bread. But these filips transform the bruschetta into a *crostino*. Often in a trattoria or ristorante, a clove of garlic stuck on the end of a toothpick will be served with the bruschette, to be rubbed over the hot bread. Unless the garlic is white and hard and has an unmusty perfume and nothing of a green heart, don't bother. In fact, even the most fresh and delicate garlic speaks louder than good oil and tends to distract from the intended simplicity. Two or three bruschette per person is the dose which begins to arouse hunger without peril of blunting it for what will come next.

Red Wine-roasted, Pancetta-wrapped Pears served with Panna Cotta di Pecorino

When *la mezzadria* – the medieval system of sharecropping – still existed in Umbria, a tenant farmer was wont to enrich his portion of the spoils with stuffs not easily tracked by his landowner. The *fattore* – administrator – kept a tally on the courtyard animals, dutifully marking births and slaughters, while grain yields were calculated before a harvest and counted out later, right down to the bushel. Hunters returning from the woods with bloodied sacks over their shoulders were met by the *fattore* or one of his squad who relieved the farmers of their spoils; and poaching was an offence punishable by beating or banishment from the farm.

Still, privateering flourished. Fruit could be bullied down from a tree, a pat or two of new cheese formed from a morning's abundant milking could be tucked inside a linen kitchen towel and set to ripen in some secret drawer. And who could know just how many baskets of mushrooms were to be dug from beneath a stand of oaks after a rain or how a piece of honeycomb was broken off in a certain way. It was this sort of cunning that enlivened the mean substance of a poor man's table. Now that nearly all the old survival methods are just memories, carving up a good pear and eating it with slivers of fresh or aged pecorino and thin threads of chestnut honey can raise up a long-ago reckoning in an Umbrian farmer. He'll offer you a slice of pear from the tip of his knife, nod his head toward the round of cheese, the loaf of bread and the honey jar on the table. And while you're helping yourself, he'll look at you and say, '*Sono buoni eh? Ma, credimi, erano più buoni quando erano rubati.* They're good, yes? But, believe me, they tasted even better when they were stolen.'

Honouring this ancient autumn rite of pairing pears with pecorino, I offer two dishes: the first is simple yet unexpectedly intriguing, a dish to be found within the text; the second is a dish I want you to have because it was Miranda's favourite. In fact, when the season came around, she would begin to ask for it – sometimes as subtly as gesturing her chin toward the basket of pears sitting on my kitchen table, other times saying outright, '*Non è ora di fare la crostata?* Isn't it time to make the tart?' The delicious thing has never had any other name but that – 'the tart'. More than once it composed the whole of a lunch between Miranda and me. Nothing but 'the tart' and some wine.

We'd begin delicately enough, cutting modest little wedges for one another. The devouring underway, we'd move the knife to a wider angle for the second cutting, wider yet for the third, until only a small desolate slice sat there in the tin. For the sake of compassion, we'd put our forks to it without the bother of lifting it to our plates. The main deed done, we'd press a finger to the crumbs, pour a last glass of wine.

The already tired fashion of transforming sweet dishes into savoury ones and vice versa is sometimes stretched to the absurd. But once in a while the idea seems valid. Case in point, trembling little moulds of cheese and cream which can be served as part of an *antipasto* (before the meal) or the *finepasto* (the end of the meal). Here we almost always have access to very young, still soft and creamy pecorino. Barring that availability, panna cotta made with grated, aged pecorino (or Parmigiano) is a lovely dish to add to one's 'easy and elegant' repertoire.

THE PEARS

TO SERVE 6

INGREDIENTS

6 ripe (but not over-ripe) Beurre Bosc pears
(almost any variety of pear can be substituted
but the naturally buttery flesh of the Bosc
is, I think, the best for this treatment). Cut a
very thin slice from the bottom of each pear
to prevent wobbling during the roasting, core
them from their bottoms with an apple corer
and stripe-peel them vertically with a vegetable
peeler (a strip of skin removed, a strip left intact
and so on around the belly of the pear). Leave
the stems intact.

40 grams cold unsalted butter

2 tbsp extra-virgin olive oil

6 1/2 cm-thick slices of pancetta, either *tesa* (in a
flat form like bacon) or *arrotolata* (the round form)

A pepper grinder

Sea salt

360–480ml of the same red wine which will
be served at supper (not an extravagance but
an assurance that the pear-roasting juices
will complement rather than fight the wine in
one's glass)

THE METHOD

Preheat the oven to 180°C/350°F.

Cut the cold butter into six equal pieces and insert
a piece into the hollow of each pear. Massage each pear
with the oil then wrap each one with a slice of pancetta
beginning at its base and securing it at the stem end with
a toothpick. In a shallow metal or ceramic flameproof
roasting dish just large enough to hold the fruit comfortably,
set the pears close together. Give a few generous turns of
the pepper grinder over the fruit, pinches of sea salt rubbed
between the palms over all. Now, into the bottom of the
dish pour a cup of the wine and place it on the middle
rack of the preheated oven. Reserve the remaining wine.

At 10-minute intervals, baste the pears with the wine in
the dish and the liquid which will be accumulating as the
heat coaxes juices from the pears. At each basting, add a
tablespoon or two of the reserved wine. Depending upon
the ripeness of the pears, roasting time will vary from 40
to 60 minutes. The pears are roasted properly when the
pancetta is crisped and the point of a sharp knife sinks
easily into their flesh. Do not overcook or the fruit will
begin to collapse into a still delicious but less lovely result.

With a slotted spoon, carefully remove the roasted pears to an oven-proof dish deep enough to hold escaping juices. Turn off the oven but place the fruit in there to keep warm.

Place the original roasting dish directly over a medium-high heat and add what may be left of the reserved wine. Allow the juices to distil and reduce until the sauce is thick but still pourable.

While the sauce is reducing, unmould a panna cotta (recipe follows) onto each of six plates, placing a pear by its side. Nap the panna cotta with the red wine sauce leaving the pear to stand as it is and serve. The goal is to get the dishes to the table while the panna cotta is still cold, the sauce still hot, and the pear at a lovely temperature somewhere in between.

PANNA COTTA DI PECORINO

TO SERVE 6

INGREDIENTS

80ml dry Marsala or dry sherry

1 envelope of powdered gelatine

600ml double cream

85 grams finely grated aged Pecorino

THE METHOD

Pour the Marsala or sherry into a small bowl and sprinkle the gelatine powder over it. Let the mixture stand, without stirring, for 5 minutes, allowing the gelatine to absorb the wine. Now give the mixture a stir.

Meanwhile, over a medium heat, warm the cream and the cheese in a large, deep and heavy-bottomed saucepan, stirring often. Watch carefully and beware overspill since, as the mixture approaches the boil, the volume of the cream will expand and rise quickly. Remove from the heat. Add the softened gelatine to the cream and stir for a full minute to be certain that it has fully dissolved in the hot, hot cream. Quickly pour the mixture into six individual moulds, preferably metal if the plan is to unmould them or into ceramic ramekins if the plan is to serve the savoury pudding in its dish.

Allow the panna cotta to cool to room temperature, then cover each mould tightly with plastic wrap, place the six puddings on a platter and store in the refrigerator overnight (4 or 5 hours is sufficient to gel the puddings but the additional resting time allows the cheese/wine flavours to ripen). Take care to place the platter distant from foods which would not benefit from proximity to the whiff of pecorino such as desserts, most especially those made with chocolate.

La Crostata di Pere e Pecorino – 'The Tart'

TO SERVE 6 TO 8

A beautiful thing to see with the roasted pears standing up to their middles in a golden cream, 'the tart' is lush yet rustic with its medieval perfumes of honey and just-cracked pepper and can be served as a *finepasto*, supplanting the fruit and cheese course or, better yet, instead of dessert.

THE CRUST

INGREDIENTS

170 grams plain flour

40 grams finely grated aged Pecorino

4 or 5 good turns of the pepper grinder

1/2 tsp fine sea salt

40 grams light brown sugar

140 grams unsalted butter, chilled, cut into 1 cm pieces

60ml *vin santo* or other ambered wine, very well chilled

THE METHOD

Pulse the flour, pecorino, pepper, salt and brown sugar two or three times in the bowl of a food processor fitted with a steel blade. Add the butter and pulse until the mixture resembles coarse crumbs. With the machine running, pour the cold wine in through the feed tube all at once and process for 4 or 5 seconds, only until the components just begin to hold together and form a dough.

Turn the mixture out onto a large sheet of plastic wrap, gathering up the errant bits and gently pressing it all into a mass. Enclose the dough in the plastic, cover the plastic with a clean kitchen towel and leave it to rest in a cool place or in the refrigerator for up to 30 minutes. Roll out the rested dough to a thinness of 5 millimetres. Transfer the rolled pastry into a buttered, 25 centimetre loose-bottomed tart pan, fitting it evenly and trimming the excess. Cover the pastry with plastic wrap and place it in the freezer for 20 minutes or in the refrigerator for an hour. Preheat the oven to 220°C/425°F.

Remove the plastic wrap from the chilled pastry shell, line it with a sheet of baking paper and fill it with dried beans (or stones gathered along the Tiber and kept for this purpose) and bake it for 10 minutes before lowering the oven's temperature to 200°C/400°F and baking the pastry for 8 minutes more or until it begins to firm and take on a pale golden colour. Remove the partially baked pastry from the oven, remove the baking paper and weight and leave to cool completely.

THE PECORINO FILLING

INGREDIENTS

500 grams of whole-milk *ricotta* (should you
find the ewe's milk variety rather than that
made from cow's milk, opt for it, keeping the
elements all in the family)

360 grams mascarpone

120 grams finely grated aged Pecorino

30ml dark honey (chestnut, buckwheat, etc.)

1 large egg plus 1 large egg yolk

THE METHOD

In the bowl of a food processor fitted with a steel blade,
process all the components to a thick creamy mass. Cover
and set aside.

THE PEARS

INGREDIENTS

A stick of cinnamon bark

6 whole cloves

6 whole allspice berries

10 whole black peppercorns

8 small, brown or green-skinned ripe but still
firm autumn or winter pears

1/2 a lemon

80ml dark honey (chestnut or buckwheat)
120ml *vin santo* or other dessert wine

For the Final Gloss
30ml dark honey
60ml late-harvest or dessert wine

THE METHOD

Preheat the oven to 200°C/400°F.

In a spice grinder or in a mortar with a pestle, grind the cinnamon, cloves, allspice berries and peppercorns to a fine powder. Cut a very thin slice from the bottom of each pear to prevent wobbling during the roasting, core them from their bottoms with an apple corer and stripe-peel them vertically (a strip of skin removed, a strip left intact and so on around the belly of the pear) with a vegetable peeler. Leave the stems intact. Rub each pear with the cut lemon. Place generous pinches of the spice powder inside the cavity of each pear and position them, upright and nearly touching, in a ceramic or metal roasting dish, just large enough to hold them. Warm the honey and paint each pear with it. Pour the wine into the bottom of the dish and roast the pears for 15 minutes, or just until a thin, sharp knife easily penetrates their flesh. The fruit suffers if roasted to a state of collapse. Remove the pears from the oven and baste them several times with the winey juices. Pour any remaining juices from the roasting dish into a small saucepan. Add the last doses of honey and wine and warm them together. This potion will be used as a final gloss for the pears once the tart has been baked. Meanwhile, allow the pears to cool.

ASSEMBLING THE TART

Preheat the oven to 190°C/375°F.

Spread the pecorino filling over the cooled pastry. Carefully position the pears over the filling and bake the tart for 15 minutes, or until the filling begins to take on a bronze skin and the pastry has crisped. Remove the tart from the oven and paint the pears with the reserved wine and honey mixture. Permit the tart to cool for 10 minutes before unmoulding it. Serve it warm or at room temperature. Present the tart with tiny glasses of the same ambered wine used in its making.

Savoury Cornmeal-crusted Tart with *Olivada*

THE CRUST

INGREDIENTS

110 grams plain flour

160 grams stone-ground coarse cornmeal

1½ tsp fine sea salt

1 tbsp fennel seeds, dry pan-roasted and coarsely crushed

120ml extra-virgin olive oil

120ml cold dry white wine

THE METHOD

Don't even think of using a food processor for this simple, less than a minute, procedure. It will do you and your hands such good to get in there and *feel* what you're doing. In a medium bowl, mix the dry ingredients by tossing them together for a few seconds until the yellow and white flours are blended. Add the crushed fennel seeds. With a fork, stir the oil and wine together in a small bowl, beating the mixture as you would an egg. Pour it all at once over the dry ingredients and mix together with that same fork or your hands until blended. Knead the mixture in the bowl six or eight times. Leave it to rest for 30 minutes in a cool place covered with a kitchen towel while you get to the *olivada*.

THE OLIVADA

INGREDIENTS

3 pitted prunes

60ml warmed Cognac or brandy

500 grams large fleshy black or purple Italian
or Greek olives, pounded lightly with a mallet
and relieved of their stones

2 fat cloves of crisp white garlic whose hearts
have not been sullied by acidic green sprouts
(better to do without the garlic than to use the
imperfect)

1½ tbsp fresh rosemary leaves chopped down
nearly to a powder

Extra-virgin olive oil (approx. 60ml)

THE METHOD

Though I pound away at this mass in a large stone mortar
with a wooden pestle, a food processor would be more
convenient if far less satisfying.

Place the prunes in the warmed Cognac or brandy
for 15 minutes until they soften and plump. Place all the
elements, save the oil, into the food processor bowl fitted
with a steel blade and pulse until a coarse paste is achieved.
With the motor running, begin to pour, drop by drop, the
good oil into the mixture until it thickens, emulsifies and
turns glossy.

Scrape the paste into a bowl and cover it with plastic wrap, leaving it in a cool place to rest while the Cognac ripens. Refrigeration simply stultifies the flavours and renders the paste like something from a tin. Why the prunes? Because the natural brine in which the olives have been aged is salty. On the tongue, one hardly notices even a whiff of prune but gets rather a sensual, richer, less-aggressive taste of olives.

TO ASSEMBLE THE TART

Generously oil a 30 centimetre metal tart tin (preferably with a removable base) and press the cornmeal pastry into it, taking care to knuckle the dough evenly over the bottom and sides of the tin. Place a sheet of baking paper over the crust, weight the paper with dried beans (or river stones collected from along the Tiber and kept for this purpose) and place it in the freezer for 15 minutes while preheating the oven to 180°C/350°F.

Bake the shell for 12–15 minutes until it begins to shrink away from the sides of the tin. Remove the baking paper and the weights and continue to bake the crust until it's golden, another 10 minutes or so. Leave the oven on. Allow the crust to cool for 10 minutes, spread the *olivada* evenly over the bottom, as extravagantly or as moderately as you wish. Remember the paste is rich. Should you end up with some to spare, spoon the *olivada* into a glass jar with a screw top and save it in the pantry. Use it over the next day or so to sauce pasta or to spread on toasted bread. Now put the tart back into the oven for 3–4 minutes, just to 'set' the paste. Take it out and leave it to cool a bit. Unmould the tart and serve it at room temperature or leave it in its tin and cut it at table.

Red Wine-braised Pasta with Shavings of 99% Cacao Chocolate

If, at the end of a good supper, you've had the orgasmic pleasure of placing a shard or two of gorgeous bitter chocolate (70–99% cacao) in your mouth, allowing it to barely begin melting before tipping your glass to sip the last of the fine red wine which you've drunk with that supper, and then – eyes closed and silent – let the two elements find their way to one another and finally to wander slowly, voluptuously down your throat, you will understand what to expect from this esoteric-sounding dish.

As the narrative recounts, cooking dried pasta in water is a relatively upstart method, it having for centuries been softened in wine or broth. There are any number of methods to cook pasta in wine but it's this unfussy way which, I think, yields the best results. Should there be a Ninuccia-type figure in your life who would dare you to produce a 15 kilo dose of the stuff, refuse.

TO SERVE 6

(As a primo or first course with other courses to follow; recipe may be doubled successfully if the pasta is to be served to six as the main plate.)

THE PASTA

INGREDIENTS

500 grams short dried pasta, preferably penne
rigate

Coarse sea salt

A bottle plus 240ml of the same red wine you'll
drink at table

125 grams plus 35 grams unsalted butter

30ml extra-virgin olive oil

25 grams finely grated fresh ginger

5 whole cloves and a stick of cinnamon bark,
pounded together coarsely

100 grams of 99% chocolate (Lindt has a good
version and is most readily available worldwide)

A pepper grinder

THE METHOD

Bring 7 litres of water to the boil, heaving in a fistful of
coarse salt just as it begins to roll. Add the pasta, stirring
well until the water resumes the boil. Quickly drain the
pasta after 3 minutes. While waiting for the water to boil,
pour 240ml of red wine in to a small saucepan and warm
it over a slow flame without letting it approach the boil;
add the 35 grams of unsalted butter, stir to melt in the
warm wine, and grind in several vigorous turns of the
pepper grinder. Keep the buttered, peppered wine warm
over a quiet flame.

In a very large sauté pan or a very large shallow pot over a medium flame, melt 125 grams of butter, add olive oil, then stir in the ginger and cinnamon/clove mixture to perfume the oil. Add the par-boiled, drained pasta. With a wooden spoon, move the pasta about in the perfumed oil to coat each piece. Turn the heat to high and, without stirring, allow the pasta to begin taking on some colour and to form a golden crust. After about 2–3 undisturbed minutes, give the pasta a good stir so that more of it can have the benefit of the heat and begin to take on colour and crust. The process of 'pan-toasting' the pasta will want anywhere from 6 to 8 minutes, depending upon the size of the pan. Now begins the dosing with the wine.

From the bottle, pour in about 60ml, give the pasta a stir and, still over a high heat, allow the pasta to drink in the wine. Give the pasta the next dose when the wine has been thoroughly absorbed. Repeat the dosing and absorbing until the pasta is properly al dente. In most cases, the entire bottle of wine will be needed to achieve this texture. Should the texture be reached before the bottle is empty, pour what remains of it into the cook's glass.

Now add the reserved buttered, peppered wine to the hot, hot pasta and toss and toss, glossing the pasta, plumping it in its final dose of wine. You'll recall that this last dose of wine has only been heated and thus its alcohol has not gone to steam – another reason not to stint on the quality of the wine in the dish or in the glass. I am not suggesting a 1998 Pomeral, for instance, but an honest red with more muscle than fruit.

Immediately ladle the pasta into warmed deep plates and, with a vegetable peeler, shave curls of the chocolate over each plate.

Schiacciata con Uve di Vino – Winemaker's Flatbread Laid with Wine Grapes and Crusted with Pepper and Sugar

A truly ancient ritual bread made once a year to celebrate the harvesting of the grapes, there are as many ways to put it together as there are women who have and who still do bake it. The single commonality is the rite which dictates that the eldest and the youngest members of a family – holding the secateurs together – cut the first of the grapes while the winemaker's wife stands at the ready with a fine white cloth in which to take the grapes and carry them to her kitchen. This ceremony signifies continuity, the passing down of 'life' from generation to generation. They actually cut a branch or an arm of grapes on which hang several bunches. This is not only for convenience, since more than a single bunch is necessary for the bread, but also because the grape-stripped branch and the attached leaves are used to decorate the finished bread.

Once the grapes are in the kitchen, the breadmaker's own fantasy and instinct prevail as long as the result is both sweet and salty, *dolce salata.* The taste of life itself.

This harvest bread is distinctly perfumed with rosemary, anise and fennel, while the grapes which are laid on it are again perfumed and then generously sugared and peppered, the sugar forming a kind of crust in the oven which, when broken in the mouth, gives forth a burst of warm luscious juices.

TO MAKE 1 LARGE FLATBREAD WHICH SERVES 6 TO 8

INGREDIENTS

1 cube fresh yeast

360ml cups lukewarm dry white wine

60 grams plus 1 tbsp dark brown sugar

600 grams plain flour

240ml plus 1 tbsp extra-virgin olive oil

3 tbsp fresh rosemary leaves, finely chopped

2 tbsp fennel seeds, crushed

2 tbsp anise seeds

A pepper grinder

1 tbsp fine sea salt

2 eggs, well beaten

750 grams white, black or red wine grapes
or table grapes (or a mixture) cut into small
bunches, washed and dried

130 grams caster sugar

THE METHOD

In a large bowl, soften the yeast in the lukewarm wine
with 1 tbsp of the dark brown sugar. Cover lightly with a
kitchen towel and allow the yeast to activate for 5 minutes.
Stir in 160 grams of the flour and, once again, cover the
bowl with a kitchen towel and allow the yeast to further
activate for 15 minutes.

Meanwhile, in a small saucepan, gently warm 240ml of oil over a low heat, adding the rosemary, fennel and anise seeds and a few generous grindings of pepper. Do not overheat the oil; cover the saucepan, set aside and allow the herbs to perfume the oil.

Now, returning to the sponge, add the remaining flour, the sea salt, 60 grams of dark brown sugar, one-half of the perfumed, cooled oil with one-half of its seeds and finally, add the eggs. Incorporate the elements with a wooden spoon or, better, your impeccably clean hands. You may never use a food processor for breadmaking again. Turn the mass out onto a lightly floured pastry marble or work surface and knead in a forceful slapping–turning motion for as long as 8 minutes or until a satiny, elastic texture is achieved. Wash and dry the bowl and pour in the 1 tbsp of oil; place the worked dough into the bowl and turn it about until it's well coated with the oil. Cover tightly with plastic wrap and then cover the wrapped bowl with a folded tablecloth or a few layers of kitchen towels. I keep a small quilt, once my son's carriage blanket, for this use. We are, after all, in pursuit of continuity here.

Allow the dough to rise until doubled. Time required depends upon the atmospheric conditions in your kitchen, the quality of your flour and the will of Destiny. The combination of yeast and wine rather than yeast and water causes dough to rise somewhat more rapidly (while giving the eventual bread a delicate crumb and an almost imperceptible sourdough flavour) so the dough may want only 30 minutes to double.

Deflate the dough with a single deft punch, place it on a large sheet of baking paper and place the baking paper on a baking tray. Flatten the dough into a free-form circle about 1 centimetre thick. Press the small bunches of grapes or single grapes pulled from their stems over the dough. Leave a 3 centimetre border of dough around the edges grape-free. Evenly pour on the remaining perfumed oil, sprinkle the bread with the caster sugar and grind pepper over the whole with an un-shy hand. Cover lightly with a clean kitchen towel and allow to rise for 30 minutes.

Preheat the oven to 200°C/400°F. Bake the flatbread for 30–35 minutes or a bit longer, until the edges are golden and swollen and the grapeskins have begun to burst. Cool the bread on the baking tray for 5 minutes then transfer it to a wire rack for further cooling. Best served warm, it can be baked several hours in advance of supper then very gently reheated at about 100°C/200°F.

La Ginuzza
A Sweet–Salty 'Cake'

I won't apologise for setting down here yet another 'androgynous' recipe which serves just as magnificently with drinks before supper as it does passed about with a last glass of wine instead of dessert. Less will I wince in telling you again of the glorious harmonies struck by the mixing of rosemary and anise. My reach is toward authenticity rather than variety for variety's sake. If you make this once, you'll make it forever. It's almost too simple, wants five minutes to mix and pat into its tin, less than half an hour in the oven. It's meant to be broken rather than cut, passed about the table or sent hand to hand among a small group standing in a meadow to watch the sunset. If stored in an airtight metal tin, it keeps longer than most love affairs. You'll give it your own name – *Ginuzza* is nothing more nor less than the diminutive of a friend who's name is Gina Maria and who is inordinately fond of the thing.

TO SERVE 8 TO 10

INGREDIENTS

185 grams plus 15 grams unsalted butter at room temperature

25 grams plus 40 grams dark brown sugar

50 grams icing sugar

110 grams plain flour

160 grams coarsely ground cornmeal

1/2 tsp baking powder

1 tsp fine sea salt

2 tbsp anise seeds

2 tbsp plus 2 tbsp fresh rosemary leaves, finely chopped

1 1/2 tsp sea salt flakes (*fleur de sel*) or coarse sea salt, pounded but not to a powder

THE METHOD

Preheat the oven to 180°C/350°F. Smear the 1 tbsp of softened unsalted butter over the bottom and sides of a 30 centimetre metal cake tin. Set aside. In a medium bowl, cream 185 grams of softened butter with 25 grams of dark brown sugar and the icing sugar until smooth. A beater is hardly necessary. In another medium bowl, combine with your hands the flour, cornmeal, baking powder, fine sea salt, anise seeds and the 2 tbsp of chopped rosemary leaves. Add the dry mix to the butter/sugar mixture and, with the fingertips, combine the elements into a mass. Turn the mass out onto a lightly floured work surface and knead three or four times, just to further render it a more cohesive dough. Lightly pat the dough into the buttered tin, knuckling and pressing it to evenness.

In a cup, combine the remaining 40 grams of dark brown sugar, the remaining 2 tbsp chopped rosemary with the sea salt flakes or the pounded coarse sea salt and sprinkle the mixture evenly over the cake. Knuckle the surface one last time so that the herb/sugar/salt is 'embedded' into the dough. Bake the cake on the middle shelf of the oven for 20 minutes or until the cake has taken on a pale but distinctly gold colour. Don't underbake. Let the cake cool in its tin for 10 minutes then turn it out onto a wire rack to cool completely at which time it will be ready to serve or to store. I prefer to divide the dose of dough into two 20 centimetre tins only because the cake is thinner, crisper, lighter that way.

Miranda's Violenza – Piquant Herbed Olive Oil

As written in the narrative, Miranda kept a five-litre jug of this 'violently' herbed oil in her pantry and used it as a marinade for meats and vegetables to be grilled over her fire or to paint same after they'd been wood-charred. She smeared it over hot roasted bread to bring forth a rather unusual sort of bruschetta. She always claimed it was the only substance better than grappa to soothe bodily wounds and bruises.

It would hardly be worth the trouble to concoct less than two litres of this at a time. Use only the most beautiful fresh sage and rosemary and only white, crisp, juicy garlic. If the purple variety can be found and it, too, is crisp and juicy and with no green heart, grab it (promise yourself to avoid the obese, acidic heads of what is sometimes referred to as elephant garlic save, perhaps, to feed it to the animal whose name it bears).

Wild fennel flowers are not readily available in even the smartest little food shops. If you live near a river, it's likely that wild fennel will be growing, here and there, along its banks. A tall, very tall stalk with a frothy yellow-flowered head, it is unmistakeable. Gather it by cutting the stalk rather than pulling it by its roots. With heavy string, tie the stalks in bunches of six or seven and suspend them, upside down, in a cool airy place to dry. A process which sometimes asks several months. The dried stalks can be used as a bed for roasting meat or fish while the dried heads, rubbed between the palms, yield a most astonishingly perfumed herb – delicate, assertive, lingering. Substitute good old fennel seed if all this foraging by a river is not part of your plan.

MAKES 2 LITRES

INGREDIENTS

2 litres of extra-virgin olive oil (please don't think that because the oil will be herbed that an inferior quality will do)

4–6 branches of fresh sage leaves, depending upon the size of the leaves (don't use dried sage; better to omit if fresh is not available)

3–4 branches of fresh rosemary (not the ornamental sort which is pretty to see but contains sparse essential oil)

2 tbsp dried fennel flowers or fennel seeds

Dried chillies (the quantity and variety are entirely a personal choice. I would use 10–12 dried ones of the variety we call *diavolini*, tiny, fierce but not vicious.)

2–3 heads of garlic (see note above)

THE METHOD

Stuff the sage branches (without tearing off the leaves), the rosemary branches (without stripping them of their leaves), the fennel flowers or seeds and the chillies (uncrushed) into the 2 litres of oil. Slap the heads of garlic with the flat of a knife and scrape the smashed, unpeeled cloves into the oil. Cork the oil, shake it, put it to rest in a cool, dark place. Give it a shake two or three times a day and in two weeks, it will be ready to use. As time passes, the *violenza* will become more so.

Note: One could scald the oil before adding the herbs but, according to Miranda, the result is far more pure and 'fresh' if time rather than heat ripens the various essences.

Zucca Arrostita
Whole Roasted Cheese and Wild Mushroom-stuffed Pumpkin

I'd been making a version of this dish for years and years before I came to live in Italy, but when I tried to build it with the local, watery-fleshed, pimply, green-skinned things called *Zucca Invernale*, the result was less than good. It was in the Lombard city of Mantua where I first found small, green-skinned squash whose flesh most resembled the native American pumpkin. One October Saturday morning there, we filled the boot of our car with twenty-two squash, having been assured by the farmer that, if stored in a cool place, they would stay firm and fine until Easter. He was right. I stuffed and roasted and scooped and fed the Thursday Night tribe on them until Miranda finally took a mallet to the few which remained by February, roasted the pieces, mixed the flesh with white wine vinegar, crushed mustard seeds, mustard oil (bought here in the pharmacy) and sugar to make *la mostarda di zucca*, a luscious condiment (typical of the city of Cremona in the region of Lombardy) through which we dragged shards of pecorino and skated crusts of bread at the finish of many suppers.

TO SERVE 6 TO 8

INGREDIENTS

1 large good pumpkin (approx. 2 kilograms in weight). Slice off the top (keep to use later) remove the seeds and strings, then carve away a centimetre or so of its interior flesh with a thin, sharp knife. Also put this flesh aside with the top. Massage the pumpkin's interior walls with fine sea salt.

45 grams plus 60 grams unsalted butter

2 large brown onions, peeled and finely chopped

The reserved pumpkin flesh

300 grams fresh wild mushrooms, (porcini, cepes, chanterelles, portobello) swiftly rinsed, then drained, dried and sliced thinly or 100 grams dried porcini, softened in 120ml warm water, stock or wine, drained and sliced thinly, the soaking liquid reserved

1½ tsp fine sea salt

A pepper grinder

720 grams mascarpone

300 grams emmentaler, grated

100 grams Parmigiano, grated

3 whole eggs, beaten with 80ml brandy or Cognac

2 tsp freshly grated nutmeg

8 slices firm-textured, day-old white bread, crusts removed, cut into 2 cm squares

THE METHOD

In a medium sauté pan, melt 45 grams of unsalted butter and saute the onions, reserved pumpkin flesh (finely diced) and mushrooms until the mass softens and the mushrooms give up their juices (if using dried mushrooms, strain the soaking liquid and add it, at this point, to the sauté pan). Add the sea salt and give the pepper grinder three or four good turns.

In a large bowl combine all other elements save the bread and remaining butter. Beat the mass with a wooden spoon, stir in the onion, pumpkin and mushroom mixture. Melt 60 grams of butter in a sauté pan and in it brown the bread, tossing the pieces about until they are crisp and golden.

Preheat the oven to 190°C/375°F. Place the readied pumpkin or squash in a large, heavy baking dish or on a baking tray. Spoon one-third of the cheese mixture into the pumpkin, add half the crisped bread, another third of the cheese, the remaining bread, ending with the remaining cheese mixture. Replace the pumpkin's hat and roast it in the oven for 1½ hours or longer – until the pumpkin's flesh is very soft when pierced with the tip of a sharp knife. Beware not to over-roast it to the point of collapse. The natural sugars in the pumpkin will caramelise and melt into the stuffing. It's least perilous to serve the pumpkin in it's roasting dish or on its baking tray, though it can be transferred to a warmed deep platter with the aid of two wide spatulas. In either case, a few autumn leaves, branches of bittersweet (or *bacche* as the wild orange berries are known here) would not be out of place. Most importantly, get it to the table quickly. Into warmed soup plates, spoon out the stuffing, scraping the spoon along the wall of the pumpkin shell for some of the good caramelised flesh.

———◆◆———

Roasted Loin of Drunken Pork

This is an 'interpreted' version of the brandy-injected leg of wild boar Miranda proffered as her 'final' solo Thursday Night supper. Along with the boar, her method asked only three elements: brandy, juniper berries and sea salt. Here we forage and dry juniper berries to use in many game preparations and shun the already-dried berries which are sometimes available commercially, the reason being that the commercial variety lack the delicacy of ours and can, even when used sparingly, trounce every possibility of achieving the desired complexity of flavours in a dish.

If one is partial to the taste of good Dutch gin with its decisive but still pastel juniper flavour, one could inject it into the pork rather than brandy. I have done this often and always with fine results. As usual, much depends on the quality of the pork (organic, corn-fed), and the quality of the gin or the brandy. One would hardly be amiss using Cognac, Armagnac or Calvados.

TO SERVE 8 TO 10

INGREDIENTS

A large injector or disposable syringe

A bottle of gin or brandy or any of the others mentioned above

A leg of fresh, young, organic pork, bone-in, weighing 2–3 kilograms

12 whole allspice berries, coarsely crushed and mixed with 2 tbsp fine sea salt

480ml dry Marsala or dry sherry

THE METHOD

Fill the injector or syringe with the gin or brandy and, with an un-shy hand, insert it deeply into the flesh of the pork, expelling all the liquid. Repeat the process over all surfaces of the meat. Place the injected meat into a deep ceramic or enamelled dish, cover tightly with plastic wrap and refrigerate. (Shockingly dangerous as it will seem, we don't refrigerate but simply retire the meat to rest in a cool place.) Several times during the first day, repeat the injection process. On the second day, once again repeat the injections, carefully covering and refrigerating the meat. On the third day, preheat the oven to 230°C/450°F. Inject the meat all over its surfaces for the last time, then score the skin in a criss-cross fashion, cutting right down into the flesh, so that the skin will roast to a good gold, hard crackle. (Should there be gin or brandy left in the bottle, resist pouring it out for the cook since it will come in handy a bit later.)

Now rub the entire leg with the allspice/sea salt mixture, place the leg on a roasting rack set in a large roasting pan and roast at the high temperature for 30 minutes. Reduce the oven temperature to 180°C/350°F and continue to roast the leg for 20 minutes per 500 grams.

Remove the roasting pan from the oven but not the leg from its rack in the pan. Leave it to rest for 15–30 minutes, uncovered. Tenting the leg with foil or covering it in any way will risk softening the crackled skin. After the leg has rested, transfer it to a cutting board. Place the roasting pan over a medium–high flame, add what's left in the gin or brandy bottle and the dry Marsala. Scrape and stir to release the clinging bits and reduce the liquid by one third.

On an Umbrian table, no sauce would be served with the meat, its succulence already assured by the liquor-plumping process. Slice the pork and its crackled skin and, if you must, drizzle with the reduced pan juices. Otherwise, serve the juices as a sauce for buttered pasta before serving the roast. (An example of 'the conducting thread' through a meal.)

Though the pork is delicious served warm, it is equally delicious served at room temperature. No rushing here to get hot, hot 'meat and gravy' to the table.

What to serve with the roast? Good bread and good wine. Resist 'apple sauce' or any such travesty. A bowl of wine-plumped, spiced dried prunes would not be inappropriate nor would a dish of fine whole-fruit Cremona *mostarda* if such is to be found wherever you are.

ACKNOWLEDGEMENTS

BOOKS ARE OFTEN MADE AS MUCH OF CALAMITY AS OF blessing. In the case of *Supper Club*, it was my splendidly perceptive editor at Hutchinson in London, Sarah Rigby, who provided rescue from the former and an abundance of the latter. If Sarah had a theme song it would be 'Amazing Grace'.